CHEZ PANISSE VEGETABLES &

CHEZ PANISSE
VEGETABLES

by

ALICE WATERS

and the Cooks of Chez Panisse

Illustrations by

PATRICIA CURTAN

HarperCollins*Publishers*

ALSO FROM CHEZ PANISSE ✒

The Chez Panisse Menu Cookbook
Chez Panisse Pasta, Pizza, and Calzone
Chez Panisse Desserts
Chez Panisse Cooking
Fanny at Chez Panisse

FIRST EDITION

Designed by Patricia Curtan

Typeset in Minion and Charlemagne by
Patricia Curtan and Bur Davis

ISBN 0-06-017147-2

96 97 98 99 00 ❖ / RRD 10 9 8 7 6 5 4 3

ACKNOWLEDGMENTS ❧

How can I begin to thank all the cooks of Chez Panisse who in so many different ways have helped us to expand our repertory? Their curiosity and audacity has enabled the restaurant to keep growing and changing. However, special thanks are due those cooks, past and present, who wrote recipes for this volume. They are listed here alphabetically. Some are chefs with over twenty years of experience, and others are young cooks who have only recently moved from jobs washing lettuce and rolling out pasta to the prep kitchens and the line, cooking to order in the café. Wherever there are vivid original turns of phrase and revealing details in our recipes they are in the voices of these hard-working and expressive cooks: Tracy Bates, Catherine Brandel, Patricia Curtan, Eve Felder, Kelsie Kerr, Jennifer Johnson, Christopher Lee, Seen Lippert, John Luther, Scott McGhee, Russell Moore, Jean-Pierre Moullé, Gilbert Pilgram, Richard Seibert, Jennifer Sherman, Peggy Smith, Fritz Streiff, Mona Talbott, Jérôme Waag, Jim Wilson, and Samantha Wood. We are also indebted to Pam Heminway, John Hudspeth, Niloufer Ichaporia, David King, and Glenn Recchia, all friends who are not cooks at Chez Panisse but who have taken the trouble to write down recipes we learned first from them.

This book would have been impossible without the special contributions of Alan Tangren. Alan is now our "forager," whose duties are to locate quality foodstuffs from farmers and markets, negotiate their purchase, and coordinate the ordering by the kitchens of both the café and the downstairs restaurant.

CONTENTS ❧

INTRODUCTION ❧

Chez Panisse opened its doors twenty-five years ago, started by an assortment of idealistic friends, all of us highly motivated but totally inexperienced in the restaurant business. Because we had not a clue about the usual ways cafés and restaurants were run, we tried from the start to do things the way we would like to have them done at a dinner party at home. We didn't know how to manage a kitchen and fill orders for dozens of different dishes at once, so we hit on a format we have stuck with ever since: one menu, no choices, one price. We tried to make it simple, feeling our way along and following our instincts. We wanted the restaurant to be popular and inclusive; but at the same time we wanted the food to be nothing but the very, very finest obtainable.

Finding the best food and doing things the simplest way sometimes feels complicated, but there is nothing very mysterious about it, nor is it something only restaurants can do. You only need to open your eyes— and all your other senses. Back when we began our search for the best-tasting food, even here amid the abundance of California agriculture, our choices were limited. There were no farmer's markets in Berkeley, no produce brokers specializing in organically grown vegetables, no commercial vendors of wild mushrooms. However, within a short time after we opened, an assortment of people began to show up at our kitchen door, drawn by our reputation for culinary curiosity. Neighbors began bringing us bunches of radishes, sorrel, and herbs from their backyard gardens—for free or in trade. A few eccentric foragers would arrive from time to time with baskets of chanterelles and morels, buckets of Pacific mussels, blackberries from the hills, and fish just hours out of the sea.

Finding steady, dependable sources of ingredients was a gradual and sometimes frustrating process, but by our tenth birthday we were able to serve mixed salad greens almost every day, grown in Berkeley gardens and picked, at the most, a few hours before we served them. Our most cherished dream was of a farm of our own. After a couple of comically misconceived experiments, we gave up trying to underwrite a new small farm, and systematically searched out the best diversified organic farm we could find within a sixty-mile radius that would contract with us to grow vegetables and welcome input from us about different varieties and when to harvest them.

Thus began our ten-year association with Bob Cannard and his Sonoma County farm. Working with Bob has been the next best thing to having our own farm. We haul the compostable vegetable waste from our kitchens up to his farm in our truck at dawn, and return to Berkeley a few hours later with branches of cherries still on the bough, boxes of radicchios with leaves like tulip petals, bunches of tender turnips, flats of freshly dug potatoes, lugs of tomatoes, buckets of tiny watercress, and much more, depending on the season. Our relationship with him makes it possible for us to cook almost as if we had a garden right outside the kitchen door. There is no substitute for the immediacy you feel when produce has been harvested and brought right to your kitchen without having languished in storage.

Of course the Cannard farm cannot grow everything we need. Over the years we have stitched together a patchwork of over forty growers of fruits and vegetables nearby. Some of them live in microclimates that have led them to specialize in just a few crops. For example, one orchardist we buy from has just a few peach trees of the variety called Faye Elberta, and every summer, for just a week or two, we get to serve these incomparable peaches to our lucky guests. Other farmers on the coast concentrate on supplying us with an assortment of tiny lettuces.

Many of our most treasured resources came to us almost accidentally. An old friend living in southern California happened upon the Chino family farm produce stand in Rancho Santa Fe near San Diego, and immediately air-freighted us the most beautiful and flavorful tiny green beans any of us had ever seen outside France. Ever since, we have bought all the Chino family produce we can. The Chinos have made an art of farming. For two generations now, they have tended their land with an inexhaustible aesthetic curiosity, constantly searching out new and old varieties of dozens of fruits and vegetables from all over the world, and planting and harvesting year round. Virtually all their produce is sold at their own stand—which looks as glorious in the winter, full of a staggering array of shades of green, from the almost black leaves of tatsoi to the glowing blanched centers of heads of curly endive, as it does in the summer, with displays of as many as seventeen kinds of tomatoes, of as many different colors.

A few principles have emerged over the years: in our opinion, the finest food is produced and grown in ways that are ecologically sound. We try to make decisions about cooking and eating that support the kind of agriculture that takes care of the land, land we hold in trust for future generations.

Good food depends almost entirely on good ingredients. Not long after Chez Panisse began to acquire a national reputation, we were invited to prepare one course of a charitable benefit banquet in New York City. We flew to the East Coast with boxes and boxes of absolutely fresh, organic, hand-picked seasonal greens from which we prepared a simple salad. One famous chef looked at our contribution and remarked, with mock censure and perhaps a little envy, "That's not cooking, that's shopping!"

Of course, he was right. The terminal handling of a vegetable in the kitchen before it is eaten is far less important for taste than what kind of variety it is, where and how it was grown, when it was harvested, and how long it has taken to get to your kitchen. Cooking is only a small part of this.

What can you the reader do to search out good vegetables to eat? If at all possible, plant a garden yourself, and above all, patronize farmer's markets. Get to know your purveyors and producers and give them feedback. There is a farmer's market movement nationwide, and now even New York City has one year-round, in Union Square. Always explore your garden and go to the market *before* you decide what to cook. Decide on your menu based on what you find there. Buy products that are fresh, local, and organic. Select produce that looks freshly harvested and at its peak. Look for vegetables that look right back at you!

Handling living food is so inspiring and energizing it makes you want to cook. You will never get tired of washing lettuce if it is beautiful to look at. There are times of the year when we can hardly wait to go to the farmer's market, in anticipation of the treasures we will find there.

When you cook, remain open to variation and taste all along the way. At the restaurant, we sometimes change the menu minutes before we open. Before you start, taste the raw ingredients and assess them: for example, if the fennel bulbs are not big and succulent, better to braise them than slice them for a raw fennel salad. Never cook slavishly, rigidly following a recipe and thoughtlessly adhering to the measurements it gives. Recipes, as formulas, are almost always approximations, anyway. For one thing, measurement by volume is notoriously inexact. Results will always vary because of the inevitable differences in ingredients and their conditions. And this variation is welcome! Trust your intuition and your own taste. Every time you cook you learn more about ingredients and combinations of flavors and you increase your mastery of a few fundamental methods and techniques.

What we have tried to do in this book is give you an album of possibilities for vegetables we know a little about and often serve at Chez Panisse. Many preparations echo sister recipes in nearby chapters—family resemblances abound in our repertory; by including so many, we have tried to suggest a recurring haphazard serendipity in our cooking. As in a family photo album, there are recipes one might think of as formal portraits: lists of precisely quantified ingredients, and step-by-step instructions in the somewhat cliché-ridden conventions of most modern cookbooks—complete with what often seem, even to a beginner cook, like redundant and obvious details ("Preheat the oven to 400°F.," "Wash, dry, and chop the parsley fine," "Season to taste"). These are side by side with recipes that are more like out-of-focus snapshots: unquantified narrative descriptions that leave much to the imagination and intuition of the cook.

Of course, the paradox is that an out-of-focus snapshot can sometimes be a better, truer likeness than the most carefully posed and costumed studio photograph. In this collection, we have left quite a few short recipes in this kind of format, hoping that you will be encouraged to try them because of their loose form, refining them to your own satisfaction by dash and splash, tasting as you go, instead of measuring them out by teaspoons and quarter cupfuls. Exact quantities should never matter as much to a cook of vegetables (or of anything else) as her confidence in her own senses.

ABOUT THE ILLUSTRATIONS

The original illustrations reproduced in this book are color linocut images drawn, cut, and printed by the artist. As in woodcut relief printing, in linoleum block printing a drawing is first transferred to the block—a layer of smooth linoleum, made from linseed oil and powdered cork, mounted on wood. The linoleum is cut with knives and gouges, removing the negative space of the image and leaving a relief surface of line or solid color. A separate block is cut for each color in the image. The images were printed by hand, one color at a time, on a 10 by 15 Chandler and Price letterpress.

AMARANTH GREENS &

Season: Spring through fall

Amaranth is a new vegetable to many of us, although it has been eaten
for centuries just about everywhere in the world. There are a great many
species of amaranth, all of them annual and mostly tropical plants that
are related to a common weed known as pigweed. The cultivated varieties are grown mostly for their edible greens, which have a distinctive,
appealing flavor somewhat like spinach. The weed amaranths are very
common, sprouting up in the cracks of sidewalks and in vacant lots, and
taste much like their domesticated cousins; there are also amaranths
grown for grain and ornamental amaranths with strikingly beautiful
flowers.

The leafy amaranths come in an enormous range of sizes, colors, and
shapes. Most cultivated varieties belong to the species *Amaranthus
gangeticus*. Leaves can be almost round or lance-shaped, from two to six
inches long. Green-leaved varieties are sometimes called *tampala*, their
name in India. There are also red-leaved varieties (the kind favored in
China), variegated varieties (one called Joseph's Coat has leaves streaked
with yellow, red, green, and brown), and very pale green varieties. Older,
larger leaves tend to have a stronger flavor than small ones.

We have never cooked with amaranth grain at Chez Panisse, but we
use the greens in much the same ways as other salad and cooking greens
and have been pleased with the results. We make salads of small red
amaranth leaves to accompany seared tuna and salmon tartare, and
cook the larger leaves both alone and combined with other greens to
serve in pasta dishes.

Unless the leaves are of the tiny beet-colored variety just picked from
the garden, amaranth is better cooked. Use the stems as well as the

1

leaves, although thicker stems may need peeling and you may not want to bother. The big, splashy leaves and stems of late-season amaranth sometimes need a preliminary parboiling. Spring and early summer amaranth needs no more than the routine washing and grooming before you get on with the cooking. You will notice that amaranth does not cook down as much as spinach.

Local farmer's markets in our part of the country often have amaranth greens for sale. The best are the ones that look the freshest and healthiest. Amaranth greens wilt quickly, so eat them as soon as possible.

The amaranths are easy to grow; seed catalogs often have a wide selection of varieties. They make a speedy and attractive addition to your kitchen garden. The Rodale Press, publishers of *Organic Gardening*, has made something of a crusade on behalf of the native American grain amaranths, one of the very few grains that are feasible for home growing. Curious gardeners are encouraged to investigate.

Wilted Amaranth Greens

Amaranth is such an interesting green that a favorite approach is to cook it quickly, although its robust flavor and texture stand up to long cooking as well. You can proceed along two lines. Sizzle a few slivers of garlic in olive oil, follow with a healthy pinch of salt, and then add the greens. Cover for a minute to let the greens wilt down, then keep tossing until the leaves and stems are tender and no longer taste raw. A second, pan-Asian treatment is to use peanut or corn oil, into which you toss finely sliced or shredded ginger, either alone or with a few slivers of garlic; a dry red chili or two; and then the salt and greens, proceeding as before.

ARTICHOKES 🍂

Season: Spring and early fall

Artichokes are the edible, immature flowers of a cultivated thistle that was introduced to America by Italian immigrants who settled near Half Moon Bay in California around the turn of the century. Italians have been practicing artichoke cultivation for at least two thousand years, and to this day they have a more highly developed expertise in its use than most Americans. For example, in Venice, in the spring, it is routine for fresh artichokes to be sold in the market already pared down to their hearts, or bottoms—large globe artichokes expertly turned by hand, as on a lathe, all the leaves cut off, leaving just the thick disk of the flower base and the immature fuzzy flowerets which form what is known as the choke. Experienced market folk turn out these hearts in seconds flat; the leaves get discarded, and the raw white artichoke bottoms arc tossed in buckets of water acidulated with lemon juice.

There are artichokes shaped like truncated cones; artichokes that are almost perfectly round; and artichokes with nasty thorns. There are green artichokes, green and violet artichokes, and purple artichokes. They are prepared at Chez Panisse in a great many ways, both raw and cooked, depending on their size and relative maturity. Larger ones are steamed whole and served with aïoli (with the leaf tips snipped off if they are very thorny); quartered, stewed, and served in salads; or cut into wedges, browned with tiny new potatoes and small, round spring onions, and finished with a persillade. Artichoke hearts are sliced very thin and baked in a gratin with thyme, cream, and Parmesan. Artichokes are trimmed and stuffed à la Provençal—with bread crumbs, parsley, garlic, and anchovies—or with onion, sausage, and mushrooms.

Especially delicious are the tender young buds of artichokes picked before their prickly chokes have developed: simmered at a low temperature in olive oil until soft, then fried at a higher heat so that the leaves open out, flowerlike, and sprinkled with persillade and lemon juice; cooked rapidly in olive oil with white wine, a few thyme sprigs, and garlic slivers until quite soft, a few drops of lemon juice and Parmesan shaved over; or sliced very, very thin and tossed, raw, with olive oil, shavings of Parmesan, and shavings of white truffle. Young artichokes can also be simmered in oil and spices, including a little hot pepper, and preserved in the same oil for an antipasto. Risotti with young artichokes, accompanied by young peas or fava beans, whole or puréed, with Parmesan grated over, breathe springtime. So does a ragout made with the same ingredients.

Artichokes produce two crops a year. After the first harvest in the spring, a second crop is ready in the early fall. The artichoke's quality varies dramatically over its life cycle. Immature flower heads are crisp and dense, but late in the season they become chokey, and start to open, a sign of overripeness. An artichoke should be harvested and eaten only in the bloom of its youth, never in its maturity. Therefore look for artichokes in the market that are unblemished, tightly closed, entirely unopened, and vibrant in color whether lime-green or bright green and purple. Look at the stem end. The scar should tell you something about how recently it was cut. Buy artichokes as fresh as you can, and don't keep them long before cooking them. Experiment with unusual varieties if you see them in your market; different varieties have distinctly different flavors.

To prepare large artichoke hearts, tear off any small leaves attached to the stem or base, and cut crosswise through the leaves where they begin to taper in toward the top, about an inch and a half above the base; younger artichokes can be cut higher up to preserve more of the tender leaves in the center. Put the artichoke cut side down and carefully trim the leaves (actually scales or bracts) away, leaving just their pale green centers. Pare away the deep green part of the head and stem. You will have only the heart left, with a length of stem still attached. Cut off all but an inch or so of the stem. With a soup spoon or a teaspoon scrape and scoop out the choke from the heart. Fresh artichokes are crisp enough so that this is an easy and simple task, and with a little practice can be done in one motion. Have ready a bowl of acidulated water into which you can immediately drop the artichokes as they are trimmed, to reduce browning from oxidation. Or lightly rub the artichoke hearts with some olive oil. The hearts are now ready for however they are to be cooked—sliced, sautéed, boiled, stuffed and braised, and so on.

Whole young artichokes are handled in a similar way. Any small leaves on the stem are torn off, and the very tops of the bracts are cut off. Break and peel off the outer layers of leaves until the tender, pale green inner leaves show. If you wish, you can pare the slightly ragged edges of the base where the outer leaves were torn off, although this is unnecessary, but do trim the end of the stem. Drop the little artichokes into acidulated water; or, if they are to be deep-fried, rub them with a cut lemon or olive oil (soaking them in water complicates their frying in hot oil).

Artichoke plants have a productive life of three to four years. They flourish in California's cool-summer coastal climate, and grow easily here in people's gardens. Like cardoons, if allowed to bloom artichokes make a striking display of purplish blue thistle flowers. The new plants are usually started from cuttings of a healthy plant; planting from seed is possible, though much more difficult. Plant artichokes away from other vegetables and flowers, three to four feet apart in good, fertile soil. Although artichokes are tolerant of drought, seedlings require deep-watering once a week. Artichokes flourish in nitrogen-rich soil.

Plant artichokes in the fall, and if they go in early enough, they will produce the next year. Several stalks are sent up by each plant, and each stalk will produce a large, central head with several smaller ancillary heads surrounding it. Harvest the central head when it stops increasing in size and its bracts are still tightly closed, cutting it so that at least one inch of stem is left on the butt. After the central head is cut, the secondary heads will continue to grow, but without ever achieving the grand size of the main head. After the first crop cut the plants back to the ground, and they will rebound to produce a nice fall crop.

ARTICHOKE AND PINK GRAPEFRUIT SALAD

Cut cooked artichoke hearts in half-moon slices about ¼ inch thick. Section a pink grapefruit and arrange the sections on a plate alternately with the artichoke heart slices. Drizzle with very flavorful extra-virgin olive oil, season with pepper, and scatter some sprigs of chervil around the artichoke and grapefruit.

PURPLE ARTICHOKES WITH BLACK OLIVES

For each person, prepare two or three of the small, purple artichokes that can be found in the spring. Remove their outer leaves and cut off their stems so that they can stand upright. Cut them crosswise, removing the top two thirds of the leaves, leaving only the tender lower third of the leaves attached to the bottoms. With a little spoon remove the chokes and fill the centers with a mixture of chopped parsley, garlic, and pitted, coarsely chopped black olives.

Put the parsley stems and a couple of bay leaves in the bottom of a nonreactive pan, cover with ¼ inch of water and a little white wine, and arrange the artichokes upright so they fit tightly. Season with salt and pepper, drizzle generously with olive oil, cover, and let stew over a low flame for about 30 minutes, until the bottoms are tender.

GRILLED YOUNG ARTICHOKES

One of the best ways to grill young artichokes is to "blanch" them first in olive oil before grilling them. Peel away the darker, outer leaves until you see only the pale green-yellow of the young, inner leaves. Cut off all but about ½ inch of their stems, and trim off ½ inch of the tops. Rub the artichokes with a cut lemon or with olive oil, to inhibit discoloring. Simmer the artichokes slowly, completely immersed in barely bubbling olive oil, until they are cooked through; then drain them on towels, and when they are cool enough to handle, open out the leaves and press the artichokes onto a hot grill, so that they flatten slightly and the leaves spread out like an opened flower. When they are nicely browned, sprinkle the artichokes with lemon juice and salt, or serve with aïoli.

ARTICHOKES BAKED WITH ANCHOVY STUFFING

Serve as a side dish to roasted meat or poultry, as a light entrée, or as a first course with aïoli and a garden salad.

4 large artichokes
Juice of ½ lemon
3 onions
6 cloves garlic
2 tablespoons olive oil
4 sprigs thyme
¼ to ½ cup white wine
Salt and pepper
¾ cup pitted niçoise olives

STUFFING
Zest of ½ lemon
2 tablespoons chopped parsley
2 salt-packed anchovies
1⅓ cups toasted bread crumbs
Salt and pepper

Splash white wine
Extra-virgin olive oil
Balsamic vinegar
A few sprigs thyme
Parsley

Pare the artichokes down to their hearts and scoop out the chokes with a spoon. Drop the hearts into water acidulated with lemon juice (or rub them with a little olive oil) to prevent them from discoloring. Set aside.

Peel the onions and garlic and slice very thin. Heat the olive oil in a sauté pan, add the onions, garlic, and sprigs of thyme, and cook slowly for 10 minutes, until the onions have softened. Add about ¼ cup of the white wine and cook 2 minutes more. Season to taste. Reserve about ¼ cup of this onion mixture and set aside. Spread the rest of the onion mixture in a small, nonreactive baking dish large enough to hold the artichokes. Scatter the olives over the onions. Preheat the oven to 375°F.

To make the stuffing, grate the zest from the lemon; chop the parsley; and rinse, fillet, and chop the anchovies. Mix together with the reserved onion mixture and the bread crumbs.

Stuff each artichoke with one quarter of this mixture and place the artichokes stuffed side down on the bed of onions and olives in the baking dish. Season generously with salt and pepper. Splash a little white wine over them and drizzle with olive oil and a few drops of balsamic vinegar. Strew with a few sprigs of thyme, cover the artichokes with parchment paper, and cover the baking dish tightly with foil. Bake for 60 to 90 minutes, until the artichokes can be easily pierced with a knife. Garnish with chopped parsley.

Serves 4.

Artichokes with Garlic, Thyme, and Parmesan

20 very small artichokes	*Salt and pepper*
5 cloves garlic	*½ lemon*
⅓ cup extra-virgin olive oil	*Reggiano Parmesan cheese*
3 or 4 sprigs thyme	

Peel the artichokes down to their pale green leaves, trim off the tops to remove any thorns, and cut off all but about half an inch of the stems. As you work, drop the artichokes into cool water acidulated with lemon juice. Peel the garlic and slice it very thin.

Put the garlic, artichokes, olive oil, and thyme in a shallow, nonreactive pan with about 1 cup of water. Season lightly, cover, and simmer moderately for about 10 minutes, until the artichokes begin to soften. Shake the pan a few times during the cooking to stir its contents. Remove the cover, raise the heat slightly, and cook until the artichokes are soft and tender, stirring occasionally. The oil, water, and seasonings should have emulsified into a delicious sauce. Adjust the seasoning and squeeze in the juice of the lemon half.

Serve the artichokes with some of their liquid and with curls of Parmesan cut over them with a vegetable peeler.

Serves 4.

Artichoke Ragout with New Potatoes

Cut new potatoes, such as fingerlings or Bintjes, into chunks the size of a small thumb and boil in salty water until tender. Clean and quarter about the same quantity of very small artichokes. Soften several small spring onions in a saucepan for a minute in olive oil and butter over a high flame. Add the artichokes and a splash of water, season, cover, and stew over a low flame until the artichokes are tender, about 10 minutes. Uncover and add the potatoes, a light drizzle of fruity olive oil, and some chopped parsley. Continue cooking a few minutes longer, until the liquid has reduced to a silky emulsion that coats the vegetables.

ARUGULA
See Lettuces and Other Salad Greens (page 193)

ASPARAGUS 🍃

Season: Spring

Spears of asparagus are the tender young shoots of the big, claw-shaped root of a Eurasian perennial, *Asparagus officinalis*, which grows into a four-foot-tall, fernlike plant with vivid vermilion berries. Asparagus spears start pushing up out of the ground in the very early spring, and are almost always harvested—here in northern California, at least—when they are between six and twelve inches above ground and quite green. However, asparagus can be prevented from turning green by being banked with earth as it grows, keeping the shoots underground. In Europe, most asparagus is blanched this way, and the varieties that are cultivated there yield extremely fat, smooth spears as big around as your thumb and completely white except for their tips, which are tinged with pink, violet, or purple. The asparagus in our markets is usually smaller in diameter, and bright green, dark purple, or green and purple. Asparagus is usually graded by size and sold in bunches. Size varies from stalks smaller than pencils to ones that are bigger than cigars. California asparagus production is at its height from March through the middle of May, with the vegetable reaching its peak of flavor and tenderness in late April and early May, although we have enjoyed local asparagus (some of it white) from a secondary harvest in the fall.

Asparagus is served whole, either grilled, steamed, or boiled, alone or in salads; or it is cut up and sautéed or stir-fried, for vegetable ragouts and pasta sauces. Early asparagus can be very thin; fatter, juicier spears come in later in the season. Thinner asparagus is better suited to sautés and sauces, although if sufficiently tender it can be grilled. Later, fatter asparagus is most often served whole, alone.

Like many vegetables, asparagus starts losing its sweetness the moment it is cut. Therefore, as always, look for the freshest specimens: they should be smooth-skinned and bright-colored, with the bloom of a living green stem; the heads should be compact and tightly formed. Inspect the butt ends—if they look desiccated, it means they were not freshly cut. Asparagus is sometimes harvested too late, after it has begun to bolt: the heads will have started to elongate and spread apart, and the tiny nascent leaves and branches to open up; the section of stalk just below the tip will appear slightly streaky and almost fluted. Asparagus like this will usually be tough, taste grassy and bitter, and may discolor when cooked. Asparagus is best eaten as soon as possible after harvesting, but to store, treat the stems as cut flowers: put the bunches in warm water, tips up, and refrigerate.

To prepare asparagus for cooking, grasp each spear with both hands and snap it; it will break at a point above which the stalk will be tender. (You can then save the butt ends for soup.) Or slice the ends off a little closer to the root end with a knife; there may be a bit less waste this way. In general, any spears served whole that are the diameter of your little finger or larger will be better for having been peeled. One way to judge whether or not smaller asparagus needs peeling is to take a bite of a raw spear: if the skin is tough enough to want peeling, it will be fibrous and strings will get caught between your teeth when you chew. You can easily peel asparagus with a swivel-bladed vegetable peeler: lay a spear flat on the counter, hold it by the tip end, just off the edge of the table, and peel downward toward the butt end. Very thick-skinned, very large asparagus must be peeled more deeply to remove all the fibrous material; some find it easier to use a fixed-blade peeler or a knife.

To boil asparagus, plunge it into boiling salted water. Cook uncovered; it is done when just barely tender when pierced with a knife through the thickest part of a stem. Start testing after a few minutes. (Bear in mind that it will keep cooking a little as it drains.) Asparagus should take on an intense green color. Cooking time will depend on the volume of water and the thickness and tenderness of the asparagus. When peeled, most green asparagus takes no more than about five minutes to cook. Fat white asparagus takes about fifteen. At the restaurant, where we handle large quantities at a time, asparagus is boiled loose in batches, in large, shallow hotel pans full of rapidly boiling water, so we can closely oversee its cooking (it can easily be tested for doneness and quickly removed and drained). When asparagus is done, quickly spread the spears out so they drain and cool rapidly to retain their appealing color.

French cookbooks usually suggest tying the peeled asparagus into bundles and boiling them upright, with the tips exposed above the water. There are specialized pots for this that have perforated inserts that can be lowered into the boiling water. Tying asparagus up in bunches is not obligatory, but it can make presentation easier. You can quickly tie up a bundle by grasping a handful of spears with one hand, securing one end of a generous length of string with your thumb, and with the other hand wrapping the string round and round the asparagus. Leave enough string at both ends to tie together into a knot. When cooked, the bunches can easily be snagged with a fork and lifted out of the boiling water, the strings cut, and the asparagus spread out on a towel to cool and drain of all excess moisture. If you tie the asparagus in bundles, leave a spear or two loose to cook along with them to serve as testers.

Sometimes (if cooking a small quantity, for example), it is more practical to steam asparagus: cooked this way it takes on little additional moisture and doesn't need careful draining—both virtues if it is to be served as a salad.

If the asparagus is going to be sautéed, it should be trimmed and then sliced diagonally, about ¼ inch thick. It will cook in just a few minutes over high heat. (Usually smaller, tender asparagus that doesn't have to be peeled is cooked this way.)

Asparagus is delicious brushed with olive oil, seasoned, and grilled over a wood or charcoal fire, and turned as it browns and caramelizes where it is in contact with the grill. At the restaurant we usually peel it and parboil it for a minute or so before grilling, although it can be grilled slowly over a low fire without any preliminary cooking—provided you keep close watch.

It takes a fair amount of space in a garden to produce a small asparagus harvest—several square feet for just one plant—and so it may be an impractical vegetable for many home gardeners. Grown from seed, it takes three or four years before it starts producing sufficiently. However, you can also buy mature roots (called crowns), plant them in the fall, and start harvesting a few spears the next spring. In many places asparagus has gone wild, and can be gathered in the spring along stream banks and in areas protected from the harshest weather. In Sicily, cooks make a delicious frittata with the tender shoots of slightly bitter wild asparagus.

GRILLED ASPARAGUS

Prepare a charcoal or wood fire in the grill about an hour before supper. The fire should be medium hot for grilling asparagus.

Snap off the tough bottom ends of the asparagus spears. Peel the spears and parboil them in salted boiling water for about 1 minute, until they are just slightly tender. Spread them out to drain thoroughly and cool to room temperature. Brush the asparagus with olive oil, salt lightly, and grill for about 6 minutes over medium heat, turning often to brown evenly. When done, arrange the asparagus on a warm platter, and season with more olive oil, pepper, and lemon juice.

Note: Alternatively, dress the asparagus with shallot vinaigrette and garnish with shavings of Parmesan cheese and slices of grilled pancetta. Or garnish with sieved hard-cooked eggs and, if you wish, a salt-packed anchovy or two, rinsed and boned and cut in tiny slivers.

GRILLED ASPARAGUS WITH BLOOD ORANGES AND TAPENADE TOAST

1 shallot	*Salt and pepper*
3 blood oranges	*1½ pounds fat asparagus*
1½ teaspoons balsamic vinegar	*(25 to 30 spears)*
½ teaspoon red wine vinegar	*4 slices country-style bread*
Extra-virgin olive oil	*Tapenade (page 317)*

Peel and chop the shallot fine and macerate for 30 minutes in the juice of ½ orange and the balsamic and red wine vinegars. Whisk in the olive oil to taste to make a vinaigrette, and season with salt and pepper. Peel just the zest from one of the oranges, chop it very fine, and add it to the vinaigrette.

Cut away all the rind and pith from all the oranges and slice them, crosswise, into thin rounds. Parboil and grill the asparagus (see above recipe). At the same time, grill the bread. When the bread is toasted, cut the slices into thirds and spread with tapenade. Arrange the asparagus on a platter with the orange slices on top. Drizzle the vinaigrette over and garnish with the tapenade toast.

Serves 4.

ASPARAGUS WITH CRISPY GINGERROOT

Snap the ends off some asparagus. If the stalks are fat, peel them. Slice them diagonally ¼ inch thick, leaving the tips whole.

Peel a knob of ginger and slice it ⅛ inch thick, and then into julienne. Over high heat, sauté the ginger for about 1 minute in clarified butter, until it is crisp and golden brown. Add the asparagus and sauté for about 2 minutes more, or until tender. Drain off any excess butter, season with salt and pepper, and serve.

ASPARAGUS AND SPRING ONIONS WITH BUCKWHEAT LINGUINE

1 pound asparagus	*3 cloves garlic*
2 spring bulb onions	*1 cup Vegetable Stock (page 321)*
(about ½ pound)	*1 tablespoon chopped chervil*
1 teaspoon olive oil	*plus 20 sprigs chervil for*
3 tablespoons unsalted butter	*garnish*
Salt and pepper	*½ lemon*
1 pound buckwheat linguine	*½ pound ricotta salata cheese*

Snap off the ends of the asparagus and peel if the stalks are thick. Slice diagonally ¼ inch thick, leaving the tips whole. Trim and peel the spring onions and slice them very thin. Peel and finely chop the garlic. Bring a pot of salted water to a boil for the pasta.

In a pan big enough for the vegetables to be sautéed, not steamed, heat the olive oil and 1 tablespoon of the butter. Add the asparagus and the spring onions, season with salt and pepper, and sauté over high heat for a few minutes, until the vegetables are slightly browned and caramelized. Cook the linguine.

When the vegetables are nearly done, add the garlic and cook 1 minute more. When the vegetables are ready, pour in the vegetable stock to deglaze the pan; add the rest of the butter off the heat, swirling the pan to thicken the sauce. Add the chopped chervil and a squeeze of lemon. Taste for salt, pepper, and lemon juice, and adjust if necessary. Drain the linguine, add to the vegetables, and toss. Serve immediately on warm plates, garnished with crumbled ricotta salata and the chervil sprigs.

Serves 4 to 6.

ASPARAGUS SOUP

2 pounds green asparagus	2 white onions
6 cups Vegetable Stock (page 321) or light chicken stock or water	1 leek
	2 red potatoes
	2 tablespoons olive oil
Bouquet garni: thyme sprigs, parsley stems, bay leaf	Parsley
	Crème fraîche

Cut or snap off the rough, rooty ends of the asparagus and simmer the asparagus in the stock with the bouquet garni for 30 minutes or so.

In a deep soup pot, stew the onions, leek, and potatoes, peeled and diced, in the olive oil and a little water. When the vegetables are very soft, strain the stock into the pot and bring to a simmer.

Chop the asparagus roughly, reserving the tips to garnish the finished soup, and add to the soup pot. Let the soup simmer for about 5 minutes, until the asparagus is just tender. Do not overcook, or you will lose freshness and color.

Purée the soup in a blender and pass through a fine sieve into a bowl. You can set the bowl in ice to cool the soup rapidly, which will help it keep a nice color. The soup should be a dense but smooth liquid. To get the right consistency, first put the vegetables with a little liquid into the blender, purée, and then thin with as much of the rest of the liquid as you need. Cut the asparagus tips in half lenthwise and parboil for 1 to 2 minutes. Serve the soup chilled or reheated to just below a boil, garnished with the asparagus tips, chopped parsley, and crème fraîche.

Serves 6 to 8.

WHITE ASPARAGUS WITH MUSTARD MAYONNAISE

Peel and trim some white asparagus. Tie the asparagus in bundles and cook in salted boiling water for at least 15 minutes, until very soft. Take the asparagus out of the water, cut off the string, and arrange the spears in a folded napkin.

While the asparagus is cooking, finely chop some shallot and mix it in a small bowl with vinegar, mustard, an egg yolk, and salt. Let it sit for a few minutes and whisk in some light olive oil to make a mayonnaise. Serve the warm asparagus with the mayonnaise.

AVOCADOS &

Season: Year-round

Botanically, the avocado is a fruit, but avocados, like tomatoes, are eaten primarily as a vegetable. (In Brazil avocados are mashed with sugar and eaten as a dessert.) The avocado is a rather bizarre fruit, since instead of getting sweeter as it ripens, it develops a very high fat content. Avocados are also unusual among fruits in being able to ripen only when they are off the tree.

At Chez Panisse, we serve avocados mainly in the spring and summer, and almost always in salads: with smoked fish, with grapefruit, with mangoes—dressed with vinaigrette flavored sometimes with lime and cilantro and sometimes with tomato, balsamic vinegar, red onions, and basil. We make salsas with cubes of avocado flesh in them. We use avocado instead of mayonnaise as the base for our version of green goddess dressing. And, occasionally, we serve guacamole.

Avocados are native to the tropics of Central America. There are hundreds of varieties of three major types: West Indian, Mexican, and Guatemalan. Most of the varieties grown commercially in California are of Mexican and Guatemalan origin, either Hass, the main spring and summer crop, or Fuerte, in the fall and winter. The former becomes very dark-skinned, almost black, as it matures, and its skin has the pebbly, lizardlike texture that must have given rise to the avocado's now largely obsolete English name, the alligator pear. Fuerte avocados are greener and shaped more like real pears, and have a thinner, smoother skin. Almost all the avocados we serve are Hass avocados. As with so many fruits and vegetables, there can be considerable variation in quality even within a single variety, but a Hass avocado is usually an ideal avocado: it ripens evenly, it peels easily, its pit is easy to remove, and it has a rich, nutty taste. If you live where avocados are grown, by all means try other varieties; some have fine flavor.

When ripe, avocados are easily bruised, so at the market try to buy them underripe, when they are still quite firm. Store them at room temperature; never refrigerate them. They will ripen quickly at home, usually within a few days (you can accelerate their ripening by leaving them in a paper bag), and you can be sure they will be relatively unhandled and unblemished when you cut into them. Ripe avocados yield to the gentle pressure of your thumb. Another way of testing ripeness is to insert a toothpick: if you can easily pierce the flesh through to the pit, it is soft and ripe.

Once the golden-green flesh is exposed to air, it starts to turn brown. It is not true that leaving the pit in contact with the flesh will retard this process. However, adding vinegar or citrus juice will. In general, serve avocados as soon as possible after you cut into them, dressed right away with vinaigrette or with lemon or lime juice squeezed over them.

Avocado, Grapefruit, and Curly Endive Salad with Citrus Dressing

6 small heads curly endive	1 orange
1 large shallot	Salt
2 tablespoons white wine or Champagne vinegar	2 grapefruit
	¾ cup extra-virgin olive oil
1 lemon	3 avocados

Wash and spin dry the curly endive. For this salad, use only the blanched hearts and save the green leaves for cooking greens.

Peel the shallot and dice it fine. Let it macerate with the vinegar, 1 tablespoon each of lemon juice and orange juice, and a pinch of salt.

Cut away the grapefruit peel, all the pith below, and the membrane around the grapefruit flesh. Then cut the sections free, carefully slicing along the membranes. Peel a little lemon and orange zest and finely chop enough to make about ¼ teaspoon of each.

When you are ready to assemble the salad, whisk the olive oil into the shallot mixture. Add the orange and lemon zest and taste. Add more olive oil or lemon juice if necessary. Cut the avocados in half lengthwise. Remove the pits. Using a sharp knife, cut the avocados into lengthwise slices about the same size as the grapefruit sections, keeping the skin on. Scoop out the slices with a large spoon. Toss the curly endive and grapefruit sections in a bowl with about two thirds of the dressing. Taste the salad and add more salt if necessary. Arrange on a platter or individual dishes. Distribute the avocado slices alongside the endive and grapefruit, season them with a pinch of salt, and drizzle the rest of the dressing over them.

Serves 6.

GREEN GODDESS DRESSING

We have adopted this euphonious appellation for a salad dressing we often make, even though our version doesn't much resemble the authentically 1950s, sweetish, mayonnaise-based dressing of the same name.

1 shallot	*½ cup cream*
1 clove garlic	*4 tablespoons chopped Italian*
2 to 3 tablespoons white wine	*parsley*
vinegar	*3 tablespoons chopped tarragon*
½ lemon	*2 tablespoons chopped cilantro*
½ lime	*1 tablespoon chopped basil*
1 or 2 salt-packed anchovies	*1 teaspoon chopped savory*
½ avocado	*Salt and pepper*
¾ cup olive oil	

Peel and chop fine the shallot and garlic and macerate in 2 to 3 tablespoons of white wine vinegar, a big squeeze of lemon, and a smaller one of lime. Add the anchovy, rinsed, boned, and very finely chopped or mashed, and the flesh of the avocado. Mash together with a fork. Whisking or stirring with a wooden spoon, gradually incorporate the olive oil and cream—as if you were making a thin mayonnaise. Use about two parts olive oil to one part cream; the avocado will smoothly absorb up to ¾ cup of olive oil and nearly ½ cup of cream. Flavor with the herbs. Taste and adjust the seasoning to your taste; the dressing probably will need salt and pepper.

Makes about 2 cups.

AVOCADO AND SMOKED TROUT SALAD

2 shallots
Juice of ½ lemon
Salt and pepper
¼ to ½ cup extra-virgin
    olive oil

1 small head curly endive or
    2 Belgian endives
1 firm, ripe avocado
1 smoked trout (about ½ pound)
A few sprigs chervil

Peel and chop the shallots fine. Put in a small bowl with just enough lemon juice to cover, and let them macerate for 1 hour. Season with salt and pepper and stir in olive oil to taste, about double the amount of shallots and lemon juice. The sweetness of the shallots and the sharpness of the lemon juice will determine the amount of olive oil.

Wash and dry the curly endive or trim the Belgian endive and separate the leaves. Cut the avocado in half, remove the pit and skin, cut into thin slices, and arrange on a serving plate, leaving room for the trout and endive.

Fillet the trout, making sure to remove all the pin bones. Gently pull the trout into pieces about ¾ inch long. Toss the trout and the curly endive or Belgian endive with the lemon and shallot dressing, reserving about a tablespoon. Drizzle the remaining dressing over the avocado and season with salt and pepper. Arrange the endive and trout next to the avocado and serve garnished with chervil sprigs.

Serves 4.

GUACAMOLE

4 ripe avocados
2 limes
3 green onions (scallions)

1 bunch cilantro
Salt
Optional: 1 jalapeño pepper

Cut the avocados in half and remove the pits. Scoop out the flesh with a soup spoon into a bowl and mash it with a fork. Juice the limes and chop fine the green onions. Chop 1 or 2 handfuls of cilantro leaves. Mix in the chopped onion and cilantro and about half the lime juice with the avocado. Season to taste with salt and more lime juice and cilantro. For a spicy guacamole, add a jalapeño pepper, seeded and finely diced.

Makes about 2 cups.

Open-face Avocado Sandwiches

Toast some good bread. Cut slices of ripe avocado (and tomato, if you like) and arrange them on the toast. Spoon over the avocado a vinai-grette made with shallots, balsamic vinegar, and olive oil. Garnish with cilantro and serve.

Salsa Cruda

Peel the papery outer skin off some tomatillos and reduce them to a purée in a mortar or a food processor. Add cubed avocado flesh, a little onion chopped into small dice, and a splash of water, if needed, to keep the consistency on the thin side. Season to taste with salt, a little fresh serrano chili pepper diced very fine, and cilantro leaves, if you wish. An excellent sauce with grilled vegetables, squash tamales, corn tortillas, or vegetable fritters.

BASIL 🌿
See Herbs (page 167)

BEANS &

In one form or another, beans are on our menus most of the year. The first tiny green beans of early summer are a revelation: tender and sweet, they exemplify the season. Alone or combined with some basil and with other vegetables, such as tomatoes, they form the backbone of many summer menus. Later in the summer, fresh shell beans start to appear, adding density and richness to the bean repertoire. When the last fresh tomato is only a distant memory, we have dry beans for wintertime comfort. Only in the spring, amidst the rush of fresh asparagus and peas, are we content to cook without beans.

There exist, in fact, thousands of named varieties of New World beans. Blue Lake snap beans, Roc d'Or yellow wax beans, pale green French flageolets, red kidney beans, fresh purple-streaked Borlotto shell beans, dry cannellini beans, and Black Turtle beans—all are members of one plant species: *Phaseolus vulgaris.* Lima beans, *P. lunatus,* and runner beans, *P. coccineus,* are closely related. (Lentils and fava beans are Old World vegetables, like the other common legumes, peas and chickpeas; all of these have their own sections in this book.) The only non-*Phaseolus* legume in this section is the black-eyed pea, *Vigna unguiculata,* which is not a pea but an Asian bean (as are soybeans and mung beans, which we don't use and haven't included). We use black-eyed peas the same ways we use the New World shelling beans—both fresh and dried. New World bean varieties are all descended from plants native to Central and South America that were staples in the diets of Native Americans. Besides being rich in protein and carbohydrates, beans also increase soil fertility, since the roots of the plants fix nitrogen found in the air.

Beans can be eaten whole, pods and all; shelled and eaten fresh; and shelled and eaten dried. All beans will go through these stages of edibility if left on the plant, but plant breeders have selected most of the commonly grown varieties for excellence at just a single stage.

GREEN BEANS 🍃

Season: Early summer through fall

Green beans come in yellow and purple as well as basic green. What these beans have in common is that they are harvested while the pod is still very tender and the seeds inside quite immature. Green beans are sometimes still called string beans, although most varieties grown today do not have tough strings along the margins of the pods that need to be pulled off. The tiniest French green beans (usually called haricots verts) may be no longer than two or three inches and as slender as matchsticks. Any that are left to grow to five or six inches will be tough and stringy. But Blue Lake and Kentucky Wonder beans are still tender and sweet at this larger size. Italian romano beans have broad, flat pods (they are also called flat beans), and can be delicious even when six to eight inches long. Yellow wax beans and purple beans are best eaten before their full color has developed, when they are still tinged with green.

As you would expect of plants that originated in the tropics, beans require a reasonably warm growing season. The first green beans appear in early summer, two months or so after the last frost. With successive plantings, they are often available until the first frost in the fall. Even without frost, production gradually dwindles with the coming of cold weather.

When buying edible pod beans, look for ones that are bright and that snap readily when you bend them. Broken open, the pods should show just a hint of the tiny seeds inside. Avoid beans that are dull or soft or limp. Since most modern varieties are relatively stringless, the presence of tough strings often means the entire pod will be tough. Varieties we like to use at the restaurant include Blue Lake, Roc d'Or, Provider, Slankette, and several kinds of French haricots verts, or fillet beans. To enjoy the fresh, sweet character of the beans, use them as soon as possible.

To prepare beans for cooking, check to see if they are stringy. If they are, snap off the top and tail of each bean, pulling down the side to peel away the strings. If not, the tops and tails can be cut off by lining up several beans to do at once. Tiny beans should be cooked whole, but larger

ones cook better and faster cut up into uniform lengths—a bias cut often looks best—or cut lengthwise into halves or quarters, a process called frenching, which you can do rather laboriously with a very sharp paring knife or more quickly with one of the gadgets sold for this purpose.

Green beans should be cooked very quickly. Drop them into a large quantity of salted boiling water, and after a few minutes test one for doneness. It should be tender but not soft. When the beans are done, drain them and serve right away with a little butter or olive oil. If you are parboiling the beans to use later, drain and spread them out to cool in a single layer on a towel or a lined baking sheet. Some cookbooks recommend that you "refresh" the beans by plunging them into ice water to cool, but treated this way they lose flavor. Beans can be parboiled several hours in advance of reheating, but don't keep them overnight: they will develop off flavors.

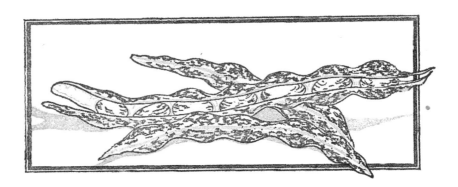

FRESH SHELL BEANS

Season: Midsummer through fall

Although fresh shell beans show up in the market by midsummer, the season really gets going at summer's end. Then there is an abundance of all varieties, but we make the greatest use of the ones called French horticultural beans. Varieties like the Italian Borlotto and the American heirloom varieties Cranberry and Low's Champion all have five- or six-inch-long ivory-colored pods streaked with red. The beans inside echo the colors of the pods, shading from green to cream, variously marked with red. Dragon Tongue beans are a flat yellow variety streaked with purple, which are also eaten whole when young, pods and all.

We also look for the long, slender pods of fresh green flageolets and black-eyed peas, and the shorter, thick pods of the white Italian cannellini types. The Chinos in San Diego grow flageolets, black-eyed peas, Cranberry beans, and cannellini and lima beans, but the ones we are most eager for are the Christmas limas. Each five- or six-inch pod contains three or four delicious giant beans, pale green flecked with brilliant red.

All these beans are at their best when fully mature but not yet dry. The condition of the pods is the surest indicator of quality. They should be fully colored and feel tough and leathery. They should also be lumpy, demonstrating that the beans within are plump and ready. Shell bean pods that are withered or discolored will not be from a recent harvest and should be avoided, along with pods that show any signs of decay.

Fresh shell beans in their pods can be stored in the refrigerator for several days. Good air circulation is important to prevent mold. Once shelled, the beans should be covered or put in a plastic bag and refrigerated no longer than overnight. Cooked beans will keep for a day or so in the refrigerator, submerged in their cooking liquid.

Fresh shelled flageolets and black eyed peas are a real luxury, because the pods are tough and the small beans are held tightly inside. But the reward is definitely worth the effort. Much easier and quicker to shell are any of the horticultural beans or the large white cannellinis.

Fresh shell beans are usually precooked before being combined with other ingredients. At the restaurant, we often simmer the beans in water to which we add half an onion, a few sprigs of thyme, and a bay leaf. Pay close attention to the cooking time; fresh beans cook much more quickly than dried ones. Test them often and remove them from the heat just as they are starting to become tender. If you let them cool slowly in the cooking liquid they will become completely tender and more flavorful.

DRIED BEANS 🫘

Season: Year-round

Dried beans are one of the mainstays of our winter menus. Imagine a winter without a savory cassoulet, or a smooth black bean soup, or pasta e fagiole. With so many different varieties, dried beans never have to be boring. The big, white cannellinis are creamy and versatile, and add much flavor to antipasto salads, bean gratins, and soups, as do the black beans and scarlet runners, the brown-speckled Jacob's Cattle, and the black-spotted Appaloosa beans. Although they call for specific varieties of dried beans, the recipes that follow can successfully be made using any of them, adjusting for different cooking times.

The first dried shell beans appear in early fall. They are almost always shelled, but if not, look for pods that are completely dry and show no signs of mold or mildew. If the beans within are not completely dried, use them right away, as they will mold quickly in storage. Otherwise, store shelled beans in a cool, dry place. Beans from the most recent crop are best; older beans may require impossibly long cooking and may not cook evenly.

Even fresh dried beans take a relatively long time to rehydrate and tenderize; exactly how long depends not only on how recently they were harvested but also on the type of bean and growing and storage conditions. Dried beans that are soaked (covered with water and refrigerated for six hours to as long as two or three days) cook much more evenly and quickly. A simple approach is to soak the beans the day before you intend to cook them. (This is what is meant when a recipe instructs you to soak the beans "overnight.") Should you forget to soak them, you can cover them with water and bring to a boil, shut off the heat, cover, and let them sit for an hour or two. Then proceed with the recipe. Dried flageolets can be cooked in an hour or so, without any preliminary soaking or boiling.

At the restaurant we usually drain off the water after soaking or parboiling beans, although many authorities advise that you simmer beans in the water they soaked in, so as to preserve nutrients. If you do simmer them in their soaking water, it is probably a good idea to wash the beans before soaking them. In any case, pick over the beans first—being especially careful with small beans like black beans and flageolets—and remove any small stones or lumps of dirt and any discolored or moldy beans. Do not salt simmering dried beans until at least halfway through the cooking, since salt inhibits water penetration, lengthening the cooking time and, depending on the bean, toughens the skin. Care should be taken to thoroughly cool cooked dried beans to room temperature, uncovered, before refrigerating; there is danger of spoilage if the beans are put covered into the refrigerator when they are still warm.

Almost every home gardener grows green beans, but it is also rewarding to grow some of the fresh shell beans, since they are still relatively rare in the market. If you don't have room for a pole bean tepee fashioned from stakes lashed together at the top, many newer varieties of shell beans and green beans produce abundant crops on small, compact bushes. Scarlet runner beans make a striking addition to an edible landscape because of their beautiful vines and brilliant red flowers.

29

PICKLED YELLOW WAX BEANS

Unlike green beans, yellow wax beans retain an appetizing color when pickled. They are delicious by themselves or as part of an aïoli platter.

½ pound yellow wax beans	*2 cups white wine vinegar or*
2 cloves garlic	*apple cider vinegar*
½ teaspoon coriander seed	*1 cup dry white wine*
1 small hot chili	*1¼ cups water*
⅛ teaspoon black peppercorns	*1 tablespoon kosher salt*
1 bay leaf	*2 tablespoons sugar*

Top and tail the beans and put them in a nonreactive container. Peel the garlic cloves and cut them in half. Add the garlic to the beans along with the coriander seed, chili, peppercorns, and bay leaf.

Put the vinegar, white wine, water, salt, and sugar in a saucepan, bring to a boil, and boil for 1 minute. Remove from the heat and pour over the beans. Cool completely at room temperature, cover, and refrigerate. The beans will be ready to eat in 48 hours, but are even better after a week.

GREEN BEAN AND CHERRY TOMATO SALAD

1 pound green beans	*3 tablespoons red wine vinegar*
1 pound cherry tomatoes (Sweet	*Salt and pepper*
100, Sungold, or Green Grape)	*¾ cup extra-virgin olive oil*
1 large shallot	*Optional: basil or other herb*

Top and tail the beans, and parboil them in salted water until tender. Drain and immediately spread them out to cool. (The beans retain more flavor if you avoid shocking them in cold water.) Stem the cherry tomatoes and cut them in half. These steps can be done in advance.

For the vinaigrette, peel and dice the shallot fine and put it in a bowl with the vinegar and salt and pepper. Whisk in the olive oil. Taste and adjust the balance with more vinegar, oil, or salt, as needed. Toss the cherry tomatoes in with the vinaigrette; this can sit for a while. Do not add the green beans until just before serving or they will discolor from the acid in the vinaigrette. For variety, the salad can be garnished with basil or some other fresh herb such as parsley, chervil, or hyssop.

Serves 6.

Note: You can vary this salad by adding cooked fresh shell beans to the mixture of green beans and cherry tomatoes. We sometimes make a more complicated, composed salad, adding boiled lobster. A concentrated reduction is made from the lobster shells, aromatic vegetables, and white wine, and then whisked into a Champagne vinaigrette to dress the beans, lobster, and tomatoes.

SUMMER BEAN RAGOUT WITH CRÈME FRAÎCHE AND SAVORY

*1 pound fresh shell beans
  (Cranberry type, lima,
  butter, etc.)
1 tablespoon olive oil
Salt and pepper*

*1 pound assorted beans (green,
  yellow wax, romano, etc.)
¼ cup crème fraîche
1½ teaspoons fine-chopped
  summer savory*

Shell the beans, and place in a saucepan with enough water to cover them by about an inch. Add the olive oil and 1 teaspoon of salt, bring to a boil, reduce the heat, and simmer until the beans are tender, about 20 minutes. Remove from the heat and transfer the beans and liquid to a shallow bowl to cool. Keep the shell beans in their liquid until ready to use.

While the shell beans are cooking, trim the other beans of their tops and tails and any strings. Parboil them for 4 or 5 minutes in a large pot of boiling salted water, or until they are tender. (They should be cooked separately according to variety in order to control cooking times.) Drain and spread them out to cool at room temperature until ready.

Before serving, drain the shell beans and put them in a large sauté pan with all the other beans. Add about ¾ cup water and cook over high heat until the beans are heated through and the liquid has almost completely evaporated. Add the crème fraîche and savory, and continue cooking until the crème fraîche has reduced a little and the beans are well coated. Season to taste and serve.

Serves 6.

GREEN BEAN AND SHELL BEAN SALAD WITH SUMMER CHANTERELLES

2 cups fresh shell beans or 1 cup dried	*Red wine vinegar*
	2 pounds green beans
1 small onion, peeled	*1 pound summer chanterelles*
1 small carrot, peeled	*Extra-virgin olive oil*
1 bay leaf	*½ pound cherry tomatoes*
Salt and pepper	*Optional: 1 lemon*
2 shallots	*1 handful basil leaves*

Put the shell beans in a saucepan, cover with water, and add the onion, carrot, and bay leaf. Bring to a simmer, and when the beans are just about cooked, season them lightly with salt. Continue to cook the beans until they are tender but not splitting apart. Remove from the heat, let them cool in their cooking liquid, drain them, and discard the onion, carrot, and bay leaf.

While the shell beans are cooking, dice the shallots and just cover with red wine vinegar, in a salad bowl. Top and tail the green beans. (A mixture of two or three varieties is nice: haricots verts, yellow wax beans, Dragon Tongue beans, etc.) Unless they are very small, either french them—cutting them in halves or quarters lengthwise—or cut them in 2-inch pieces on the bias. Parboil the beans in rapidly boiling salted water until they are just cooked through but not soft. Drain and spread out to cool.

Clean the chanterelles, brushing away loose dirt and trimming the bases of their stalks. Cut them in slices. Heat 2 or 3 tablespoons of olive oil in a sauté pan, add the mushrooms, and cook over medium-high heat for several minutes, until they are beginning to brown. If the pan goes dry, add a splash of water; this will draw more moisture out of the chanterelles. When the chanterelles are lightly browned and tender, pour off and save any juice remaining in the pan.

Whisk the chanterelle juices into the vinegar and shallot mixture, and then whisk in enough olive oil to make about ¾ cup of vinaigrette. Season with salt and pepper. Taste and adjust the seasoning, adding more vinegar if necessary. (Fresh lemon juice will also brighten the flavors.)

To the salad bowl add the shell beans, the fresh beans, the chanterelles, and the cherry tomatoes, sliced in half. Toss everything together, and adjust the seasoning, adding a handful of chopped basil leaves.

Serves 8.

Fresh Shell Bean Gratin

2 to 3 pounds fresh shell beans
    (cannellini, Cranberry,
    Pinto, flageolet, etc.)
Salt
6 tablespoons olive oil
½ onion
4 cloves garlic

1 or 2 sage leaves
Optional: 1 small bunch greens
    (broccoli raab, chard,
    mustard, turnip, etc.)
2 medium tomatoes
½ cup Toasted Bread Crumbs
    (page 319)

Shell the beans. Yield will vary according to variety, but you want to end up with about 3 cups shelled beans. Cook them with just enough water to cover by an inch. (Fresh shell beans absorb very little water.) When they have come to a boil, add salt and 2 tablespoons olive oil, and lower the heat to a simmer. Cook until the beans are tender, about 30 minutes. If you use more than one kind of bean, cook each kind separately, since cooking times will vary. Drain the beans and save their liquid.

While the beans are cooking, dice the onion and cook it in 2 tablespoons olive oil with the garlic cloves, peeled and cut into slivers; the sage leaves, chopped; and some salt. Cook over low heat until soft and translucent. If you wish, cook a small bunch of greens with the onion; add a little of the bean water along with them, if you do. When the onion is cooked, add the tomatoes, roughly chopped, raise the heat, and cook for a minute or two more.

Combine the beans in a gratin dish with the onions, tomatoes, and greens. Add enough bean water to almost cover. Taste, correct the seasoning, and pour the rest of the olive oil over the gratin. (You can prepare the gratin to this point in advance, even the day before, and refrigerate it.) To finish the gratin, cover the top with the toasted bread crumbs, and bake in a preheated 350°F. oven for 45 minutes. Check it occasionally and moisten with more bean water if the gratin seems to be drying out too much.

Serves 4 to 6.

Note: A gratin of dried shell beans can be made in a similar manner. In a gratin dish, combine cooked beans, tomato, mirepoix, garlic, and chopped thyme and parsley. Season well and moisten with bean liquid or stock. Cover with bread crumbs, drizzle with olive oil, and bake. Check the gratin periodically during the baking; dry beans tend to require more liquid than fresh beans.

Soupe au Pistou

Soupe au pistou is the Provençal version of minestrone. The colorful garlic-basil purée called pesto in Italy is known as pistou in Provence. To give this soup an especially Provençal flavor, add a leftover roast lamb bone to the broth.

1 pound (1 cup shelled) fresh shell beans (Cranberry, Borlotto, Dragon Tongue, etc.)	*2 tomatoes* *Salt and pepper* *¼ pound orzo, conchiglie, or orrechiette pasta*
1 onion	
Bouquet garni: Thyme, parsley stems, cracked peppercorns, bay leaf	PISTOU
	6 cloves garlic
1 pound green beans	*2 cups basil leaves*
2 green zucchini	*Reggiano Parmesan cheese*
2 yellow summer squash	*Extra-virgin olive oil*

Shell the beans and cook them for about 30 minutes in 2 quarts salted water with the onion, cut in quarters, and the bouquet garni.

While the beans are cooking, cut the green beans, zucchini, and yellow squash into chunks roughly the size of the tip of your little finger, so each spoonful of soup will have a variety of different vegetables. Peel, seed, and chop the tomatoes. Strain any juice from the seeds through a sieve into the bean broth.

When the shell beans are tender, drain them, reserving the liquid. Remove the bouquet garni and the onion quarters and discard. Bring the bean broth back to a boil and lower the heat. Season with salt. Add the green beans to the broth, and when it has returned to a simmer, add the zucchini and yellow squash. When the broth returns to a simmer again, add the shell beans and diced tomatoes and let it all cook together gently for 20 minutes. Add the pasta after 10 minutes. The broth should be busy with vegetables, but add some more liquid if they get too crowded.

To make the pistou, pound the garlic cloves to a purée in a mortar, add all the basil leaves, roughly chopped, and keep pounding and working until you obtain a paste. Add a small handful of grated Parmesan and thin out with some olive oil.

When the pasta is cooked, taste the soup and adjust the seasoning. Let the soup sit for an hour and reheat it before serving. Bring the pistou to the table in its mortar. Serve the soup with a generous spoonful of pistou in each bowl and pass a bowl with more grated Parmesan.

Serves 6.

FRESH SHELL BEAN PURÉE ON GRILLED BREAD

Late-season beans, full-flavored and starchy, are best for this purée; quantities will vary depending on the variety of bean. The results will always be delicious if you are generous with the best olive oil you can afford.

*1 pound fresh shell beans
(scarlet runner, cannellini,
Cranberry, Pinto, flageolet,
etc.)
2 or 3 cloves garlic*

*Salt and pepper
A few sprigs savory or rosemary
¼ to ½ cup extra-virgin olive
oil
Grilled country-style bread*

Shell the beans and discard the pods. In a saucepan, cook the beans in lightly salted water until they are nearly falling apart. Drain them of all but a cup of their liquid. To the beans in the saucepan, add the garlic, peeled and sliced; a little salt; the savory or rosemary; and about ¼ cup olive oil. Cook and stir over low heat until the beans soften and begin to form a paste. Add more water if necessary. This will take from 10 to 30 minutes. Taste during the cooking and remove the herb sprigs when the beans have taken on enough flavor. (This is especially important with rosemary, which can become overpowering.) The garlic will soften and you can mash it into the beans; purée the beans and garlic in a food processor for a more uniform texture. Finish the purée with as much olive oil as your conscience allows and adjust the seasoning.

Serve the purée on grilled country-style or levain bread toast that has been oiled and rubbed with a little garlic.

Makes about 2 cups purée.

Note: A favorite version of this purée is made with fresh fava beans (see page 142). Like this recipe, it is often served on grilled bread—as an hors d'oeuvre, as an accompaniment to a green salad, or as part of an antipasto plate with vegetable salads and prosciutto.

Fresh Black-eyed Peas and Rice

Hoppin' John is what this dish is called in the American South.

1 cup long-grain white rice	*2 pounds (about 2 cups shelled)*
2¼ cups water	*fresh black-eyed peas*
Salt and pepper	*Unsalted butter*
	A few sprigs savory

Put the rice in a saucepan with the water and bring to a boil in the usual manner of cooking rice. Salt the water and add the black-eyed peas. Cover and simmer for 20 minutes, until the rice is just cooked; the peas will be tender as well. Stir in a little butter and some freshly chopped savory leaves. Taste for salt; add a few grinds of pepper. This is very good served with roast chicken and the roasting juices from the bird.

Serves 4.

Fresh Black-eyed Peas with Pancetta and Caramelized Onions

Cut pancetta into lardons and brown in a sauté pan. Remove the pancetta and pour off most of the rendered fat. Slowly sauté thinly sliced sweet summer onions in the pan, stirring frequently, until they are well browned and caramelized. Remove the onions and set aside.

Sauté some chopped garlic in the pan (add a little rendered fat if needed) until it just sizzles, then deglaze the pan with chicken stock. Add shelled black-eyed peas, a few sprigs of fresh thyme, and enough additional chicken stock to just cover the peas. Cover and simmer gently until the peas are tender, about 15 to 20 minutes.

Just before serving, add the pancetta and caramelized onions and a generous grinding of pepper. Taste for salt and correct the seasoning. Serve with Corn Bread (page 122).

BLACK BEAN AND ROASTED TOMATILLO SOUP

2 cups dried black beans	*½ bunch cilantro*
4 tomatillos	*½ jalapeño pepper*
Olive oil	*3 cloves garlic, peeled*
Salt and pepper	*1½ onions*

Soak the beans overnight. When you are ready to cook, drain them. Preheat the oven to 350°F.

Peel the dry skin off the tomatillos, cut them in quarters, and toss lightly with olive oil and salt and pepper. Place them in a heavy-bottomed, ovenproof dish just big enough to hold them in a single layer, and roast for 15 minutes in the oven, until they are soft. While they are roasting, pluck the cilantro sprigs off their stems and reserve to garnish the finished soup. Wrap the cilantro stems, the jalapeño pepper, and the garlic in a cheesecloth sack.

Slice the onions very thin; in a soup pot, cook them in olive oil, seasoned with salt and pepper, until they are soft and translucent. Add the drained beans, 3 quarts water, and the cheesecloth sack. Bring the pot to a boil, then simmer over medium heat, skimming off any foam that rises to the surface.

When the tomatillos are done, put them through a food mill or purée them in a blender until smooth. Continue to simmer the beans until they are very tender; this takes somewhere between 1½ and 3 hours, depending on all the bean variables—their variety, age, dryness, etc. When they are done, remove the cheesecloth bag of seasonings and squeeze the liquid out of it back into the soup. Pass the soup through a food mill or purée it in a blender in small batches until very smooth. It may need to be thinned out a little. Reheat the soup, adding the roasted tomatillo purée to taste, and seasoning with salt and pepper. Serve garnished with the reserved sprigs of cilantro.

Serves 8.

Note: Tomatillos are closely related to the Cape gooseberry, and not, as one might assume, to the tomato. The firm green fruits are covered with papery outer skins. The tomatillo is native to Mexico, where it is prized for its sharp, clean taste and much used in sauces, soups, and stews.

Beans Cooked in the Fireplace

In Tuscany, where there is a tradition of cooking on the open hearth, beans are cooked in a glass flask. That famous dish inspired us to use our fireplace for bean cookery.

3 cups dried Borlotto beans (or other dried beans)	*2 teaspoons salt*
1 large yellow onion	*1 teaspoon pepper*
1 medium carrot	*1 bay leaf*
1 slice smoked bacon	*5 or 6 sprigs thyme*
2 tablespoons duck or goose fat, or olive oil	*A few leaves of sage or rosemary*
1 large ripe tomato or several small canned tomatoes	*6 cups chicken stock*
	Parsley
	3 cloves garlic

Soak the beans overnight in the refrigerator. Peel and finely dice the onion and the carrot. Dice the slice of bacon very fine (rind removed).

In a saucepan, cook the vegetables and the bacon slowly in the fat or oil until soft but not browned, about 10 minutes. Peel, seed, and dice the tomato. Add the tomato to the vegetables and bacon and cook for 3 or 4 minutes more. Drain the beans and add them to the saucepan along with the salt, pepper, bay leaf, herbs, and chicken stock. Bring to the boil, shut off the heat, and transfer to a deep ovenproof gratin dish or tureen.

Place the tureen in the fireplace, uncovered, near the coals so as to effect the slightest possible simmer in the tureen. Cook until the beans are soft and creamy but not falling apart, about 3 hours. Stir the pot occasionally to ensure even cooking. Cover the pot about halfway through the cooking to help keep the beans moist, but leave the lid ajar to allow smoke from the fire to flavor them. Check the pot from time to time, and if the contents have begun to go dry, add a little more liquid as needed.

Finely chop enough parsley to make about ¼ cup. Peel and chop the garlic cloves and chop again together with the parsley. When the beans have finished cooking, remove the tureen from the fireplace and stir in the garlic and parsley. Cover and let the pot stand in a warm spot for 10 minutes before serving.

Serves 8 to 10.

Tuscan Bean and Farro Soup

2 cups dried cannellini or
   kidney beans
1 yellow onion
1 small leek
1 small carrot
3 cloves garlic
¼ cup olive oil
2 medium tomatoes
1 sprig thyme
6 sage leaves

1 bay leaf
1 pinch red pepper flakes
1 small piece prosciutto or
   smoked bacon
6 cups chicken stock
Salt and pepper
1 cup farro (see page 321)
2 cups water
Extra-virgin olive oil

Soak the beans overnight. The next day, peel and dice the onion, the white part of the leek, the carrot, and the garlic. Stew the diced vegetables in the olive oil in a nonreactive pot until the vegetables are translucent. Peel and seed the tomatoes. Drain the beans and add them to the pot. Add the tomatoes, herbs, pepper flakes, prosciutto or bacon and stew for 5 minutes or so.

Add the stock, bring the soup to a boil, and lower the heat to a slow simmer. Partially cover the soup and cook for about 1¼ hours, stirring occasionally. Add 2 to 3 teaspoons salt after about an hour.

While the beans are cooking, put the farro and 2 cups salted water in a saucepan. Cook at a simmer, covered, until the grains are soft and tender but not falling apart, about 45 minutes. Drain. When the beans are cooked, stir in the farro. Simmer for another 10 minutes; be careful not to overcook. Serve the soup with extra-virgin olive oil drizzled on top and a few grinds of pepper.

Serves 8.

Cannellini Beans and Wilted Greens

This makes an excellent side dish with roasted or grilled poultry, and it is also a fine sauce for a sturdy pasta, such as taccozette or penne. When the beans are tender, roughly mash about half of them, to thicken the sauce, and then stir in the cooked pasta. Add a little more bean liquid if the mixture is too thick.

2 cups dried cannellini beans
Bouquet garni: celery, thyme, parsley, bay leaf
1 onion
1 carrot
6 cups water or chicken stock
Salt and pepper

1 large bunch chard, kale, spinach, mustard greens, or turnip greens (about 1 pound)
6 cloves garlic
5 to 6 tablespoons olive oil
1 tablespoon chopped rosemary leaves
Extra-virgin olive oil

Soak the beans overnight. The next day drain them and put them into a heavy-bottomed pot with the bouquet garni. Add the onion and carrot, peeled. Cover with water or stock and bring to a boil. Reduce to a simmer, skimming off any foam that forms on the surface. Cook the beans until very tender, from 45 minutes to 2 hours, depending on the age of the beans and how long they were soaked. Salt the beans generously once they start to soften. When fully cooked, remove from the heat.

While the beans are cooking, wash, trim, and chop the greens.

Finely chop the garlic cloves and gently sauté them in the olive oil with the rosemary, about 1 minute. Add the beans and about 1 cup of their cooking liquid, and simmer about 5 minutes, until some of the beans have crumbled apart. Add the greens to the beans, and stew together, uncovered, until the greens are wilted and tender. Add more of the bean liquid, if needed, to keep the vegetables moist and a little soupy. Taste for seasoning and grind in some pepper. Serve with extra-virgin olive oil drizzled over the surface.

Serves 6 to 8.

White Bean and Wilted Greens Soup

1 medium yellow onion	2 medium tomatoes
1 small carrot	6 cups chicken stock
3 cloves garlic	3 teaspoons salt
¼ cup extra-virgin olive oil	1 bunch spicy greens (rocket,
2 bay leaves	mustard greens, or turnip
1½ cups cannellini or Great	greens)(about 1 pound)
Northern beans	Olive oil
A small piece of prosciutto, with	12 sage leaves
rind, or smoked bacon	Reggiano Parmesan cheese

Soak the beans overnight. Peel and cut the onion and carrot into small dice; peel and chop the garlic very fine. In a nonreactive soup pot, stew the vegetables, covered, with the olive oil and a splash of water, until they are translucent. Add the bay leaves, drained beans, and prosciutto or bacon, and cook for a few minutes more. Peel, seed, and chop the tomatoes, add them to the beans, and stew for another minute or so.

Pour in the stock and bring the soup to a boil. Lower the heat to a simmer and cook for about 1¼ hours, stirring occasionally. Add the salt after about an hour. The beans should be fully cooked, soft but not falling apart. Add the greens, washed and cut into 1-inch strips, and simmer, uncovered, for another 20 minutes, stirring occasionally.

Meanwhile, heat some olive oil in a small frying pan. Fry the sage leaves in the oil for a few seconds, a few at a time (more than a few seconds, and they turn black). Drain on a paper towel or absorbent cloth. When the soup is done, ladle it into soup bowls and serve, garnished with a few shavings of the Parmesan and the fried sage leaves.

Serves 6.

BEANS, FAVA (BROAD BEANS) &
See Fava Beans (page 139)

41

BEETS AND BEET GREENS ❧

Season: Summer, fall, and winter

Unlike other root vegetables, the beet (*Beta vulgaris*) has intense, highly saturated, jewel-like colors. Besides the familiar red-purple of the common round beet, there are golden beets the color of carnelian, pink beets, and white beets, and even two-toned beets—the Chioggia variety, for example, which resembles a red-and-white bull's-eye in cross section. Nor are all beets round. There is a dark red beet with an elongated, cylindrical root that is perfect for making uniform slices. There are variations in flavor as well as in size and color: Chioggia beets are quite mild in flavor, while the larger red beets will be much stronger, with a little bitterness to them. What all beets have in common is a remarkably high sugar content for a vegetable: the root of the sugar beet, the white variety grown for processing into pure sugar, is about 8 percent sugar by weight. Beets belong to the goosefoot family, and their closest relatives —chard, spinach, lamb's-quarters—are cultivated for their leafy greens. Not surprising, then, that beet greens can be delicious. They have a thick, fleshy texture and a mild flavor well suited to slow braising (they are not sharp and pungent like turnip greens). Some beet varieties are grown for their edible greens alone.

At Chez Panisse, we like to serve lightly pickled beets as a key element in many a composed salad. Their sweet and earthy flavors complement salty meats like prosciutto and some pâtés, and are good with other root vegetables—especially with celery root or carrots in a lobster salad. In general, we prefer to roast beets until tender, rather than boiling them, because they lose less flavor (and color). Red beets start bleeding their vivid juice as soon as they are cut. Added to a consommé during its clarification, for example, they will dye the liquid a brilliant ruby red. However, the other, less highly pigmented varieties do not bleed and stain, which makes them usable in vegetable ragouts and other mixtures. The tiniest, marble-size beets we steam whole, unpeeled, with their tops still attached.

Beets are most abundant from June through October, usually marketed with their tops still attached. Late, large beets, which can be quite tender if properly grown, are usually topped and stored, and they keep well from late fall throughout the winter. Choose medium-size specimens that have firm, fine-textured flesh. In the spring, beets tend to bolt, and those in the market then can be tough and woody. The best quality beets always have firm, regularly shaped roots. Misshapen roots are often evidence of a struggle to grow or of bolting, and they may be tough and bitter. Tops should be brilliant green, with no wilting or yellowing. For the most tender cooking greens, select small bunches with small, bright green leaves and narrow ribs.

Beets keep best wrapped loosely in the refrigerator. Tops wilt fast, and turn yellow and slimy. If you are not using the beet roots right away, cut off the greens a little above the root and cook them up within a day or two. The roots will keep well for another week or so.

For any recipe, beets must be cooked until they are completely tender but not mushy. If they are even a little undercooked, they may retain an unpleasant bitterness and ruin an otherwise well-made dish.

Home gardeners can easily and quickly grow beets from seed; the vegetables will be ready to eat within two months. The first thinnings from the plot will give you tiny, sweet, tender greens for steaming, and when the first roots start forming, you can pick and steam them whole with their greens. Mature plants have such beautiful foliage you may be reluctant to harvest them at all.

BEET SALADS

Preheat the oven to 400°F. Use a combination of Chioggia, red, and golden beets. Remove their tops, leaving about ½ inch of stem. Wash the beets thoroughly and put them in a baking pan with a splash of water. Cover tightly with foil and bake for 45 minutes to 1 hour, until they can be easily pierced through with a sharp knife. Uncover and allow to cool.

Peel the beets and cut off their tops and the bottom tails. (The red beets will color the other beets unless they are dressed separately.) Cut them in halves or quarters, depending on their size; sprinkle generously with vinegar, and season with salt and pepper. Add a pinch of sugar if the beets are at all bitter. Do not add any oil until the beets have sat for about ½ hour and have had a chance to absorb the flavor of the vinegar. The beets will never be as good if the oil is added too soon. The vinegar brightens and accentuates the beet flavor; the oil should be added sparingly, for balance only. Adjust the seasoning. Prepared this way, the beets are ready to be combined with other ingredients in composed salads and antipasto plates. Here are a few suggestions:

Beets, sherry vinegar, orange zest, and tarragon. A tiny bit of crushed garlic is good too.

Beets, sherry or balsamic vinaigrette, with blood orange sections, and mâche.

Chioggia beets, white wine vinegar, shallots, fennel, and watercress or garden cress.

Beets, white wine vinegar, and chives; with smoked trout or whitefish tossed with crème fraîche and lemon juice.

Beets, balsamic vinegar, shallots, and toasted walnuts.

RED AND GOLDEN BEETS WITH BLOOD ORANGE, ENDIVE, AND WALNUTS

2 pounds red and golden beets
½ cup shelled walnuts
2 blood oranges
2 tablespoons red wine vinegar
2 tablespoons orange juice
Zest of ½ orange
¼ cup olive oil
Salt and pepper
¼ pound Belgian endive

Preheat the oven to 400°F. Trim and wash the beets and roast them, tightly covered, with a splash of water. While the oven is on, put the walnuts on a baking sheet and toast them in the oven for about 5 minutes. With a sharp paring knife, trim off the top and bottom of each orange. Pare off the rest of the peel, making sure to remove all of the pith. Slice the oranges into ¼-inch rounds.

Make a vinaigrette by mixing together the vinegar, orange juice, and the zest, finely chopped, and stirring in the olive oil. Season with salt and pepper. When the beets are cool enough to handle, peel them and slice into rounds. Toss them gently with the vinaigrette, and arrange the beets on a plate with the orange slices and Belgian endive leaves. Drizzle over any vinaigrette remaining in the bowl, and garnish with the toasted walnuts.

Serves 4 to 6.

BEET, CUCUMBER, AND CELERY RELISH

4 medium-size red or golden beets
1 large shallot
2 teaspoons white wine vinegar
Salt and pepper
2 cucumbers

2 stalks celery
1 tablespoon red wine vinegar
4 tablespoons extra-virgin olive oil
1 tablespoon chopped chervil

Preheat the oven to 400°F.

Trim and wash the beets. Put them in a small baking dish with a generous splash of water, cover tightly, and roast in the oven for 30 minutes to an hour, until they are cooked through.

Meanwhile, peel the shallot, cut it into very small dice, and let it macerate in a bowl for 20 minutes in the vinegar with a pinch of salt. Peel and seed the cucumbers, and cut into ⅛-inch dice. Peel the celery, cut into ⅛-inch dice, parboil for about 30 seconds in boiling salted water, and drain.

When the beets are thoroughly cooked, allow them to cool, uncovered. Peel them, trimming off the rest of the stems, and cut them into ⅛-inch dice. Put the beets in a bowl, add the red wine vinegar, 1 tablespoon of the olive oil, and the chervil; season with salt and pepper. (The beets are kept apart until serving to keep them from coloring the other ingredients red. If you use any golden beets, they can be combined and seasoned with the rest of the relish.)

Add the cucumber, celery, the remaining olive oil, and the golden beets (if used) to the bowl with the shallot and vinegar. Taste and adjust for seasoning and consistency, adding more vinegar, salt, and olive oil if needed. To serve the relish, spread the dish to be garnished first with the cucumber mixture and then sprinkle the beets on top. This garnish is particularly delicious and beautiful with grilled salmon.

Makes about 2 cups.

Beet Chutney

Serve this chutney as an accompaniment to Indian-style braised chicken, guinea hen, or lamb with Saffron Rice (page 319), along with Cucumber Raita (page 128); the chutney will heat up your palate and the raita will cool it off.

4 medium red beets
2 tablespoons olive oil
1 tablespoon finely chopped
    fresh ginger
2 teaspoons finely chopped
    serrano peppers
1 tablespoon peanut oil

1 teaspoon salt
½ teaspoon pepper
1 tablespoon finely chopped
    cilantro
1½ teaspoons red wine vinegar
1 teaspoon lime juice
¼ teaspoon cayenne

Preheat the oven to 400°F. Roast the beets in the oven with the olive oil and a splash of water, seasoned with salt and covered tightly. When they are cooked through, after 30 minutes to an hour, cool and peel them, and cut them into ⅛-inch dice.

Combine the beets with the ginger, serrano pepper, peanut oil, salt and pepper, cilantro, red wine vinegar, lime juice, and cayenne. Taste and adjust for salt, vinegar, and spiciness.

Serves 4.

Beet-Green Pasta

Beet greens cooked this way can also be served as a side dish, without the pasta.

½ cup currants
3 to 4 bunches beet greens
    (about 2 pounds)
1 small bunch fresh mint
    (about ⅛ pound)
2 medium red onions

2 to 3 cloves garlic
1 bay leaf
½ cup extra-virgin olive oil
1 pound dried fedelini pasta
Salt and pepper

Cover the currants with boiling water, let them soak for 15 minutes, and drain them. While they are soaking, wash the beet greens, strip the leaves from the stems, and cut the leaves into chiffonade. Chop the stems into 2-inch lengths. Stem the mint (use a smooth-leaved variety, if possible), wash the leaves, and chop them into chiffonade.

Put on a pot of salted water for the pasta. Peel the onions and the garlic and chop them both fine. Sauté them with the bay leaf over medium heat in ¼ cup of the olive oil for about 5 minutes or until they are translucent. Add the beet leaves and stems and the currants and cook 5 minutes more, covered. Meanwhile, when the water has come to a boil, add the pasta. Uncover the beet greens, season with salt and pepper, and add the mint leaves. When the pasta is cooked, drain it and toss well with the sauce, moistening it with a ladle of the pasta water and the rest of the olive oil. Serve immediately.

Serves 4 to 5.

Note: For a slightly more piquant dish, add a splash of vinegar and a pinch of cayenne.

BOK CHOY 🍃
See Cabbage (page 61)

BROCCOLI AND BROCCOLI RAAB ❧

Season: Early spring, fall, and late winter

Broccoli is the dense, unopened budding sprouts of a member of the cabbage family. (*Brocco* means sprout in Italian, and *broccoli* means little sprouts.) Broccoli belongs to the very same species (*Brassica oleracea*) as kohlrabi, cauliflower, brussels sprouts, kale, collard greens, and all the cabbages. There are both short- and long-season varieties of the familiar large green-headed kind, and several varieties so different in appearance as to make them virtually different vegetables: Italian sprouting broccoli produces small, dark green heads over a relatively long period; Romanesco, a non-sprouting long-season variety, produces conical chartreuse-colored heads with spiraling flowerets; and there are several purple-headed varieties that almost look more like cauliflower than broccoli.

Broccoli raab, or *rapini*, on the other hand, is more closely related to the turnip, another *Brassica*, than to broccoli. It is grown for its greens, which rather resemble sprouting broccoli that has started to flower, and it can be used the same way—quickly sautéed with olive oil and a little garlic, for example. It is one of the tastiest and most neglected members of the *Brassica* family, and it has a nutty and slightly bitter flavor all its own.

At the restaurant, broccoli is boiled or steamed and served by itself or as an accompaniment to other vegetables, in salads, pastas, or on pizzas; or it is sautéed as part of a vegetable ragout. Long-cooked broccoli—with garlic, olive oil, and lemon juice (and sometimes enlivened with hot pepper and anchovies)—is a classic garnish for savory dishes.

Commercially, broccoli is available year-round and is surprisingly consistent in appearance. But broccoli is a cool-season vegetable, and is best in fall, late winter, and early spring. In the summer its flower heads become fibrous, and it loses the hardy, vigorous, green appearance—and flavor—of winter and spring broccoli.

In the market, look for broccoli that is firm, with tightly bunched-up flower heads. It should taste clean, bright, and crisp. Avoid broccoli that has started to go limp or lose its deep green color. The appearance of any yellowing or tiny yellow flower buds is a sure sign of age and poor quality. When buying broccoli raab, choose tender fleshy stems with the flower heads still closed.

Larger heads of broccoli need to be trimmed and peeled before cooking. Pick off the leaves along the stem. Use a vegetable peeler or a paring knife to peel off the tough outer skin from the large stem, cutting away as little flesh as possible. Cut the flowerets from the main head just where they join the main stem; they may need to be broken or cut into smaller pieces. The peeled stem can be cut into baton-shaped pieces and cooked along with the flowerets. Sprouting varieties may not need peeling, but can be trimmed to even the stems.

If broccoli needs to be precooked, for a stir-fry, for example, it should be parboiled or steamed. To parboil broccoli, drop it into a large quantity of rapidly boiling salted water. Don't cover the pot. It will be done in a few minutes, when the stems can be easily pierced and the color is still vivid. "Refreshing" the vegetable, by plunging it in ice water, is an effective way to retain maximum color but is deleterious for flavor and texture. Allow broccoli to cool at room temperature and, if possible, avoid refrigerating it after cooking. Broccoli can also be steamed, covered, over simmering water.

Broccoli is easy to grow and will bear over a long season. It should be planted to mature in cool weather. Harvest broccoli, cutting several inches below the head, when the head is firm and tight and has stopped enlarging. Cutting the central head causes the smaller peripheral heads to grow, and sprouts can be harvested from the plant over quite a long period. Do not let any of the sprouts start to bud out and flower, or the plant will stop sprouting.

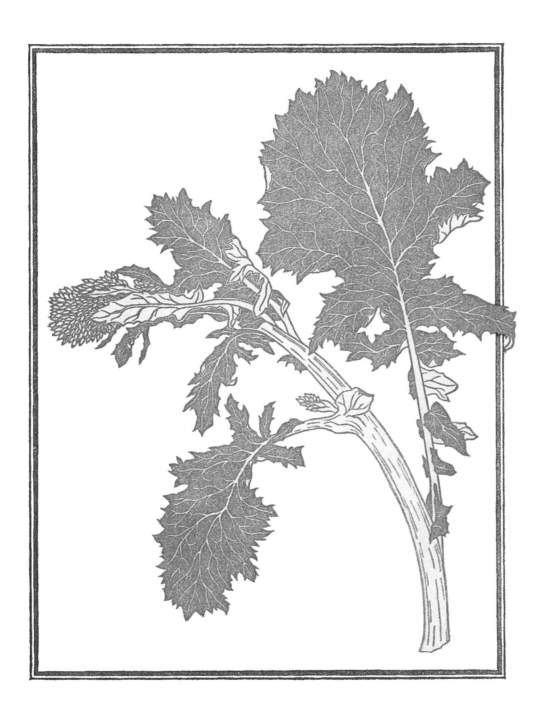

Spicy Broccoli Vegetable Sauté

We serve this Indian-inspired dish with Saffron Rice (page 319) and Cucumber Raita (page 128); it is one of the more interesting all-vegetable dishes we offer. The combination of vegetables may vary, but broccoli is usually one of the main ingredients.

1 pound broccoli	*3 tablespoons clarified butter*
1 pound cauliflower	*(or peanut oil)*
½ pound baby turnips	*2 small dried chili peppers*
1 small onion	*Optional: 4 curry leaves*
2 carrots	*Salt and pepper*
1 small knob fresh ginger	*½ teaspoon cumin seed*
1 serrano pepper	*1½ teaspoons mustard seed*
4 cloves garlic	*1 teaspoon black onion seed*
	A few sprigs cilantro

Tear off any broccoli leaves; trim, peel, and slice the stems; break the flowerets into small pieces. Trim the cauliflower and break it into small flowerets. Trim and slice the baby turnips. Peel and dice the onion fine. Peel and slice the carrots, parboil for about a minute, and drain them. Peel the ginger and cut it into julienne, about 2 teaspoons. Chop the serrano pepper very fine. Peel and chop fine the garlic, about 2 teaspoons.

Heat the clarified butter in a large sauté pan. When it is hot, add the cauliflower and sauté until it has browned slightly. Add the dried chili peppers and the curry leaves, if you have them. Continue to sauté over medium heat, adding in succession the turnip slices, broccoli flowerets, and onion, tossing regularly so everything cooks evenly. Salt and pepper the vegetables and add the cumin seed, mustard seed, and black onion seed. Keep tossing, letting the seeds pop; this removes their bitterness and releases more flavor. Add the carrots, the julienned ginger, and the chopped serrano pepper and garlic. Taste and adjust the seasoning; the dish should be spicy. Garnish with the cilantro sprigs and serve.

Serves 4.

Fedelini with Sprouting Broccoli and Hot Pepper

The sprouting broccoli can be served without the pasta as a side dish or at room temperature, as part of an antipasto plate, or chopped and served on grilled bread.

1½ pounds sprouting broccoli	Salt and pepper
1 medium red onion	2 pinches red pepper flakes
4 cloves garlic	Red wine vinegar
1 pound fedelini (or spaghetti) pasta	1 lemon
Extra-virgin olive oil	⅔ cup Toasted Bread Crumbs (page 319)

Put a large pot of water on to boil. Cut the broccoli into ½-inch flowerets. Peel the onion and slice it very thin. Peel and finely chop the garlic.

Put the pasta on to cook.

Heat 4 tablespoons of extra-virgin olive oil in a large sauté pan over medium heat. When it is hot but not smoking, add the broccoli. Season with salt and pepper, and when the broccoli begins to soften, add the sliced onion and red pepper flakes. Sauté over medium to high heat until the vegetables are brown and tender. The broccoli should still be slightly crunchy and should not taste steamed. Add the garlic and remove from the heat, tossing and stirring so the garlic doesn't burn; if it starts to brown, add a splash of water. Add a few drops each of red wine vinegar and lemon juice. Taste the broccoli; it should be assertively seasoned with a balance of heat and acid. When the pasta is done, drain and add to the broccoli, adding enough olive oil to coat the pasta thoroughly. Toss together and serve, sprinkled with the toasted bread crumbs.

Serves 6.

Note: This dish works equally well with ordinary broccoli or cauliflower, or with such hardy greens as mustard, kale, or escarole substituted for the broccoli. It can also be more aggressively flavored, either by adding several salt-packed anchovies, rinsed, filleted, and chopped, at the same time as the garlic, or by adding 4 ounces thinly sliced pancetta with the onion.

BROCCOLI RAAB PASTA

1 large onion	*Red pepper flakes*
6 to 8 cloves garlic	*Salt*
2 bunches broccoli raab	*½ to ¾ pound penne pasta*
(about 1½ pounds)	*Red wine vinegar*
Extra-virgin olive oil	*Pecorino romano cheese*

Peel and thinly slice the onion. Smash, peel, and thinly slice the garlic. Wash the broccoli raab, removing the heavy stems, and chop the leaves and sprouts coarsely. Put a large pot of water on to boil.

Liberally cover the bottom of a sauté pan with the olive oil and sauté the onion over high heat. When the onion has begun to wilt and brown a little, add the garlic and pepper flakes, to taste, and salt. Toss briefly, then add the broccoli raab and a splash of water. Lower the heat and cook until tender, stirring or tossing frequently. Meanwhile, cook the pasta. Taste the broccoli raab for seasoning and add a generous amount of extra-virgin olive oil and a splash of red wine vinegar. Toss with the freshly cooked and drained pasta, and garnish with grated cheese.

Serves 4.

LONG-COOKED BROCCOLI

2 pounds large-headed broccoli	*Salt and pepper*
8 cloves garlic	*3 salt-packed anchovies*
2 cups water	*1 lemon*
½ cup olive oil	*Pecorino romano or Reggiano*
½ teaspoon red pepper flakes	*Parmesan cheese*

Pick off the coarse leaves from the broccoli stems and peel away their tough skin with a vegetable peeler. Slice the broccoli stems and flowerets crosswise into ⅛-inch-thick slices. Put the slices in a shallow saucepan about 3 inches deep. Peel and slice the garlic and add to the pan with the water, olive oil, and red pepper flakes. Season with salt and pepper.

Bring to a boil, cover, and simmer for 50 to 60 minutes, until the broccoli is tender and beginning to crumble, and the liquid is nearly evaporated. If the pot goes dry before the cooking time is up, add a little more water.

Rinse, fillet, and roughly chop the anchovies. When the broccoli is done, add the anchovies, squeeze the lemon over, and toss everything together well. Serve on a warm platter and garnish at the table with a grating of the cheese.

Serves 4.

Pizza with Broccoli Raab, Roasted Onion, and Olives

1 medium yellow onion
Salt and pepper
Olive oil
Optional: 2 sprigs thyme
1 bunch broccoli raab
1 clove garlic

1 pinch hot pepper flakes
Pizza dough for 1 pizza
½ cup grated mozzarella cheese
16 niçoise olives, pitted
1 lemon

Preheat the oven to 375°F.

Dice the onion and toss in a small ovenproof sauté pan with a pinch of salt and enough olive oil to coat lightly, and the leaves of the thyme. Put the pan in the oven and roast, stirring occasionally, until the onion is cooked and golden, about 30 minutes.

While the onion is roasting, wash and drain the broccoli raab, remove the heavy stems, and roughly chop the leaves and sprouts into coarse chiffonade. There should be enough to make about 2 cups. Peel and finely chop the garlic. Heat a large sauté pan and coat it with olive oil. Add the broccoli raab, season with salt, pepper, and the hot pepper flakes, and fry over high heat until the broccoli raab is tender. Add the garlic and fry, tossing, for a few seconds.

When the onions are done, take them out of the oven and turn the heat up to 450° to 500°F. Put a pizza stone in the oven. Roll out or shape a 12- to 14-inch disk of pizza dough and slide it onto a floured pizza peel or the back of a baking sheet. Lightly brush the dough with olive oil, leaving a ½-inch border dry. Evenly sprinkle the cheese on the oiled surface, spread the onions over, and top with the broccoli raab and the olives. Drizzle about 1 tablespoon olive oil over the pizza. Slide the pizza onto the preheated stone in the oven and bake from 5 to 10 minutes, until the crust is brown and crisp. Remove the pizza from the oven, sprinkle a few drops of lemon juice over it, slice, and serve.

Makes one 12-inch pizza.

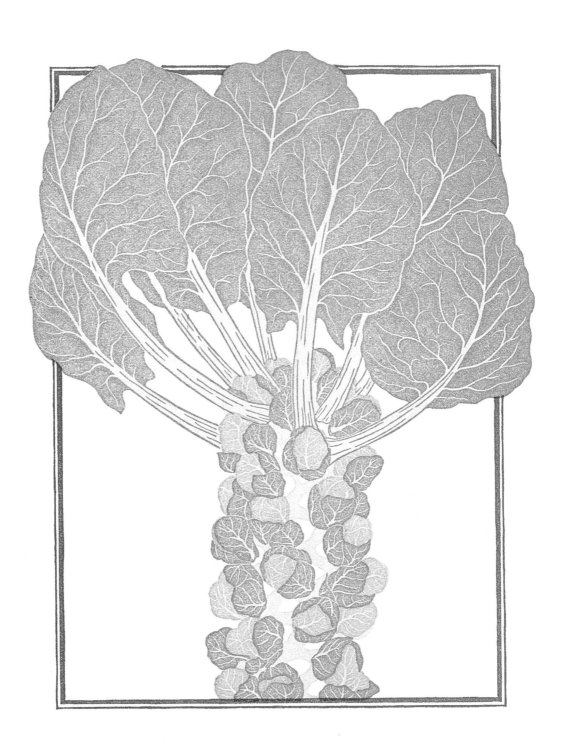

BRUSSELS SPROUTS &

Season: Late fall and winter

Brussels sprouts are a variety, *gemmifera*, of the cabbage species *Brassica oleracea*. Because of selective breeding done in the thirteenth century in Belgium, brussels sprouts do indeed look like tiny, perfectly formed cabbages. They grow on a heavy stalk, several feet tall, with a few large leaves at the top. As with cabbage, there are both red and green varieties.

Brussels sprouts taste best cooked quickly. At Chez Panisse we often cut out the core at the stem end of each sprout and separate the leaves, so that all they need is a quick wilting in butter or olive oil. Cooked this way, they seem like a different vegetable entirely, and are delicious tossed with pasta or as a side dish. The very tiniest sprouts, less than three quarters of an inch in diameter, can be parboiled or steamed whole.

Even though new, short-season varieties have been developed, brussels sprouts do not develop their delicate sweet, nutty flavor until cold weather comes. Their prime season is late fall and early winter, especially after the first frost.

At some markets you can buy the entire dramatic-looking stalk and pluck the sprouts off when you get home. Look for stalks that have small sprouts; they will be sweeter than the larger ones. Choose those that feel firm and heavy. Avoid any that have any wilting or yellowing leaves, or that do not form a tight head.

To prepare the sprouts for cooking, pull off any loose leaves around the stem. Trim the stem close to the bottom of the sprout, but unless you will be separating the leaves, be careful not to cut too close to the bottom leaves. To use the individual small leaves, cut out the core of the sprouts with a small, sharp paring knife and carefully tease the leaves apart with your fingers. If the innermost leaves cannot be easily separated, slice them thinly. Rinse the leaves or whole sprouts carefully in cold water and drain before using.

Brussels sprouts are not good candidates for small gardens. They need lots of space in the garden over a growing season as long as five months. But if you have the space and the patience, you will be rewarded with a harvest that can last into the winter.

BUTTERED BRUSSELS SPROUTS

Cut the brussels sprouts in half vertically and parboil or steam them until just tender, about 4 minutes. Drain and toss with softened butter. Season with salt and pepper and serve.

SAUTÉED BRUSSELS SPROUTS

Slice the sprouts thin, about ⅛-inch thick. Heat a sauté pan, add a small amount of olive oil or unsalted butter, and sauté the sprouts for a few minutes. Add about ¼ inch of chicken stock to the pan and continue cooking until tender. Season with salt, pepper, fresh chopped thyme, and a squeeze of lemon juice. The idea here is to end with an emulsified liquid that just coats the sprouts.

BRUSSELS SPROUTS LEAVES WITH BACON

Cut out the stems and separate the sprouts into leaves. Thinly slice the tightly compact centers. Sauté some diced onion and pancetta or bacon in olive oil until softened. Add the sprout leaves, season with salt, and moisten with a little white wine and water or chicken stock. Cover and simmer for 10 to 15 minutes, until tender. Taste for seasoning, grind black pepper over, and serve.

Brussels Sprouts with Toasted Walnuts

Sauté sliced sprouts in browned butter. Add toasted walnuts and a little chicken stock, and cook until just tender. Season with salt and pepper and a squeeze of lemon.

Brussels Sprouts Pasta

Cut the stem out of each sprout and separate it into its leaves. Thinly slice the tiny hearts if you can't tease apart all the leaves. Slice red onion very thinly and chop some garlic. Start cooking the pasta (a sturdy dry type, such as farfalle or penne; orrechiette is good because it has the same size and shape as the brussels sprouts leaves).

Heat a sauté pan, add a little olive oil, toss in the sprout leaves, salt and pepper them, and sauté for about a minute over very high heat. Then add the sliced onions and a pinch of hot pepper flakes, and continue to sauté until the sprouts are tender and a little browned, 2 to 5 minutes. Remove from the heat, add the garlic, and toss. If the garlic appears to be browning, add a splash of water to the pan. Squeeze a little lemon onto the sprouts, and when the pasta is done, add it, drained, to the sauté pan and toss everything together. Taste and adjust the seasoning. Serve drizzled with good extra-virgin olive oil. If you want, toss the pasta with some toasted bread crumbs, but if the sprouts are very sweet and tasty, don't bother.

CABBAGE ❧

Season: Year-round; best in late fall and winter

Over the centuries that cabbage has been cultivated, plant breeders have propagated an astonishing variety of strains. Cabbages come in many shades and combinations of green, red, purple, and white. Some form heads like cannonballs, and some are grown for their leaves or their flowering tops. The heads can be round, cone-shaped, or flat. The leaves can be smooth and shiny or crinkled. Cabbages can take six months to mature, or they can be ready to eat in three. And all this variability is found in just one species, *Brassica oleracea*, which includes the common red and green heading cabbages, savoy cabbage, broccoli, brussels sprouts, cauliflower, kale, collard greens, and kohlrabi.

Cooked well, cabbage has wonderful texture and lots of spicy, sweet flavor. Because it can provide food in the winter when there may be few other vegetables to be had, and because it can be grown in most of the temperate climate zones of the earth, cabbage has developed a lingering reputation as a commonplace, even coarse, food. But it is worthy of the most refined preparations. At the restaurant we serve it with foie gras and caviar. Its sweetness complements the richness of duck and pork. It is surprisingly good with fish, wrapped around salmon and steamed, for example, trapping juiciness and flavor. Braised, steamed, or stir-fried, it is a treat by itself. Fermented and transformed into sauerkraut, it is a new vegetable altogether.

Most of the Asian cabbages belong to another very large species, *B. rapa*. Its many permutations include napa, or Chinese, cabbage, whose large, mature heads make wonderfully tender coleslaw; mizuna greens, which we sometimes use at the restaurant as a salad green; and many kinds of bok choy. In the early summer, when we find young bok choy at the market, we cut the heads in two and grill them. Another variety of bok choy we are particularly fond of at Chez Panisse grows into flat rosettes of thick roundish leaves so dark that it merits its English name, flat black cabbage (also known in local markets by its Japanese name, tatsoi or tat-soi). When wilted quickly, it has a fine texture and a spicy, fresh flavor, and it retains its lustrous dark green color.

Early-maturing cabbages of all kinds find their way to market in early summer. But the best of the main crop cabbages come at the end of summer and last until truly cold winter weather begins. In California and the South, cabbage can be harvested throughout the winter and into early spring. The only time of year likely to be without cabbage is late spring, when bolting is the most likely and can halt production.

When considering most types of cabbage at the market, look for heads that are tight, firm, and heavy for their type, with shiny, crisp outer leaves. Savoy cabbage is an exception: it forms looser heads because of its puckery texture and has more of a matte finish than the other kinds. The leaves should show no signs of yellowing or other discoloration. The best cabbages for quick cooking and tender coleslaw are ones with thin leaves.

Loose-leaf Asian cabbages, such as bok choy and flat black cabbage, should look bright and fresh, with no wilting or discolored leaves. The stems should be firm, with no signs of splitting.

Remove any loose or wilted leaves from cabbage, whether it is to be cooked or eaten raw. The heads should be rinsed in running water to remove any dirt.

There are few vegetables that grow so robustly and look so abundant. For that reason alone, cabbages should be front and center in any home garden. If you have had only market cabbages, developed for good keeping and shipping qualities, you owe it to yourself to try some of the other, tastier varieties. Early Jersey Wakefield, a cone-shaped heirloom English variety, is still considered the standard for flavor. The newer Dutch variety, Grenadier, is also good. For red cabbage, try the non-hybrid Lasso or the Japanese-bred Scarlet O'Hara.

Braised Red or Green Cabbage

1 red or green cabbage	1 bay leaf
1 medium onion	Salt and pepper
3 tablespoons duck fat	½ cup water
1 tablespoon sherry vinegar	1 apple

Remove the outer leaves from the cabbage. Cut it in half, remove the core, and slice the cabbage very thin. Peel the onion and slice very thin.

In a large pan, heat the duck fat, add the onion, and cook for 5 minutes. Put in the cabbage, vinegar, bay leaf, salt and pepper, and water. Cover and simmer for 20 minutes. Peel and grate the apple, add it to the cabbage, and cook for another 5 minutes. Taste and correct the seasoning, and serve.

Serves 4 to 6.

Red Cabbage with Chestnuts

1 pound chestnuts	½ cup sweet white wine
1 small red cabbage	Salt and pepper
Duck fat or butter	Sherry vinegar

Score the chestnut shells with a knife and parboil them. Drain and peel off the shells and skins. Finish cooking in a little water or chicken stock until just soft enough to be eaten but still firm. Drain, let the cooking liquid cool, return the chestnuts to the liquid, and set aside.

Cut the cabbage as you would for coleslaw, in strips ¼ inch wide. Cook it in duck fat or butter. When it has started to soften, add the wine.

Break the chestnuts into small chunks and sauté them separately in duck fat or butter until golden brown. Add the chestnuts to the cabbage and season with salt and pepper and a few drops of the vinegar to brighten the flavor. Continue cooking until the cabbage is very soft, keeping it moist as needed with the chestnuts' cooking liquid. Serve with roast duck or pork or with a Thanksgiving turkey.

Serves 6 to 8.

Note: If you wish, flavor the dish with a little Cognac or port, Pineau des Charentes, or cassis.

BRAISED CABBAGE WITH HALIBUT

1 medium head savoy cabbage
1 bay leaf
A few sprigs thyme
1 cup chicken stock, vegetable
  stock, or water
1 cup dry white wine
6 tablespoons butter
Salt and pepper

18 small potatoes (Yellow Finns
  or red creamers)
2 tablespoons olive oil
Optional: 2 strips bacon
2 pounds halibut (or rock cod)
  fillet
1 small bunch Italian parsley

Preheat the oven to 400°F.

Cut the cabbage in half through its core and cut each half into 2-inch wedges. Pack the wedges tightly in a baking dish with the bay leaf and half the thyme. Pour in ½ cup each of the chicken stock and the white wine. Make thin slices of about 3 tablespoons of the butter and arrange them evenly on top of the cabbage; cover and put the dish into the oven for about 45 minutes, until the cabbage is tender. Cut out and discard the cores, chop the cabbage roughly, and return it to its own juices. Taste for seasoning, add salt if necessary, and set aside.

At the same time, roast the potatoes: Rinse them and pat dry with a towel. Put them in a baking dish and toss with olive oil, salt, and the rest of the thyme. Cover and bake 30 to 45 minutes, until done. Slice them in half and add to the cabbage. Increase the oven temperature to 500°F.

If you want to include the bacon, cook it now: Cut it into ¼-inch pieces and sauté over medium heat until crisp. Drain and add to the cabbage and potatoes.

Slice the halibut into 6 pieces of roughly equal weight (5 to 6 ounces) and thickness (about 1 inch). Season the pieces of fish on both sides with salt and place them in a baking dish large enough to hold them in one layer without crowding. Distribute the remaining 3 tablespoons of butter over the fish, moisten with the remaining white wine and chicken stock, and bake in the oven for 5 to 7 minutes, until the fish is just cooked through. At the same time reheat the cabbage and potatoes in the oven, uncovered. Chop enough parsley leaves to make about ¼ cup.

To serve, arrange the cabbage, potatoes, and bacon around the fish on a warmed platter and pour over the pan juices from both baking dishes. Grind pepper over, sprinkle with the chopped parsley, and serve immediately.

Serves 6.

STUFFED SAVOY CABBAGE

1 savoy cabbage (2 to 3 pounds)	*1 cup milk*
1 onion	*2 sprigs thyme*
1 clove garlic	*4 sprigs parsley*
¼ pound bacon	*4 to 5 sage leaves*
¾ pound fresh lean sausage meat	*Salt and pepper*
	2 cups homemade tomato sauce
4 slices country-style bread	*1 handful parsley leaves*

Remove the outer leaves of the cabbage and trim the core but leave the cabbage whole. Bring a large pot of salted water to a boil, plunge in the cabbage, and simmer for 15 minutes. Carefully remove the whole cabbage with a skimmer and let it drain, upside down, in a colander or on a dry towel.

Prepare the stuffing: Peel and chop the onion, peel and slice the garlic, and cut the bacon into small dice. Heat a sauté pan and add the bacon. When it has started to render some fat, add the onion and garlic, and cook, stirring occasionally, until they have started to brown. Add the sausage meat and cook over low heat for 10 minutes.

Preheat the oven to 375°F.

Cut the crusts off the bread and tear it into small pieces, pour the milk into a bowl, and soak the bread in it for 5 minutes. Squeeze the milk out of the bread and add the bread to the sausage mixture. Chop the herbs and add to the stuffing. Season to taste with salt and pepper.

Delicately open up the cabbage by peeling the leaves back to create a cavity in the center. Season with salt and pepper and pack the stuffing into the center of the cabbage. Fold the leaves back, completely encasing the stuffing, and tie the cabbage with string to help it keep its shape. Put it in a large baking dish, pour the tomato sauce around it, cover, and bake for 1 hour. Check after 30 minutes, and add some water or white wine if the tomato sauce has been reduced too much. Cut off the string and serve the cabbage in its baking dish or on a platter surrounded by the sauce, with parsley leaves scattered over it.

Serves 4 to 6.

CABBAGE AND BEAN SOUP WITH DUCK CONFIT

This is one of many versions of *garbure*, the long-cooked cabbage and bean soup from southwestern France. This very hearty winter meal is meant to serve a hungry household.

*1 pound dried shell beans
(navy or white, or flageolets)
1 cured ham hock
4 onions
3 carrots
1 piece bacon, about 4 ounces
Bouquet garni: Sprigs of thyme
and parsley, a bay leaf, green
leek tops
3 cloves garlic*

*2 leeks
3 small potatoes
4 small turnips
1 medium head green cabbage
2 tablespoons duck fat
2 cups light chicken stock or
water
4 preserved duck legs
(duck confit; see Note)
6 to 8 slices country-style bread*

Soak the beans in water to cover for 2 hours. Drain them and put them in a large pot with the ham hock; 1 whole onion and 1 whole carrot, peeled; and the bacon. Add the bouquet garni and water to cover, and bring slowly to a boil. Reduce the heat and simmer, uncovered, for about 1 to 1½ hours, until the beans are tender. When they are done, let them cool in their liquid.

Meanwhile, peel and slice the remaining onions and the garlic; trim, wash, and slice the leeks; peel the potatoes, turnips, and remaining carrots, and cut them into quarters. Trim and core the cabbage, cut it in half, and slice thick.

In a large, heavy skillet, melt the duck fat, add the onions, garlic, and leeks, and cook them over medium heat for 5 minutes, stirring frequently. Cover with the chicken stock or water, bring to a boil, and add the potatoes, turnips, carrots, and cabbage. Reduce the heat and simmer for 25 minutes.

Remove the ham hock, the onion and carrot, the bacon, and the bouquet garni from the pot of beans. When the other vegetables are done, add them and their liquid to the beans. Cut the bacon into small pieces and shred the meat from the ham hock and the duck legs. Add the bacon, ham, and duck to the soup and simmer for another 10 minutes. Serve ladled over a slice of toasted country-style bread in the bottom of each soup plate.

Serves 6 to 8.

Note: Duck that has been disjointed, salted, and simmered until very tender while submerged in fat, and finally preserved in fat, is known as duck confit. We have given a recipe in *Chez Panisse Pasta, Pizza, and Calzone*, by Alice Waters, Patricia Curtan, and Martine Labro, but duck confit can be purchased in some specialty food stores.

CABBAGE WITH DUCK FOIE GRAS

1 small duck foie gras	*1 shallot*
Salt and pepper	*¼ cup port*
1 medium green cabbage	*½ cup duck or chicken stock*

Slice the foie gras into 8 slices, ½ inch thick, season with salt and pepper, put on a plate, cover with plastic wrap, and refrigerate.

Remove the outer leaves from the cabbage but leave it whole. Bring a large pot of salted water to a boil, put in the cabbage, and simmer for 10 minutes. Remove the cabbage carefully, refresh under cold water, and drain, inverted in a colander or strainer. Pull the cabbage leaves off the core, separating them carefully, and pat very dry.

Peel the shallot, chop it very fine, and put it in a small saucepan with the port. Bring to a boil, add the duck stock, and reduce by half.

Take the foie gras out of the refrigerator, heat a nonstick sauté pan, and cook the slices over high heat for a few seconds on each side. Let them drain on paper towels. One by one, wrap each foie gras slice in 1 or 2 cabbage leaves, put the stuffed leaves in a single layer in the pan with the sauce, and simmer for 2 minutes. Put two cabbage packages on each plate, pour the sauce over, season with salt and pepper, and serve with grilled or toasted country-style bread.

Serves 4.

WILTED FLAT BLACK CABBAGE

Separate, wash, and dry the flat black cabbage (tatsoi) leaves. In a sauté pan, heat a little olive oil—or a shallot or garlic vinaigrette—and cook the leaves briefly, for just a few minutes, until the leaves are wilted but the stems are still crisp. Season and serve.

Cabbage Salad with Apple and Celery Root

1 small green cabbage	*Salt and pepper*
1 bunch watercress	*2 tablespoons hazelnut*
½ small celery root	*(or walnut) oil*
1 Granny Smith apple	*1 tablespoon olive oil*
1 shallot	*Chives and chervil for garnish*
1 tablespoon sherry vinegar	

Pull off and discard the outer leaves of the cabbage. Cut it in half, re-move the core, and slice into chiffonade. Wash and dry the watercress, removing the larger stems. Peel the celery root, cut into thin slices, and then into julienne. Peel and core the apple and cut into small dice.

Prepare a vinaigrette: Peel and dice the shallot and combine with the sherry vinegar, salt and pepper, and the two oils in a large salad bowl. Add the cabbage, watercress, celery root, and apple to the vinaigrette and toss thoroughly. Serve the salad scattered with chopped chives and a few sprigs of chervil.

Serves 4.

Note: Vary this recipe by adding raisins, chestnuts, or thinly sliced raw mushrooms with the other ingredients.

Spicy Coleslaw

This is an excellent coleslaw to serve with breaded and fried oysters.

2 small heads cabbage	*Juice of 1 lime*
(preferably savoy)	*2 to 3 teaspoons white wine*
½ small red onion	*vinegar*
2 to 3 jalapeño peppers	*⅓ to ½ cup extra-virgin olive oil*
A few sprigs cilantro	*Salt and pepper*

Tear off and discard the outer leaves of the cabbages. Quarter the heads and remove their cores. Slice the quarters crosswise, into ⅛-inch-thick strips. Slice the onion lengthwise as thin as possible. Cut the jalapeño peppers in half, remove their seeds and veins, and slice the peppers very thin. Coarsely chop the cilantro.

Combine all the sliced vegetables in a large bowl and toss with the lime juice, 2 teaspoons of the white wine vinegar, the olive oil, and salt and pepper to taste. Taste again and, if necessary, add more jalapeño and vinegar. Serve at room temperature.

Serves 6.

WARM CABBAGE, ONION, AND APPLE SLAW

1 medium yellow or red onion	*Oil*
1 medium red or green cabbage	*Salt and pepper*
2 large crisp, sweet apples	*Vinegar*

Peel and slice the onion very thin. Trim the cabbage, core it, cut in half, and slice into fine chiffonade, as for coleslaw. Peel, core, and slice the apples very thin.

In a large sauté pan, heat a little oil and begin to sauté the onions. When they are translucent and just beginning to brown, add the apples. Sauté about 1 minute so everything is sizzling, and add the cabbage, the seasoning, a dash of vinegar, and a little water. Stir on a hot flame just long enough to barely cook the cabbage. It should retain a little crunch and the sweetness of fresh cabbage.

Serve with pork, roast chicken, or duck; a savory grain and legume pilaf or roast potatoes; or by itself, cold.

Serves 8 to 10.

Note: You might add herbs and mushrooms to this stir-fry, or go in another direction with such spices as cinnamon or allspice. Try a variety of oils and vinegars. For sweetness, add a little balsamic vinegar or sugar.

COLD CHINESE CABBAGE WITH CILANTRO

Macerate finely diced shallots in white wine vinegar for 15 minutes or so. Slice Chinese, or napa, cabbage very thin, toss with the shallots and vinegar, some good olive oil, and salt and pepper. Let the cabbage sit about 10 minutes so it starts to wilt. Add a handful of fresh cilantro leaves and serve.

CARDOONS 🌰

Season: Late spring through late fall

Cardoons are often found growing wild around the Mediterranean, and
they are widely appreciated in Italy and France as a cultivated vegetable.
But although they have established themselves in the wild in northern
California, they are not well known in the United States. They require
several steps in their preparation, but their wonderfully mild, herbaceous flavor makes them well worth the trouble.

Just looking at a cardoon plant will probably not induce hunger. The
young plants form rosettes of long, spiny leaves that may be several feet
across. A mature plant looks like a hugely overgrown thistle, six feet tall
or more, with large purple and blue artichoke-like flowers at the tips of
the stalks. Although cardoons (*Cynara cardunculus*) are closely related
to artichokes, the choice edible part of the cardoon is the large leaf stalk,
not the flower head. The subtle flavor slightly resembles that of artichokes but otherwise is impossible to categorize.

In the market, cardoons are usually sold as stalks cut from the plant,
several feet long, often trimmed of their leaves. Sometimes you will see
the entire center rosette of young stalks for sale, leaves still attached,
looking rather like a mutant head of celery.

The season for cardoons starts late in spring, with young stalks cut
from plants that have overwintered. It continues through the summer
and fall, when you are more likely to find the hearts of plants that have
been started in the spring. In order to produce tender stalks, some
growers blanch the plants during the growing season by hilling up the
soil at the base of the plants or wrapping them with paper or burlap.

Small or medium stalks will be tenderest and need the least preparation time. If you can, cut into a stalk to make sure it is solid. Those with

hollow interiors should be avoided, because they are usually old and tough, and there will be little flesh left after trimming. When buying either individual stalks or whole heads, look for cardoons that seem firm and not wilted, with healthy-looking leaves.

Cardoons will keep for several days, wrapped and refrigerated.

To prepare cardoons for cooking, trim the leaves and any spiny skin off the stalks. Cut the stalks into manageable lengths, about three inches long, and immediately put them in a basin of cold water acidulated with lemon juice or vinegar. (Like artichokes, cardoons discolor rapidly when they are cut and exposed to air.) One by one, peel the skin off the cardoon pieces and tear off the largest strings, as you would from celery stalks, returning each piece to the water as you finish. Some cooks find peeling and stringing easier after a preliminary parboiling in salted, acidulated water. In any event, most preparations require a parboiling before the final cooking. The innermost stalks are sometimes tender enough to be eaten raw.

Although cardoon plants take up a lot of space, they are a handsome addition to an edible landscape, especially when in flower. Stalks can be harvested from the plants as they grow through the season. Several domestic mail order seed companies sell cardoon seed, although for a selection of varieties you will probably have to look to European seed sources.

CARDOON, CANNELLINI BEAN, AND ARTICHOKE RAGOUT

2 cups dried cannellini beans	1 piece (3 ounces) salt pork or bacon
1 small onion	Salt
1 small carrot	6 medium artichokes
2 cloves garlic	1½ pounds cardoons
4 tablespoons olive oil	3 tablespoons chopped parsley
1 bay leaf	3 teaspoons chopped garlic
4 sprigs thyme	Extra-virgin olive oil
1 medium tomato	Reggiano Parmesan cheese

Soak the beans overnight in the refrigerator. The next day, drain them. Chop the onion, carrot, and garlic, and cook them gently in 2 tablespoons of the olive oil until softened. Add the beans, the bay leaf, and 2 sprigs of the thyme; the tomato, peeled, seeded, and chopped; about six cups of water; and the salt pork or bacon. Bring to a boil, reduce to a simmer, skim the top, and cook slowly, covered, for 1½ to 2 hours. After about an hour, when the beans have begun to soften, add about 2 teaspoons salt. Continue cooking until the beans are creamy and their skins are soft, but not disintegrating.

While the beans are cooking, peel and trim the artichokes down to their hearts, dropping them into cool water acidulated with lemon juice (page 4). Cut them into ½-inch-thick wedges, and cook them, covered, in a shallow nonreactive pan with ½ cup water, 1 tablespoon of the olive oil, and the remaining thyme, and season with salt. Simmer for about 8 minutes, until the artichokes begin to soften, shaking the pan a few times to stir its contents. Uncover, raise the heat slightly, and continue cooking, stirring occasionally, until the artichokes are soft and tender. The water should be nearly evaporated. Remove the thyme.

Trim the cardoons and cut them into 4-inch lengths. Cook them slowly, covered, in a nonreactive pan with 1 cup water, the remaining tablespoon of olive oil, and about 2 teaspoons salt, for 35 to 40 minutes, until they are soft and tender. Add more water if the pan starts to go dry, but the liquid should be nearly evaporated by the time the cardoons are cooked. When they are cool enough to handle, peel away the strings from the cardoons as you would with celery and cut the cardoons crosswise into ½-inch slices.

When the beans are cooked, remove the piece of salt pork or bacon and the thyme sprigs, add the cooked artichokes and cardoons, and simmer together for 10 minutes or so. Mix together the chopped parsley and garlic and stir into the beans. Serve, with a drizzle of olive oil and a little grated Parmesan, either by itself or with roast pork or lamb.

Serves 8 to 10.

BAGNA CAUDA

Another delicious way to eat cardoons when they are young and tender is dipped in *bagna cauda*, the Italian "hot bath" for raw or barely cooked vegetables—a simple sauce of half extra-virgin olive oil, half butter, salt, pepper, chopped anchovies, and lemon zest, all gently heated together. String and parboil the cardoons, cut into sticks (or serve them raw, if they are exceptionally tender), and serve warm or cold with the warm sauce.

CARDOON GRATIN

Trim the cardoons and cut them into 3-inch lengths. Simmer them in a nonreactive pan, well covered with water flavored with salt, olive oil, and lemon, for 35 to 45 minutes, until tender. When cool enough to handle, peel away the strings from the cardoons, as you would with celery.

Arrange a thick layer of cardoons in a buttered earthenware gratin dish. Just cover with cream, or a mixture of cream and stock, season with salt and pepper, and sprinkle with grated Parmesan. Bake in a pre-heated 375°F. oven until browned and bubbly. Serve garnished with chopped parsley and chervil.

CARDOON FRITTERS

Choose cardoons with white, tender-looking hearts. Strip the strings from the stalks (just as one would do with celery) and then parboil the cardoons in salted, acidulated water. Drain them when just tender. Cut the stalks into 3-inch by 1-inch sticks. Dredge them in flour, shake off the excess, then dip them in egg and finally in fine bread crumbs. Deep-fry them in peanut oil at 360°F., until golden brown. Drain on towels and serve.

Note: You can also make cardoon fritters in batter. Trim the cardoons, string and parboil them, and cut into sticks, as described above. Dry the cardoons and marinate in a mixture of olive oil, lemon juice, and chopped parsley. Dip the slices in fritter batter and deep-fry in peanut oil heated to 375°F., until lightly browned. Drain on towels, salt, and serve. If you like, batter-fry thinly sliced and seeded Meyer lemons to serve with the cardoons.

CARDOONS À LA GRECQUE

Cardoons can be served as part of a marinated vegetable salad cooked à la grecque—with, for example, artichokes, cauliflower, and fennel. Follow the Fennel à la Grecque recipe (page 153).

CARROTS &

Carrots, onions, leeks, and fennel are the aromatic vegetables that flavor most of the cooking we do at Chez Panisse. Carrots are closely related to parsley and fennel, and they contribute a sweet, rich character to stocks, marinades, soups, and sauces. But their particular charms are most apparent when they are cooked alone or with a few other vegetables.

In late spring, when the first tiny carrots come in from local farms, they are wonderful all alone, boiled and buttered, or tossed with fava beans and peas to accompany the first local salmon. These tiny carrots are also good lightly pickled and served as part of an antipasto plate.

The greatest abundance of fresh sweet carrots comes in middle to late summer. This is the time to use them in minestrone, or to make carrot and cilantro soup, or to serve them in Provençal or Moroccan-style salads.

In the fall and winter, carrots fade into the background but never disappear. Large sweet carrots, either late-harvested from nearby California farms or from storage, are perfect for cold weather braises or roasted along with other winter root vegetables.

Most of us recognize the ordinary long, cylindrical, tapered orange carrot, the Imperator variety, which is seen at every supermarket and corner grocery. But check the farmer's market for small, globe-shaped carrots like Planet and Thumbelina, and the more cone-shaped Chantenay types. Also look for the many varieties of Nantes carrots, medium French varieties that are uniformly cylindrical. The Chino family farm has supplied us with slender tapered carrots in colors ranging from pure white through bright yellow and orange to dark reddish purple.

When you shop, look for firm, crisp carrots with smooth, unblemished skin. Avoid those with soft or discolored spots, and any that look withered. If the tops are still attached, they should be bright green and not wilted or blackened.

Carrots keep better with the tops removed. Store carrots loosely wrapped in the coldest part of the refrigerator. Tiny new carrots should be used in a day or two, but larger ones will keep well for at least a week.

Resist the urge to peel the first small carrots of the season; much of their flavor is in the skin, which does not have the bitterness of more mature carrots. Leave up to an inch of the stems attached to the top; the stems are tender and edible and add a look of freshness. Even large carrots need only the thinnest possible layer of peel removed; this is most easily done with a swivel-bladed vegetable peeler. Carrots can be peeled ahead of time, wrapped in a damp towel, and refrigerated overnight. If they are not wrapped, they will oxidize and turn dark. Sometimes older carrots have a tough core, which can be removed after cutting the carrots in quarters lengthwise.

Carrots are useful in a kitchen garden, where they can be harvested at all stages of development. The large Imperator varieties need very deep, fine soil, but the shorter round or conical types can be grown in ordinary good garden soil. Mixing carrot seeds with a few radish seeds will help you remember where the relatively slow-germinating carrots are planted, and the radish seedlings will break the crust of soil to help the tiny carrot plants come up. As the radishes are harvested, more space will be available for the developing carrots.

Moroccan Carrot Salad

This salad benefits from marinating in its dressing for an hour or so. It has been served at Chez Panisse as part of a memorable antipasto quintet: the other elements were a salad of fennel marinated with lemon, a green salad, Pickled Spring Onions (page 219), and Wilted Mustard Greens and Prosciutto (page 214).

Peel baby carrots, leaving ¼ inch of stem attached. Cut them in half lengthwise and boil until tender in salted water with a crushed clove of garlic. Drain and cool to room temperature. Toss them with a little ground cumin, paprika, and salt, and a pinch each of cinnamon and cayenne. Toss together with lemon juice, olive oil, and chopped parsley, and set aside to marinate for at least an hour before serving.

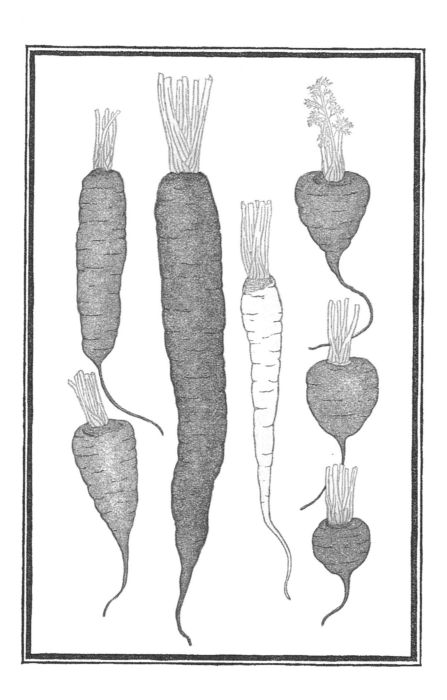

SPICY CARROT SALAD

2 pounds carrots
1 clove garlic, peeled
1 teaspoon salt
2 tablespoons red wine vinegar

1 tablespoon lemon juice
¼ teaspoon cayenne
¾ cup olive oil
2 tablespoons chopped cilantro

Peel the carrots and cut into julienne—quick work with a Japanese mandolin. Mash the garlic clove with the salt, and mix it with the red wine vinegar, lemon juice, and cayenne. Whisk in the olive oil. Taste for seasoning and add more acid, salt, or cayenne if needed. Toss with the carrots, add the chopped cilantro, and serve.

Serves 4.

CARROT AND CILANTRO SOUP

1 white onion
3 tablespoons butter
1 bunch carrots (about 2
    pounds)
2 or 3 potatoes (about ½ pound)
Salt and pepper

1 to 1½ quarts chicken stock
1 bunch cilantro (about ¼
    pound)
1 small red onion
1 or 2 jalapeño peppers
Juice of 1 lime

Peel and slice the onion and put it on to stew in the butter over low heat, covered. Peel the carrots and potatoes and cut them in large chunks. Once the onions are fairly soft, add the carrots and potatoes, salt generously, and continue to stew, covered, for about 10 minutes more. Add chicken stock to cover, and simmer until the vegetables are entirely cooked. Take the pot off the heat.

Reserve a handful of cilantro leaves for salsa and throw the rest of the cilantro into the soup pot. Purée the soup in a blender or food processor (or pass through a food mill), and strain through a medium sieve. Adjust the seasoning with salt and pepper. Make a little salsa to your taste with the onion and jalapeño peppers, chopped; the lime juice; and the reserved coriander leaves, coarsely chopped. To serve the soup, bring back to a simmer, ladle into bowls, and garnish with the salsa.

Serves 6.

Oven-roasted Carrots and Turnips

4 medium carrots or
  2 bunches baby carrots
6 medium turnips or
  2 bunches baby turnips

¼ cup olive oil
Salt and pepper

Preheat the oven to 400°F.

Prepare the carrots and turnips so they are about the same size and shape. First peel and trim the carrots. If you have medium carrots, cut them in ⅛-inch slices, on the diagonal. If you have baby carrots, wash and drain them first before peeling, then cut them lengthwise, in halves or in quarters, leaving a little of their tops attached.

If you have medium turnips, pare off their skin and tough outer layer, halve or quarter them lengthwise, and slice into ⅛-inch-thick pieces. If you are roasting baby turnips, taste one first—if the skin isn't tough or strong-tasting, you need not peel them. Check for dirt or grit that might be trapped in the tops, wash in cold water if necessary, and drain thoroughly. Cut them lengthwise in halves or in quarters, leaving about ¼ inch of their tops attached.

In a large bowl, toss the carrots and turnips together with the olive oil, and season generously with salt and pepper. (Taste a raw vegetable to check the seasoning.) Spread the vegetables evenly in a baking pan in a single layer, and roast, uncovered, stirring and tossing occasionally, until the vegetables are cooked through, for 20 to 45 minutes.

Serve as a side dish with roasted meats or chicken, or on top of creamy polenta for a hearty vegetarian meal, sprinkled with fresh chopped herbs.

Serves 4 to 6.

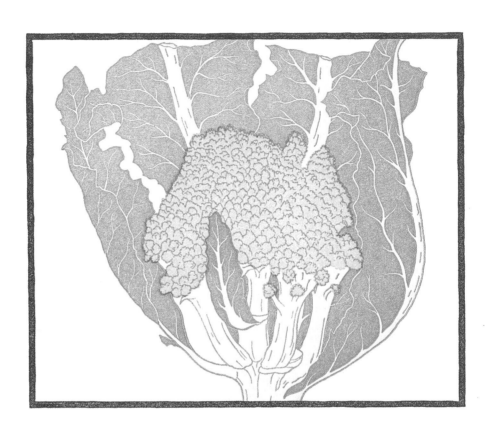

CAULIFLOWER 🍃

Season: Year-round; best in fall and early winter

Cauliflower is one of the vegetables that were bred from the original parent of the species *Brassica oleracea* to exploit and emphasize a particular characteristic of the plant. Others included in this book are broccoli, brussels sprouts, cabbage, and kale. Cabbage was bred to form tight heads of fleshy leaves, brussels sprouts to form miniature cabbage-like leaf rosettes along a main stem, and so forth. In the case of cauliflower, it is the bunched flower stems that make up the edible part of the plant. These masses of flower stalks form the recognizable curd of a head of cauliflower, generally a single domed mass or a mass with a spiraling snail-shell shape. In addition to the common large, white heads, there are varieties that produce smaller heads of purple cauliflower, or of pale chartreuse green, which are not always clearly different from some of the purple broccolis.

Like other members of the cabbage family, cauliflower matures during the cool part of the year. In most parts of the country, locally grown cauliflower is plentiful in fall and early winter. There may be a secondary crop in late spring. In coastal California, however, the cool, moist conditions that produce the best cauliflower occur through much of the year, and the season ebbs only in late summer.

At the restaurant when we have particularly mild, sweet, fresh cauliflower, we like to serve it very simply, perhaps with Bagna Cauda (page 73); steamed and served with brown butter, parsley, sieved egg, and bread crumbs; or as a smooth cream of cauliflower soup. But the mildness of cauliflower is also good when set against other more assertive flavors. In the winter its color and freshness make cauliflower a welcome part of an antipasto. One of our favorite pastas combines cauliflower with garlic, anchovies, olive oil, and hot pepper flakes.

Before the days of factory farming, shoppers could evaluate cauliflower by the color and the condition of the leaves left attached to the head. If these leaves are bright green and not wilted, the cauliflower is fresh. This is still true at farmer's markets, where the leaves also serve to cushion the heads and prevent bruising. But in most larger markets, cauliflower is sold stripped of its leaves and tightly wrapped in plastic, resisting any attempts to check its quality. Nevertheless, good cauliflower will have fine-grained, compact curds and will not show any discoloration. Avoid cauliflower that looks coarse textured or "ricy," which is an indication of advanced age. Fresh cauliflower should exhibit no spots or browned areas. Check the head closely, as sometimes these discolorations will have been shaved off by the produce seller.

Cauliflower will keep several days, covered and refrigerated. Before using, trim off any discoloration. To flush out any aphids that may be hiding within the flowerets, soak the cauliflower in cold water to which you have added salt and vinegar. As a rule, the shorter the cooking time, the better tasting the cauliflower. To ensure quick cooking, separate the head into flowerets. If the cauliflower is tender and fresh, the stems will not need peeling. After cooking, serve cauliflower as soon as possible, so it will maintain its fresh character. Serve purple types raw if you want to preserve their color; they turn green when cooked.

Cauliflower is very exacting in its cultural requirements. If your garden has well-drained, rich soil, and you can be assured of cool, even temperatures for a period of months, give it a try. An early variety such as Snow Crown would be best to experiment with. Or try Violet Queen, a purple-headed early variety.

WARM CAULIFLOWER WITH AÏOLI AND ANCHOVIES

Steam cauliflower flowerets until just tender and drain. While they are still warm, spoon over Aïoli (page 162) and garnish with Cured Fresh Anchovies (page 256) or salt-packed anchovy fillets. Serve with grilled lamb or, cooled to room temperature, as part of an antipasto plate.

Note: See Fennel à la Grecque (page 153) for another way to prepare cauliflower for a salad and antipasto.

PICKLED CAULIFLOWER

1 clove garlic	*1 sprig thyme*
½ pound small onions	*1 small chili pepper*
1 pound cauliflower	*2 cups tarragon vinegar*
1 bay leaf	*1 teaspoon coarse salt*

Peel the garlic and onions. Remove the stem and leaves from the cauliflower and separate into flowerets.

Put the flowerets, garlic, onions, herbs, and chili pepper in a hot sterile glass canning jar. Measure the tarragon vinegar into a saucepan, add the salt, bring to a boil, and boil for 1 minute. Remove from the heat and pour over the cauliflower; the cauliflower should be covered with vinegar. Put on the lid, tighten the band, and let cool. Store in a cool, dark place for a month. Keeps 2 to 3 months. Refrigerate after opening.

Makes 1 quart.

FRENCH CREAM OF CAULIFLOWER SOUP

1 large cauliflower	*4 tablespoons crème fraîche*
(2 to 3 pounds)	*Salt*
1 onion	*Nutmeg*
2 tablespoons unsalted butter	*Chervil*

Cut off the stem of the cauliflower and any green leaves. Break up into flowerets. Wash them in cold water. Reserve a handful of flowerets to garnish the soup.

Peel and slice the onion thin. In a soup pot, stew the onion slices and the flowerets in the butter with a little water for 15 minutes, stirring occasionally, without letting them brown. Add water to cover and cook for 25 minutes, covered, over medium heat. Meanwhile, parboil the reserved flowerets in boiling salted water for 8 minutes or so, keeping them crunchy.

Purée the soup in a blender and reheat gently to just under boiling. Add the crème fraîche and season with salt and nutmeg to taste. Serve the soup very hot, garnished with the whole flowerets and a few sprigs of chervil.

Serves 4 to 6.

Cauliflower Soup with Salmon Caviar

Break up a head of cauliflower, stem and all, and boil, covered, in salted water until tender. Drain and reserve the cooking liquid. Roughly purée the cauliflower in a food processor with a little of the cooking liquid. Thin it with milk to the desired consistency, return to the saucepan, and simmer for about 5 minutes, but do not boil. Add some finely chopped Italian parsley and simmer for 2 minutes more. Serve this soup tepid or at room temperature—or chilled, in the summertime—garnished with a generous spoonful of salmon caviar, a dollop of crème fraîche or kefir cheese thinned with cream, and a sprinkling of green onions or chives. If you like, serve with butter-fried croutons.

Whole-wheat Pasta with Cauliflower, Walnuts, and Ricotta Salata

2 heads cauliflower	1 pinch red pepper flakes
1 medium onion	White wine vinegar
4 cloves garlic	½ lemon
1 pound whole-wheat pasta	½ cup toasted walnuts
Extra-virgin olive oil	4 ounces ricotta salata or feta
Salt and pepper	cheese

Put a large pot of water on to boil. Cut the cauliflower into small flowerets. Peel the onion and slice it very thin. Peel and finely chop the garlic. Put the pasta on to cook.

Sauté the cauliflower in olive oil in a large sauté pan. When the cauliflower begins to soften, season with salt and pepper and add the sliced onion and red pepper flakes. Sauté over medium to high heat until the vegetables are brown and tender. The cauliflower should still be slightly crunchy and should not taste steamed. Add the garlic and remove from the heat, tossing and stirring so the garlic doesn't burn; if it starts to brown, add a splash of water. Add a few drops each of vinegar and lemon juice and the toasted walnuts. Taste and correct the seasoning. When the pasta is done, drain and add to the cauliflower, adding enough extra-virgin olive oil to coat the pasta thoroughly, toss together, and serve, with the cheese crumbled over the dish.

Serves 6.

CELERY AND CELERY ROOT &

Season: Celery, year-round; Celery root, fall through winter

Leafy celery and celery root are varieties of the same plant, *Apium grave-olens*, which is thought to be native to southern Europe. The first culti-vated celery appears to have been used medicinally, and it was not until the seventeenth century that it was used for food—and then only for seasoning. Eventually, plant breeders produced two distinctly different crop plants. One, celery root (also known as celeriac), was bred for its dense, fleshy root. The other, bunch celery, was bred for its closely bunched heads of pale green, succulent stalks. Until relatively recently, the varieties grown to produce edible stalks had to be blanched: wrapped in paper to shield them from the sun and to prevent them from toughening and turning green. However, the newest strains of bunch celery are nearly stringless and do not require blanching. Celery root, on the other hand, produces tough, dark green stalks; but the prize, so to speak, lies underground. A well-grown celery root is about the size of a grapefruit, lumpy, and brown, with a few green stems growing out the top and a few straggling roots growing downward from the sides and bottom of the main root.

Because celery tastes so strong and herbaceous, especially the leaves, it is used rather cautiously in the Chez Panisse kitchen, most frequently as part of a bouquet garni to flavor a meat or a poultry stock. Some-times, though, the tender, inner stalks of celery are used raw as an ele-ment in a midwinter salad with such vegetables as fennel, endive, and turnips, all sliced very thin. Occasionally we serve braised celery as an accompaniment to roasted meats and poultry.

In most of the country, fresh bunch celery is best from midsummer through fall. In California, celery is also abundant in midsummer, with a second season lasting throughout the winter. The best Florida celery comes in late winter and early spring. No matter where it comes from, good celery is easy to spot in the market. Look for bunches with pale green stalks and fresh-looking leaves. Open the bunch slightly. The inside surfaces of the stalks should be smooth, not rough or puffy. The heart should be pale and show no signs of discoloration. Avoid bunches that are dark green or that have stalks that look thin and stringy.

Celery keeps well in a plastic bag in the refrigerator, where it will stay fresh for several days. The outer stalks and leaves are best for cooking, and the inner stalks are best for eating raw. If you are using individual stalks, trim off a half inch from the top of the bunch and about an inch from the base. The stalks should separate easily, and can then be rinsed and drained. If you are cooking a bunch of celery whole, trim off the top half inch, but shave just an eighth inch or so from the base. Then pull the bunch apart slightly and hold it under cold running water to rinse away any sand from the heart.

Because of its milder flavor, we use celery root more than bunch celery. We often serve it raw, either by itself or combined with other root vegetables, cut into julienne and dressed with a mustard-flavored mayonnaise. It also makes a fine soup, puréed together with artichokes, chestnuts, fennel, or other cold season vegetables. Celery root is delicious as a purée or baked as a gratin to accompany grilled or roasted meat, sometimes combined with other root vegetables, such as potatoes, turnips, or parsnips. And celery root is particularly tasty when cut into slices or little batons and deep-fried.

Since celery root has a long growing season, the best is not available until the fall. But because of its very good keeping qualities both before and after harvest (celery root left underground remains good to eat after the tops die back after the first frosts), good-quality celery root can be enjoyed throughout the wintertime. Choose the small roots that are heaviest for their size: they are more likely to be dense and tender. Good, fresh celery root will feel firm and have vibrant green leaves on the stem ends. Larger, softer, lightweight roots may be pithy or even hollow.

For storage, cut off the stems and put the celery root in the coldest part of the refrigerator in a loosely tied plastic bag. Kept this way, just above freezing, it should stay fresh for a week or two.

Celery root must be peeled for all preparations. Slice off the top and bottom of the root and then peel away the sides to remove the tough skin and the many small roots attached to it. As soon as it is peeled, submerge it in acidulated water to prevent it from discoloring. If it is not

going to be used right away, put it back in the water after it has been sliced, diced, or julienned and refrigerate it.

Celery can be attractive in the garden, but it must have rich, moist soil in perfect tilth. If these conditions are not met, or if the soil is allowed to dry at any time during the growing season, results can be bitter. As we said, most varieties of bunch celery won't need blanching, especially those variously called Utah or Pascal, but some gardeners still suggest hilling the soil around the base of the plants. For celery root, the varieties called Mentor and Brilliant are often recommended.

CELERY ROOT, POTATO, AND OLIVE OIL GRATIN

4 large Yellow Finn or russet potatoes	*3 or 4 sprigs thyme*
	Salt and pepper
1 large celery root	*½ cup white wine*
2 yellow onions	*½ cup chicken stock*
Extra-virgin olive oil	*1 tablespoon butter*

Peel and slice the potatoes and celery root ⅛ inch thick. Cover with water until ready to assemble the gratin. Peel and slice the onions ¼ inch thick. Sauté in about 2 tablespoons olive oil until golden brown, about 10 minutes.

Preheat the oven to 375°F.

Drain the potatoes and celery root, removing as much water as possible. Strip the leaves off the thyme sprigs. Place half the onions in a gratin dish, season with salt and pepper, and half the thyme leaves. Arrange half of the potato and celery slices over the onions and season with salt and pepper. Make another layer with the rest of the onions, and finish with a top layer of potatoes and celery root. Evenly overlap the celery root and potato slices on the top layer for a finished look.

Pour the white wine and chicken stock over the vegetables; the liquid should come about halfway up. Drizzle generously with olive oil and dot with the butter. Season with salt and pepper and the rest of the thyme leaves, and bake, covered, for 30 minutes. Uncover and press the vegetables evenly down with a spatula, allowing the juices to baste the top layer. Continue baking, uncovered, for 30 minutes more, or until the potatoes are cooked through.

Serves 6.

CELERY ROOT AND POTATO PURÉE

*3 pounds Yellow Finn or red
    potatoes
Salt and pepper
1 medium celery root*

*¼ pound unsalted butter
About 1 cup milk or cream
White wine vinegar*

Peel the potatoes and cut them into 1½-inch chunks. Cover with water in a large pot, add some salt, bring to a boil, and cook until very tender, about 20 minutes. Drain.

Peel the celery root and cut it in 1-inch dice. Put it into a saucepan with the butter and enough water to barely cover. Cook, covered, for 20 to 25 minutes, until the celery root is tender. If necessary, add additional water to keep the celery root from sticking to the pan. The celery root will be nearly puréed.

Warm the milk or cream in another saucepan. Pass the celery root and the potatoes through a food mill or ricer. Add enough warmed milk or cream for the purée to reach the consistency you want. Season with salt and pepper and a splash of white wine vinegar to heighten the flavor of the celery root.

Serves 6 to 8.

CELERY ROOT RÉMOULADE

*1 medium celery root
Salt and pepper
Juice of 1 lemon
3 tablespoons Dijon mustard*

*½ cup homemade mayonnaise
2 tablespoons heavy cream
Parsley*

Peel the celery root and cut it into julienne about ⅛ inch thick, either by hand, with a knife or a mandolin, or with the special attachment of a food processor.

In a bowl, dissolve a pinch of salt in the lemon juice, grind in some pepper, and stir in the mustard, mayonnaise, and cream. Toss in the celery root. Taste and correct the seasoning and let stand for at least 15 minutes before serving. Mound it on a plate and sprinkle with parsley leaves.

Serves 3 to 4.

CHARD 🌰

Season: Late spring through winter

Chard is appreciated in various parts of Europe, but for some reason it is often called Swiss chard here in the United States, where it is not as well known as it deserves to be. Both its dark green leaves and their wide, thick ribs can be eaten, each cooked in different ways. The leaves can be steamed, parboiled, or sautéed, and added to soup, stuffed with meat or vegetable fillings, or used to line a pâté mold. The crisp-textured stems are delicious steamed, stewed, or gratinéed.

Most varieties of chard have medium to very dark green leaves growing from their broad white stems (or ribs). The leaves may be more or less ruffled and are rarely perfectly flat. Rhubarb chard, however, has ribs that are a brilliant red, and strongly resembles beet greens. Not surprisingly, both chard and garden beets derive from the same species, *Beta vulgaris*. France and Italy are the countries of origin for some of the choicest chard varieties, such as Paros, with curly leaves resembling those of savoy cabbage, and Argentata, which sports very dark green leaves surrounding silvery white stems.

In the colder parts of the United States, the season for chard starts in late spring and continues until late fall. In many parts of the South, and in California, chard is grown and harvested throughout the winter as well. But the chard planted in late spring seems to produce the largest and most tender leaves.

In the market, the best and most flavorful chard will have fresh, crisp, and intensely green leaves. The ribs should be stiff and free of any brown spotting. Avoid bunches that have been bundled too tightly: the leaves will be bruised. In the case of chard, baby leaves are not a guarantee of quality. In fact, the largest leaves will often be the most tender.

Unless the chard is very small and immature, it is best to separate its leaves from their ribs before cooking. This is easily accomplished by loosely folding the leaf in half along the stem, grasping the folded leaf with one hand, and pulling the rib away with the other hand. This will go very quickly once you get the hang of it. Once stripped off, the leaves are ready to be washed, drained, and used as the recipe directs. Some fastidious cooks like to peel the ribs, pulling away the strings as if from celery stalks, but this is rarely necessary. (The ribs should be washed and drained before proceeding, of course.) The ribs will look neater if their edges are trimmed a little. Chard that has been prepared for cooking can be covered or wrapped in plastic and kept refrigerated for several hours until needed.

Few vegetables look more handsome growing in a kitchen garden than chard. Both green and red varieties add terrific color and texture. A couple of plants will not take up much room, and by harvesting only the outer leaves from the plants as they mature, you can ensure a steady supply throughout the entire season from a single planting.

Sautéed Chard with Lemon and Hot Pepper

Stem the chard, wash and drain the leaves, and cut them into a rough chiffonade. Sauté in olive oil, covered, for 5 minutes or so, until the leaves are wilted and tender. Remove the cover and cook away the excess moisture. Season at the last minute with a pinch of red pepper flakes according to taste, and with salt and pepper, and squeeze lemon juice over just before serving.

Chard Stem Gratin

Chard stems are delicious. Remove their strings, if necessary, then parboil until tender, drain, and arrange in a gratin dish with bits of fried pancetta, some chopped garlic, chopped flat-leaf parsley, and a seeded, coarsely chopped tomato. Cover with a bit of béchamel sauce or cream and gratinée in a preheated 450°F. oven or under the broiler until golden.

BRAISED CHARD

Separate the leaves and ribs of a large very fresh bunch of red or green chard. Wash, drain, and cut the leaves into a rough chiffonade. Slice a large sweet onion and start it stewing in some olive oil in a pot large enough to hold all the chard leaves. After the onion softens, add the chard leaves, season with salt and pepper, cover, and stew for 20 to 30 minutes, stirring every so often. Although additions such as garlic, pancetta, or lemon can be made, the chief virtues of chard cooked this way are its own sweet flavor and a meltingly tender texture.

CHARD GRATIN

2 pounds young red or green chard
1 clove garlic
3 tablespoons unsalted butter
2 cups milk

2 tablespoons flour
Whole nutmeg
Salt and pepper
¾ cup Toasted Bread Crumbs (page 319)

Preheat the oven to 375°F.

Wash the chard and cut off the thick ends of the stems. Parboil the chard for 1½ minutes in lightly salted boiling water. Drain, squeeze out the water from the leaves, and chop them into ¾-inch pieces. Peel the garlic and chop it very fine.

Melt the butter over medium heat in a large, nonreactive skillet and add the chard. Turn the chard in the butter as it begins to wilt, add the garlic, and continue cooking slowly, uncovered, for 7 or 8 minutes, until the leaves have begun to soften. Warm the milk in a small saucepan.

Sprinkle the flour over the chard and stir to distribute the flour evenly. Cook for 1 minute more and then begin to slowly add the milk, about ¼ cup at a time. Continue adding the milk in small amounts as it is absorbed by the chard until the milk is completely incorporated.

Season with a light grating of nutmeg, salt, and pepper; transfer to a buttered gratin dish. The layer of chard should be about 1 inch thick. Cover evenly with the bread crumbs and bake for 35 minutes, until the crumbs have browned nicely.

Serves 4.

CHARD, SPINACH, AND ESCAROLE PASTA

Greens cooked this way make an excellent side dish without the pasta.

1 bunch chard (about 1 pound)	*1 tablespoon chopped fresh*
2 pounds spinach	*thyme*
1 large head escarole	*1 cup red wine*
2 large red onions	*1 pound linguine*
3 or 4 cloves garlic	*½ cup stock or water*
¼ cup olive oil	*2 tablespoons capers (see Note)*
1 bay leaf	*Salt and pepper*

Stem the chard and the spinach, if necessary. Remove the core from the escarole and separate the leaves. Wash all the greens and cut into chiffonade. Peel and coarsely chop the onions. Peel and chop the garlic very fine. Put a pot of salted water on for boiling the pasta.

Heat a heavy casserole over medium to high heat; add about half the olive oil and the onions, bay leaf, and thyme; cook, covered, until tender, about 5 minutes. Uncover, and continue cooking about 5 minutes more, or until the onions are very brown, just short of burning. Add the red wine and deglaze the pan, cover, turn the heat to low, and simmer for 3 to 4 minutes.

Put the pasta on to cook. Uncover the onions and add the garlic. After a minute or so add the greens and the stock. Cook for 5 minutes, add the capers, and season to taste with salt and pepper.

Drain the pasta and add to the casserole with the greens. Pour a little olive oil over, toss well, and serve.

Serves 6.

Note: Use either large salt-packed capers, rinsed and coarsely chopped, or brine-packed ones, leaving them whole if they are small.

CHERVIL
See Herbs (page 168)

CHICKPEAS &

Season: Fresh, summer; dried, year-round

Depending on where you live, the edible seeds of the legume *Cicer arietinum* may be called chickpeas or garbanzos, their Spanish name. Chickpeas are native to the eastern Mediterranean and the Middle East, from whence they were introduced into North Africa and Spain, and, eastward, into India and Central Asia. In the course of exploring these cuisines at Chez Panisse, we have used chickpeas in tagines and couscous from Morocco, in salads from Spain and Mexico, and in breads and curries from India. Chickpeas harmonize particularly well with seasonings of cilantro and cumin.

One of our cooks grew up in Kabul, Afghanistan, and fondly remembers the markets there where you can buy crunchy chickpeas roasted in hot sand (like beer nuts, he says), potatoes and onions deep-fried in chickpea batter, and slices of gelatinized cooked chickpeas served with cilantro and vinegar.

In Provence—closer to home, so to speak, for much of the cooking we do—chickpeas are served both hot and cold in salads. One Provençal cook we know soaks her chickpeas in mineral water, cooks them with the usual aromatic vegetables, and dresses them, while still warm, with a paste of garlic, parsley, olive oil, and salt and pepper pounded in a mortar. Chickpea flour is used in Provence to make a kind of crêpe, called *soca*, and a bread called *panisse*. We felt obliged to try and make *panisse* once, but we didn't achieve an authentic result.

During the summer, we sometimes find fresh chickpeas at the markets in San Francisco that cater to ethnic cooks. These can be shelled and cooked in the same way as other fresh shell beans.

Most often we use the familiar dried chickpeas: round, buff-colored, and the size of very large peas. They are available in bulk at natural food stores and, increasingly, in supermarkets. (There are varieties grown in other parts of the world that are pale green, brown, or black.)

Because they are very hard and dense, dried chickpeas must be soaked in water overnight before cooking. Chickpeas are said to be difficult to cook properly in hard water, and some cookbooks recommend that you soak and cook them in rainwater. If you know that your water has a high calcium content, it is probably wise to cook your chickpeas in bottled water. There is no sure way to tell how old chickpeas are, but as with many other dried legumes, the fresher they are, the faster and more evenly they cook. Sort through them before soaking, as small stones and dirt clods are sometimes harvested along with the beans.

Once soaked, chickpeas should be simmered in water for one to two hours, until they are tender. Salt them toward the end of the cooking, once they have softened. Chickpeas that are to be served whole can be peeled, although this is seldom done. Simmer them until just barely tender, from forty-five minutes to an hour. Drain them and submerge again in cold water. Rub them between your hands and skim the skins from the surface of the water as they rise to the top. Remove the chickpeas from the water and continue cooking as the recipe directs. Cooked chickpeas can be kept for several days in their cooking liquid in the refrigerator.

Don't even think about growing chickpeas at home. They yield only two or three beans in each pod, and require an enormous amount of space. Furthermore, the only named variety we have found listed in a seed catalog, the Black Kabouli, is purported to attract thunderstorms when it is flowering!

Spanish Chickpea Soup

2 cups dried chickpeas
6 to 7 cups chicken stock or water
1½ large yellow onions
1 carrot
A few sprigs thyme
1 sprig marjoram
2 bay leaves
One 2-inch piece orange zest

1 small bunch parsley
Salt and pepper
½ stalk celery
2 tablespoons olive oil
1½ teaspoons paprika
1 teaspoon red wine vinegar
1 pinch cayenne
2 tablespoons extra-virgin olive oil

Soak the chickpeas overnight in water. Drain and put them in a large pot and cover with the chicken stock or water. Add half an onion and half a carrot, peeled, and a bouquet garni made with the thyme, marjoram, bay leaves, orange zest, and most of the parsley (save a few sprigs to chop for a garnish). Bring to a simmer and cook until the chickpeas are tender, 1 to 2 hours, depending on the age of the chickpeas. Check after 1 hour and season with salt. When the chickpeas are cooked, discard the onion and carrot, taste for salt, and adjust as necessary.

While the beans are cooking, peel and chop the remaining onion and carrot and the celery into ¼-inch dice. Sauté in the olive oil until the vegetables are thoroughly cooked. Season with salt and stir in the paprika, red wine vinegar, and cayenne. Add the vegetables to the chickpeas and their liquid, and simmer together gently for 20 minutes. Remove and discard the bouquet garni.

Purée one third of the soup in a blender or food processor and pass through a medium-mesh sieve. Return the purée to the rest of the soup, check the consistency, and thin out with a little water, if necessary, and taste and adjust the seasoning. Serve garnished with the extra-virgin olive oil and chopped parsley.

Serves 6 to 8.

Note: A Sicilian version of chickpea soup is garnished before serving with peeled, seeded, and diced tomatoes sautéed in olive oil with onions and garlic, red pepper, and rosemary.

CHICKPEA SALAD WITH PICKLED ONIONS

Rapidly fried or grilled squid, with aïoli, is a particularly good addition to a chickpea salad. Usually with green beans added as well, that salad has become a traditional part of the menu at our annual Bastille Day garlic celebration.

2 cups dried chickpeas	*Salt and pepper*
About ½ cup extra-virgin	*2 stalks celery*
olive oil	*1 clove garlic*
1 small onion	*4 large basil leaves*
1 carrot	*12 mint leaves*
1 jalapeño pepper	*2 Pickled Red Onions*
2 sprigs thyme	*(page 219)*
2 bay leaves	*Red wine vinegar*

Soak the chickpeas overnight in cold water. Before cooking, rinse them thoroughly in running water.

In a large pot, heat a little of the olive oil and sauté the onion, cut in quarters; the carrot, peeled; and the jalapeño pepper, halved and seeded. Add about a quart of water and the thyme sprigs and bay leaves, and bring to a slow boil. Add the chickpeas, return to a boil, and then reduce the heat to a gentle simmer. Cook until they are soft throughout, between 1 and 2 hours. Check after 1 hour and season with 2 teaspoons salt.

Drain the cooked chickpeas and remove the onion, carrot, pepper, and bay leaves. Toss the chickpeas with just enough olive oil to lightly coat them. Taste and season with salt and pepper. Let the chickpeas cool.

Peel and thinly slice the celery, chop the garlic fine, and chop the herbs, and add to the chickpeas. Combine with pickled red onions, and let the salad stand for 5 minutes before correcting the seasoning as needed with more oil, vinegar, or salt and pepper.

Serves 6.

CHICKPEA AND FARRO SOUP

4 cups dried chickpeas	*2 cups cooked Farro (page 321)*
3 bay leaves	*Extra-virgin olive oil*
3 sprigs thyme	*1½ large onions*
Zest of 1 orange	*3 stalks celery*
½ head garlic	*Cayenne*
2 carrots	*A few sprigs rosemary*
2 tablespoons salt	

Soak the chickpeas overnight, drain them, and rinse them thoroughly under running water. Wrap 2 of the bay leaves, the thyme, and the orange zest in cheesecloth and add to a large pot with the chickpeas, the garlic, and the carrots, peeled. Add enough water to cover, bring to a boil, and simmer for 1 to 2 hours. The cooking time will vary according to the age and provenance of the chickpeas. Check after 1 hour and season with the salt. When done, the chickpeas should be completely tender and hold their shape.

While the chickpeas are cooking, prepare half the recipe for Farro, finished with olive oil, and reserve. Chop the onions and celery very fine; in another large pot, cook them gently in olive oil with a little salt and the remaining bay leaf until they are soft.

When the chickpeas are done, remove the carrots, the garlic, and the aromatics wrapped in cheesecloth. Reserve about one quarter of the chickpeas and the liquid, and pass the rest with the remaining liquid through a food mill into the pot with the onions and celery. Add the whole chickpeas and their liquid, and bring to a simmer. The soup should be quite thick, but it can be thinned with hot water at this point, if necessary. Add the farro and continue to simmer for 5 minutes. Taste and adjust the seasoning with salt, pepper, and a pinch of cayenne. Serve drizzled with fruity olive oil or olive oil infused with orange zest, and sprinkle with a little chopped rosemary.

Serves 8.

Moroccan Chickpeas

Serve this chickpea dish on a bed of couscous, along with such vegetables as small white turnips, young carrots, and spring fava beans, sautéed and highly spiced. Chopped preserved lemon is a delicious and authentic accompaniment, and so is a dollop of Harissa (page 241).

2 cups dried chickpeas	*1 pinch ground saffron*
1 small carrot	*1 teaspoon ground turmeric*
1 yellow onion	*½ teaspoon cayenne*
1 small bunch cilantro	*2 ripe tomatoes*
One 2-inch knob fresh ginger	*Salt*
One 1-inch piece cinnamon stick	

Soak the chickpeas overnight in cold water. Peel the carrot and onion and chop roughly. Drain the chickpeas and cover with fresh water. Bring to a boil, skim off the foam, and turn down to a simmer. Add the carrot and onion. Cut off the stems of the cilantro and reserve the leaves to garnish the finished dish. Tie the stems in a bundle and add to the chickpeas along with the ginger, peeled, and the cinnamon, saffron, turmeric, and cayenne. Keep the chickpeas submerged in water as they cook, but do not add more water than necessary, so as not to dilute the flavorful broth.

Peel, seed, and coarsely chop the tomatoes. After 30 to 45 minutes, when the chickpeas are about three quarters cooked, add the tomatoes and salt to taste. Continue to simmer until the chickpeas are very soft and the broth has thickened slightly, about 1 hour. Remove and discard the cinnamon, ginger, and cilantro stems. Taste for seasoning, garnish with the reserved cilantro leaves, and serve.

Serves 6.

CHICORIES 🐚

Season: Mid-fall to late spring

Chicories are all Old World members of the daisy family, closely related to lettuces and dandelions, which they resemble. Escarole, Belgian endive, curly endive, and radicchio are only a few of the many types found in the market. These leafy vegetables are all varieties of either *Cichorium intybus* or *Cichorium endivia*. Nomenclature is confusing, to say the least. *Cichorium*, of course, gives us chicory; and *endivia*, endive. But what we call Belgian endive, following the French, is the characteristically tight-headed white forced variety of *Cichorium intybus*, which the British call chicory (and the Belgians call witloof). And the shock-headed, leafy green fright wig the French call *chicorée* or *chicorée frisée* is a variety of *Cichorium endivia* that we call curly endive (or frisée). The red varieties that originated in Italy are called radicchio both here and there (or *cicorie*), but the cabbage-shaped kind is properly called by the more specific name Rossa di Verona, while the looser, romaine-shaped radicchio is called Rossa di Treviso. Red chicory can also be forced in the winter to produce tight heads shaped exactly like Belgian endive, but colored Burgundy-red at the tips and along the leaf margins. One of the most beautiful sights at the restaurant is a basket of tiny spring radicchios looking like parrot tulip leaves all creamy and speckled with maroon.

Further inconsistency extends to pronunciation: at Chez Panisse, we are about equally divided between those of us who say EN-dive to rhyme with jive, with the accent on the first syllable, and those who prefer to echo the French and say on-DEEVE or ON-deeve. Both are correct. However, customers unfamiliar with the Italian chicories, which have only recently become widely commercialized in the United States, sometimes do not know that the *ch* in the word *radicchio* is not pronounced like the *ch* in peachy, but like the *ch* in Pinocchio.

Like lettuces, chicories are variously shaped—loose-leaf or headed, tapered or round, leaves whole or finely divided, curly- or smooth-edged. Their colors can be intense, ranging from pure whites and pale yellows, to bright greens, to the maroon-red hues of radicchio. Whereas lettuces are generally prized for a certain delicacy of flavor and texture, the chicories are valued for a certain wild bitterness, common to them all. Some varieties—especially Belgian endive, radicchio, and escarole—though crisp and delicious raw, have a sturdiness that makes them also highly suitable for braising or grilling.

At Chez Panisse we make a great many dishes with chicories. Their refreshingly bitter flavor and substantial crunchy texture combine well with richer foods in composed salads: with nuts, apples, and cheese; with smoked fish or caviar and crème fraîche; and with duck confit or pigeon and pigeon liver toasts. One of the best chicory salads is made with a red wine and balsamic vinaigrette enriched with highly reduced essence of pigeon roasting juices. We often serve spoonfuls of salmon caviar or fresh white bean paste on the separated leaves of Belgian endive instead of on croutons. The tougher leafy chicories make particularly good warm wilted salads, tossed with a little garlic in hot olive oil, or with duck or bacon fat, and splashed with vinegar. Radicchio is often grilled and served warm or at room temperature with salsa verde or an anchovy vinaigrette, or is added to risotti. Belgian endives are sometimes browned very slowly in butter and served alongside grilled fish and meat, or are baked in a gratin with bacon and a little Parmesan, or are braised with mushrooms and cream.

Chicories love to grow in cool, moist weather, so they are most often sown in late summer, to mature in the cool months of fall. In mild climates the heads can often be harvested throughout the winter. They are less successful grown in the spring, unless sown very early, because with the first sign of hot weather they quickly become impossibly bitter and tough. Belgian endive is an exception, but its leafy tops are chopped off and discarded at the end of the growing season, and it is the sizable roots that are harvested and stored in order to be forced indoors during the winter, producing the pale, tightly bunched leaf-stem clusters known as chicons.

The outer leaves of any chicory in the market should be bright and crisp, with no wilting or browning. The hearts of leafy varieties such as Batavian, escarole, Sugarloaf, and curly endive should be pale yellow,

almost white. The stem ends should not be brown or dried out. Flavor should be pleasantly bitter, balanced by a sweetness that can be surprising if tasted within a few hours of harvest. Cooking intensifies both the bitterness and sweetness, so don't expect to rescue a bitter radicchio by grilling it. Parboiling it in boiling salted water may help.

The outer leaves of the tightly headed varieties such as Belgian endive and some radicchios may be your only guide to their quality. Exposed to light, Belgian endive quickly gets bitter and starts turning pale green, so choose only perfect specimens that are tightly compacted and pure white, with tips of the palest yellow. Reject radicchio that shows any browned or withered outer leaves.

All chicories should be refrigerated as soon as possible after purchase. Wrapped loosely in a towel and put in a plastic bag, they will keep fresh for a day or two. It is especially important to keep Belgian endive wrapped and refrigerated so it will be protected from light. Belgian endive bruises easily and browns quite rapidly, so it is best to wash it and cut it up just before serving or cooking. Leafy chicories for a salad can be washed and dried ahead of time, like lettuce. Belgian endive and radicchio often need only be wiped with a damp towel.

The leafy chicories, especially curly endive, will be at home in a kitchen garden, but be careful not to harvest them too soon, as the inner, blanched leaves are the best. Thinnings can be used in mesclun-type mixtures of salad greens, but only when you want a bitter accent, and only in small quantities. The larger, heading varieties are suitable for gardeners who can spare the room during a longer growing season. Experimentation with indoor Belgian endive cultivation should certainly be considered by the adventurous.

LONG-COOKED ENDIVES

A simple way to cook Belgian endives. Count 1 big or 2 small endives per person. Cut them in half lengthwise and steam, cut side down, until they have become slightly translucent but are still firm at the base. Finish in a nonstick pan over a low flame with butter and salt and pepper. They are ready when completely soft. The long cooking and the sweet butter bring a nice balance to a somewhat bitter winter vegetable. Serve with a flavorful white fish, such as bass, or with a pork roast.

BRAISED BELGIAN ENDIVE

Trim 6 endives and slice them in half lengthwise. Season well with salt and pepper. In a heavy-bottomed skillet, heat some butter and brown the cut side of the endives over a high flame. Do this in batches, adding butter each time. The pan will brown, which is fine—just don't allow it to blacken; if it does, wash it out before the next batch. Place the endives, browned side up, in a gratin dish just large enough to hold them in a single layer. Pour chicken stock into the dish to a depth of about ½ inch. Cover tightly and bake in a preheated 400°F. oven for 20 minutes or until quite tender.

Serves 6.

Note: For a richer, more savory version, the halved endives can be wrapped in thinly sliced pancetta or bacon before browning. This requires a slower flame and browning on both sides. The butter will still be needed to keep the meat from sticking. This makes a fine first course all by itself, or it can be a delightful accompaniment to roasted or grilled meats and birds.

BELGIAN ENDIVE SALAD WITH CAVIAR AND CRÈME FRAÎCHE

3 to 4 Belgian endives
4 tablespoons extra-virgin
  olive oil
1 lemon

Salt and pepper
½ cup crème fraîche
¾ cup salmon caviar

Trim the endives (ideally half red and half white), separate into leaves, and toss in a salad bowl with the olive oil and a few drops of lemon juice. Add salt, pepper, and more lemon juice to taste. Put the leaves on a platter or chilled plates. Evenly drizzle the crème fraîche over the endive (if the cream is too thick to drip gently from the spoon, it may need to be thinned out with a little pouring cream). Spoon the caviar over the salad and serve.

Serves 4.

Note: Replace the caviar with thin slices of smoked salmon or with flaked, boned fillets of smoked trout.

Belgian Endive Risotto with Taleggio and Walnuts

6 Belgian endives
1 medium yellow onion
2 quarts chicken stock
3 tablespoons olive oil
1¼ cups Arborio rice
Salt and pepper

⅓ cup dry white wine
2 tablespoons butter
2 to 3 ounces Taleggio cheese
2 tablespoons chopped toasted
  walnuts (see page 108)
Parsley

Trim the endives, slice them in half lengthwise, and then cut them crosswise into ½-inch-thick slices and set aside. Peel and chop the onion into small dice. Heat the chicken stock.

In a heavy-bottomed saucepan, heat the olive oil and cook the onion over medium heat until it is translucent but not brown, about 5 minutes. Stir in the rice and a pinch of salt. Cook over low heat for about 3 minutes, stirring often, until the rice has turned slightly translucent. Keep stirring, turn up the heat, and pour in the white wine. The pot will boil violently and the wine will almost completely evaporate. Add just enough hot stock to cover the rice, stir well, and reduce the heat.

Keep the rice at a gentle simmer. As it absorbs liquid, add more stock, a ladle or two at a time, to keep the pot simmering at a level just above the rice, stirring before and after every addition. After 15 minutes, the rice kernels will be nearly cooked but still slightly crunchy in the middle. Stir in the endive and the butter and continue cooking for 3 to 5 minutes. Taste for texture. If the rice is not quite cooked and appears to be becoming sticky, add a little more broth.

The finished risotto should be creamy and almost pourable, neither dry nor soupy. The rice should be somewhat chewy and firm, neither crunchy nor so cooked that the kernels have split. Just before serving, stir in the Taleggio and taste for seasoning, adding salt and pepper to taste. Garnish with the walnuts and parsley and serve immediately.

Serves 6.

Wilted Escarole

Wash and trim the escarole. Cut the leaves into wide strips. Sauté in olive oil, covered, until wilted and bright green, about 2 to 3 minutes. Season with salt and pepper, add a splash of vinegar, and serve.

HEARTS OF ESCAROLE WITH APPLES AND ROQUEFORT

Throughout the season, salads of chicory and fall fruits—persimmons, apples, pears, figs—appear often on our menus; many are garnished with toasted walnuts, pecans, or almonds.

1 head escarole or other chicory	*1 tablespoon sherry vinegar or*
1 Sierra Beauty apple	*white wine vinegar*
¼ cup shelled walnuts	*Salt and pepper*
3 to 4 tablespoons extra-virgin	*2 ounces Roquefort cheese*
olive oil	

Preheat the oven to 350°F. Trim the escarole, discarding any tough outer leaves, wash thoroughly, and spin dry. Peel, core, and slice the Sierra Beauty apple (or use another favorite eating apple). Toast the walnuts in the oven for about 5 minutes. Take the walnuts out of the oven and rub them in a towel to remove the loose skin, which may be bitter.

Whisk together the olive oil and vinegar, and season with salt and pepper. Toss the escarole and apple together with the dressing. Sprinkle with the Roquefort cheese, crumbled, and the toasted walnuts.

Serves 4.

CURLY ENDIVE, RADICCHIO, AND FUYU PERSIMMON SALAD

1 shallot	*1 radicchio*
1 tablespoon red wine vinegar	*3 small heads curly endive*
A splash of sherry vinegar	*6 ripe fuyu persimmons*
Salt and pepper	*6 tablespoons olive oil*

Peel and finely dice the shallot and put it in a salad bowl with the vinegars and a pinch of salt.

While the shallot is macerating, fill up the sink or a large bowl with cold water. Peel the radicchio, discarding the outer leaves; tear the remaining leaves into bite-size pieces and toss them into the water. Remove the outer leaves of the curly endive, saving only the pale green and white, tender hearts. (Reserve the outer leaves for cooking greens.) Cut out the tough core and add the leaves to the sink. Gently agitate the greens and let them sit in the water for a few minutes. Scoop out the leaves from the water with your hands without disturbing the sand and dirt at the bottom of the sink. Dry the leaves in a salad spinner.

Peel and slice the persimmons into ¼-inch wedges. Whisk the olive oil into the shallot and vinegar and taste for acidity, adjusting as necessary. Add the persimmon slices to the bowl, season with salt and pepper, and toss. Add the chicories, season with salt and pepper, and gently toss again, mixing all the ingredients. Taste the salad and adjust the seasoning if necessary. Serve on a platter or chilled plates.

Serves 6.

CURLY ENDIVE SALAD WITH FIGS AND WALNUTS

This salad is especially good with a duck liver crouton. It can also be made with young dandelion greens or mâche instead of curly endive. For more on salads, see Lettuces and Other Salad Greens (page 193).

2 heads curly endive — *¾ cup shelled walnuts*
(about 1 pound) — *12 very fresh, ripe figs*
2 shallots — *½ cup extra-virgin olive oil*
2 tablespoons balsamic vinegar — *Salt and pepper*

Preheat the oven to 350°F.

Tear off the tough outer leaves of the curly endive, saving only the pale green and white, tender hearts. (Reserve the outer leaves for cooking greens.) Cut out the core and plunge the leaves into a sink or basin filled with cold water. Gently agitate the greens and let them soak for a few minutes. Scoop out the leaves and dry them in a salad spinner.

Peel and chop the shallots very fine, cover with the vinegar, and macerate for 20 minutes. Spread the walnuts on a baking sheet and toast them in the oven for 5 to 8 minutes. When cool, rub any excess skin off the walnuts—between your hands or in a towel.

Chop 6 of the figs very fine (peel them first if they are tough-skinned) and add them to the shallots. Whisk in the olive oil and season with salt and pepper. Just before serving, quarter the rest of the figs, and toss with the curly endive, walnuts, and just enough dressing to coat all the elements. If the figs are very tender, dress them apart and arrange them around the greens. Serve immediately.

Serves 6.

Warm Curly Endive Salad with Spring Onions

Thoroughly wash and dry some curly endive. Make a vinaigrette with red wine vinegar and a little balsamic vinegar, some finely mashed garlic, salt, and olive oil. Slice sweet young red onion very thin, and in a large sauté pan, sauté it quickly in a little olive oil until limp and a little browned. Add the curly endive and the vinaigrette and toss quickly over heat until the endive is just starting to wilt. Grind some pepper over the salad and serve it by itself—or as a main dish with a grilled pork chop.

Chicories Grilled over the Coals

Almost any chicory can be grilled. The loose-headed radicchio called Rossa di Treviso can be left whole if it is small; other radicchios, Belgian endive, escarole, and curly endive should be halved or quartered, depending on their size; if they are larger than, say, a clenched fist, they should be quartered. Dip the pieces in a basin of water and let them drain in a large colander. The water they retain helps prevent them from burning over the coals. Brush them lightly with a vinaigrette made with balsamic vinegar, extra-virgin olive oil, a few sprigs of thyme, and a little crushed garlic. Season the chicories with salt and pepper and place them on a grill over a medium-hot fire. Turn the chicories often on the grill as each side begins to brown lightly, basting with the vinaigrette as you turn. Total cooking time will vary from 20 to 30 minutes, depending on the variety. The small, leafy ones, such as Treviso and Rossa di Verona take less time than the firm-headed varieties, such as Castelfranco and Belgian endive. When they have finished cooking, the chicories should be deeply browned and crisp on the surface, and completely cooked through and soft. They are good as accompaniments to grilled meats or fish; in pastas or risotti; on pizza, with anchovies; or alone or with other grilled vegetables, warm or at room temperature, with spring Salsa Verde or Salsa Rustica (page 174).

GRILLED RADICCHIO RISOTTO WITH BALSAMIC VINEGAR

1½ medium heads radicchio
4 tablespoons olive oil
Salt and pepper
1 medium yellow onion
2 quarts chicken stock

1¼ cups Arborio rice
⅓ cup dry white wine
2 teaspoons balsamic vinegar
4 tablespoons butter

Trim the radicchio, tearing off any bruised or damaged leaves and cutting off any root or stem. Cut the radicchio into 9 wedges and toss with 1 tablespoon of the olive oil and a little salt. Grill the radicchio wedges over a medium fire until they are wilted and lightly colored but not charred. When they are cool enough to handle, chop them coarsely and set aside.

Peel and cut the onion into small dice. Heat the chicken stock. In a heavy-bottomed saucepan, heat the remaining 3 tablespoons olive oil and cook the onion over medium heat until it is translucent but not brown, about 5 minutes. Stir in the rice and a pinch of salt. Make sure that the rice is lightly coated with oil and cook over low heat for about 3 minutes, stirring often, until it has turned slightly translucent. Keep stirring, turn up the heat, and pour in the white wine. The pot will boil violently and the wine will almost completely evaporate. Add just enough hot stock to cover the rice, stir well, and reduce the heat.

Keep the rice at a gentle simmer. As it absorbs liquid, add more stock, a ladle or two at a time, to keep the pot simmering at a level just above the rice, stirring before and after every addition. After 15 minutes, the rice kernels will be nearly cooked but still slightly crunchy in the middle. Stir in the radicchio, the balsamic vinegar, and the butter and continue cooking for 3 to 5 minutes. Taste for texture. If the rice is not quite cooked and is becoming sticky, add a little more broth. Taste for seasoning, adding salt and pepper to taste.

The finished risotto should be creamy and almost pourable, neither dry nor soupy. The rice should be somehat chewy and firm, neither crunchy nor so cooked that the kernels have split. Serve the risotto immediately, garnished with more black pepper freshly ground over it.

Serves 4 to 6.

CORIANDER (CILANTRO) ❧
See Herbs (page 167)

CORN &

Season: Summer

The first fresh sweet ears of the summer's corn crop reach us in June from farmers in southern California. The Chino family takes justifiable pride in the corn they send us early in the summer from their farm outside San Diego; they grow as many as fifteen or twenty kinds, never tiring of experimenting with new and old varieties and hybrids. When the first corn arrives, by air freight, we sometimes offer it in the café by the ear, grilled on the cob. (One pun-loving maître d' used to insist on listing corn-on-the-cob on the menu as "Buccaneer corn"—because we sold it for a dollar an ear.) We use fresh sweet corn for a myriad of preparations: corn soup, corn soufflés, corn custards, corn salads. We combine corn with other summer vegetables to make succotash. We make corn and pepper relish and a relish for salmon with corn kernels, red onion, chervil, parsley, cucumbers, and olive oil.

The old-fashioned wisdom about corn-on-the-cob says to put your pot of water on to boil before you go out to the garden to harvest the ears. There is a good reason why: Traditional, open-pollinated sweet corn starts converting its sugar into starch immediately after it is picked. Modern hybrid corn varieties have been bred to reduce the need for such a drastic approach to corn cookery. The newest hybrids are known as Super Sweet, or SH2 hybrids, and Sugary Enhanced, SE (or EH) hybrids; not only are they many times sweeter than previous varieties, they are crisper, and they measure their loss of sweetness in days and weeks, instead of minutes and hours. They have such names as How Sweet It Is, Candy Store, and Kandy Korn, and they appear to be displacing many of the previous Normal Sugary hybrids. This is not necessarily a blessing, for although they are extremely sweet, they strike many corn lovers as having insufficient corn flavor. Ears of Super Sweet corn stored for a week or more taste distinctly odd, being both cloyingly sweet and somehow stale-tasting at the same time. Even when they are very fresh, some eaters find them much too sweet.

The earlier generations of hybrids included some wonderful varieties that still turn up in markets: the white Silver Queen, the bicolored Peaches and Cream, the yellow Early Sunglow, to name a few. And you may find heirloom varieties of open-pollinated corn for sale. Home gardeners often choose to grow an unhybridized sweet corn variety called Golden Bantam, which is still considered a benchmark of corn flavor years after being introduced.

No matter what the variety, it is still safe to say that the fresher the corn the better. If you don't have a corn patch of your own, buy locally grown corn straight from the farmer—at a produce stand on the side of the road or at a farmer's market. At the market, look closely at the ears. The ones picked most recently will have fresh-looking cuts at their stems and will still look—and feel—moist, plump, green, and vibrant. The brown silk peeping out at the top will look a little sticky. Kernels should look shiny and healthy. Do not panic if you see the occasional worm. Obviously you do not want worm-infested corn, but it can be reassuring to know that the farmer has not gone overboard with the pesticides.

Another surprise that sometimes greets corn shuckers is a kind of corn smut, or fungus, that may produce what are called "galls" on the ears. A corn fungus gall is a swollen, convoluted, creamy-colored excrescence with a texture resembling a mushroom's. In Mexico, this corn fungus is known as *huitlacoche*, and it is prized as a delicacy, gently cooked, wrapped in crêpes or tortillas.

If you cannot serve it immediately, corn should be stored in the refrigerator, unhusked and wrapped in a damp towel.

Corn should be shucked at the last minute, and any wispy corn silk pulled away from the bare ears. If it is to be boiled and served on the cob, it will be ready in no more than about two minutes in rapidly boiling water. Do not salt the water; salt toughens the kernels during cooking. If a recipe calls for fresh corn kernels, shuck the corn and cut off the stem end; holding the ear by its tip and resting it firmly on the cutting board on its base, slice the kernels off the cob with a sharp knife.

The other way we use corn at the restaurant is in the form of cornmeal, the white or yellow ground dried corn that we make into polenta and corn bread year-round. If you can find it, stone-ground cornmeal milled from organically grown corn has a robust corny flavor superior to that of mass-produced cornmeal.

Corn is a summer crop that needs lots of warm weather, water, and fertilizer. The foggy summers in the Bay Area make corn a dicey proposition in our backyard gardens, although some rapidly maturing varieties do well. Gardeners in sunnier zones should take care that the soil temperature has reached about 60°F. before planting, and that the nights are warming up. Sow the seeds about an inch deep and a foot apart, with three feet between rows. To ensure successful pollination, there should be a block of corn plants at least four feet square. Keep the soil irrigated and fertilize the corn once or twice while it is growing.

GRILLED CORN-ON-THE-COB

To prepare corn for grilling, peel back the husks but do not tear them off. Tear out and discard the corn silk, and then pull the husks back over the cobs. (Some cooks moisten the husks with water before grilling, which helps keep them from burning, especially over a very hot fire.) Put the cobs on a hot grill over a medium-low fire for 7 to 8 minutes, turning every few minutes. Before serving, check one to make sure it is done. Serve with sweet butter and salt. Or serve with lime wedges and a mixture of salt and cayenne to sprinkle on the corn.

CORN AND SUMMER CHANTERELLES

Clean and slice some chanterelles and sauté in a little butter. Season with salt and pepper. When they have begun to brown and are nearly done, add some chopped garlic and parsley, and continue cooking gently another minute or two. Add fresh sweet corn kernels cut from the cob and a splash of water. Cook until the corn is just done, taste for seasoning, and add a nut of butter off the heat. (You can also incorporate cooked fresh shell beans in this sauté.) This is very good with grilled or roast pigeon or chicken.

CORN PUDDING SOUFFLÉ

This type of pudding soufflé is a preparation that is both more substantial and less risky than a traditional soufflé. We make many versions to serve as first courses: with green garlic instead of corn, with zucchini, with wild mushrooms. One interesting variation incorporates boiled lobster tail baked in the soufflé, and is served with a reduced lobster sauce made from the shells.

8 ears sweet corn	*4 eggs*
2 cups half-and-half	*Salt and pepper*
6 tablespoons unsalted butter	*A pinch cayenne*
4 tablespoons flour	*½ cup heavy cream*
2 sprigs thyme	*1 handful basil leaves*

Shuck the corn and slice the kernels off the cobs. Set aside half the kernels to be added to the soufflé mixture later. Cut each corn cob into several pieces and put them in a saucepan with the other half of the corn kernels. Pour in the half-and-half. Bring to a simmer over very low heat, remove from the heat, and scrape the cobs with the blunt side of a knife to squeeze out all the cream and corn juices. Purée the corn and the half-and-half in a food processor or blender and strain through a medium-fine strainer.

In a heavy-bottomed saucepan, melt 3 tablespoons of the butter, add the flour, and cook over a low flame for a few minutes, stirring to keep the flour and butter from browning. Add the thyme and slowly pour in the puréed corn and half-and-half, whisking all the time to prevent any lumps from forming. Once all the purée has been added, let the mixture cook for 20 to 30 minutes over low heat, stirring frequently to keep it from sticking to the bottom of the pot. Remove and allow to cool to room temperature. Take out the thyme sprigs.

Preheat the oven to 400°F. Lightly butter 6 ramekins.

Melt the remaining 3 tablespoons butter and whisk into the soufflé base mixture when it has cooled; add the reserved corn kernels. Separate the eggs and beat the egg yolks into the base, one by one. Season with salt, pepper, and cayenne.

Beat the egg whites until they form soft peaks and gently fold them into the soufflé base. Ladle the mixture into the ramekins and place them in a baking dish. Pour in enough hot water to come halfway up the sides of the ramekins. Place the dish with the ramekins in the oven. The little soufflés should take about 30 minutes to cook, but check after 20 minutes in case there are hot spots in your oven. When done, the soufflés should be puffed up and golden brown on top. Immediately remove them from the oven, take them out of the water bath, and allow them to cool. It is normal for the soufflés to fall, but they will rise again. They can be made up to this point several hours in advance of serving.

Eight minutes before the soufflés are to be served, turn them out of their ramekins and place them, right side up, on a shallow baking dish. Pour a little of the heavy cream on the tops of the soufflés and pour the rest around the sides. Put the baking dish back in the oven for about 6 minutes, or until the cream is bubbling slightly and the soufflés have swelled up. Cut the basil leaves into chiffonade. Remove the soufflés from the oven and place each one on a warmed serving plate. Pour the cream from the baking dish over the soufflés, garnish with the chiffonade of basil leaves, and serve.

Serves 6.

WHITE CORN SOUP

1 large white onion	*Salt and pepper*
6 tablespoons unsalted butter	*5 ears white corn*
Optional: Half a pig's foot	*Nasturtium flowers or chervil*

Peel and dice the onion. In a deep soup pot, put the butter, the onion, the half a pig's foot (a pig's foot imparts a uniquely gelatinous richness to this soup), and a big pinch or two of salt and pepper. Stew over low heat, stirring occasionally, until the onions are very soft and starting to fall apart, about 30 minutes. If the onions begin to dry out and stick to the pan, add a little water. While the onions are cooking, slice the corn kernels from the cobs.

When the onions are ready, add a quart of water, bring to a boil, add the corn, and simmer 3 to 5 minutes, until the corn is just cooked. (Do not overcook!) Take the pot off the fire, remove the pig's foot, and purée the soup in a blender. Pass through a medium-fine sieve to obtain a uniform, slightly thick texture. Season to taste. Serve with freshly ground pepper and garnish with nasturtium petals cut into chiffonade, or garnish with chopped chervil.

Serves 4 to 6.

CORN SOUP WITH SALSA

1 medium onion	*3 cups fresh corn kernels*
¼ small carrot	*4 cups chicken stock*
2 cloves garlic	*1 teaspoon salt*
2 tablespoons unsalted butter	*2 tablespoons half-and-half*
1 sprig thyme	*1 cup Corn and Roasted Tomato*
1 bay leaf	*Salsa (see recipe below)*
1 small piece prosciutto or	
smoked bacon	

Peel and finely dice the onion, carrot, and garlic, and stew slowly in the butter with a little water, covered, until the onion is translucent. Add the thyme, bay leaf, and prosciutto or bacon, and stew for 3 or 4 minutes more. Add the corn and cook for another minute or so.

Pour in the stock, add the salt, bring the soup to a boil, and shut off the heat. Cover and let stand for 3 minutes. Remove the thyme, bay leaf, and pork, and purée the soup in a blender for 3 minutes. Strain through a medium-mesh sieve, add the half-and-half, reheat the soup to just below a boil, and serve, garnishing each bowl with a spoonful of the Corn and Roasted Tomato Salsa.

Serves 6.

Note: Other garnishes to consider are roasted red peppers, puréed or chopped; or chopped hot chilies and cilantro, with or without crème fraîche.

CORN AND ROASTED TOMATO SALSA

1 large ripe tomato	*2 tablespoons extra-virgin*
1 sprig thyme	*olive oil*
2 sage leaves	*2 tablespoons fresh corn kernels*
	Salt and pepper

Preheat the oven to 375°F. Peel and seed the tomato, and cut into ½-inch dice. In a small baking dish, toss the tomato with the thyme and sage and 1 tablespoon of the olive oil. Put the dish in the oven and roast for 20 minutes, stirring occasionally. Remove from the oven, allow to cool, and remove the thyme sprig and sage leaves. Toss together with the remaining tablespoon of olive oil and the corn, and season to taste. Serve as a garnish for corn soup, with corn chips, or with grilled fish.

Makes about 1 cup.

CORN AND PEPPER RELISH

This makes a delightful relish for shellfish—such as fried softshell crab, grilled shrimp, and lobster salad.

2 shallots or 1 small red onion	*8 ears white corn*
1 small bulb fennel	*Olive oil*
2 sweet bell peppers (different colors, if possible)	*Salt and pepper*
	⅛ teaspoon cayenne
Juice of 1 lemon or ¼ cup white wine vinegar	*1 small bunch cilantro or parsley (about ¼ pound)*

Peel and dice the shallots or the onion. Trim off and discard the tops and the outer layer of the fennel. Cut the fennel in small dice. Stem and core the peppers and cut into small dice. In a bowl, combine these vegetables with the lemon juice or vinegar and allow to sit for at least 15 minutes.

Cut the corn kernels off the ears with a sharp knife (you should have about 4 cups), and sauté them in about 1 tablespoon of olive oil until slightly softened, about 2 minutes. Cool the kernels and add them to the pepper, fennel, and shallots. Season with salt, pepper, and cayenne and enough olive oil to just coat the vegetables. Just before serving, finely chop 2 or 3 tablespoons cilantro or parsley and stir into the relish.

Makes about 6 cups.

CORN AND GREEN BEANS

Slice corn kernels off the cob with a sharp knife. Top and tail some slender green beans. To a pot of boiling water, add the beans; after a minute or two, when they are just about cooked, add the corn. After another minute or two, drain the vegetables and put them in a warm bowl with a little butter, salt, pepper, and some chopped parsley or basil.

POLENTA

Polenta is the Italian name for the coarse yellow cornmeal mush we serve at Chez Panisse. It is either cooked "hard"—cooled, solidified, cut into the appropriate shapes, and either grilled or deep-fried; "soft"—served straightaway, warm, thick but still pourable; or as polentina ("little polenta")—basically a chicken soup, thickened with a little polenta. Obviously, the amount of stock or water determines the final consistency.

The ratios of cornmeal to liquid are approximate, but represent a good starting point. In fact, polenta almost always requires additional liquid. The cooking qualities of cornmeal may vary from batch to batch—even if it is the same brand. And in our kitchen, personal preference plays a large part in the way it is cooked. Some cooks prefer a little residual mealiness and cook the polenta quite fast, in about 20 minutes, stirring the whole time. Others like creamier polenta and nurse it along for over an hour.

Firm polenta is cooked with a starting ratio of 3 parts liquid for 1 part polenta; for soft polenta, the ratio is 4 to 1. Otherwise the method is the same. Allow about ¼ cup cornmeal and ¼ teaspoon salt per serving. Bring salted water or chicken stock to a boil in a heavy-bottomed pot and gradually add the polenta, stirring all the while with a whisk. Keep whisking until the starch from the cornmeal starts to emulsify with the liquid and the polenta starts to thicken; lower the heat to very low, switch to a wooden spoon, and continue to cook slowly for about 30 to 40 minutes, stirring very frequently so the polenta doesn't stick to the bottom and burn. About midway through the cooking you will probably have to start adding more liquid, a ladleful or two at a time, to keep the polenta from getting too thick. Once the cornmeal is fully cooked, turn off the heat and let it sit for 10 minutes. Then stir in butter, and season with salt and pepper. When adding butter to soft polenta, use your own judgment; start with about 2 tablespoons butter per cup of cornmeal; it can absorb a great deal more.

Hard polenta destined to be deep-fried needs little, if any, butter; polenta that will be grilled benefits from a certain amount to keep it "fluffier"; too much, though, and it will crumble. To prepare hard polenta, pour the cooked polenta onto an oiled sheet pan or a baking dish or platter and spread it out uniformly with a spatula, about ¾ inch thick. Allow to cool and set up at room temperature for an hour. Cover with plastic wrap and refrigerate for at least another hour before cutting it: in finger-size batons for deep-frying, or in squares or triangles for grilling or baking.

POLENTINA SOUP

Stew some diced white onion in duck fat or butter. When it is soft, add some sliced garlic, cook a little more, and add flavorful chicken stock and a bouquet garni (thyme, parsley, bay leaf, a leaf or two of sage). Bring it all to a rolling boil, whisk in cornmeal (from ¼ cup to ½ cup per quart of liquid, depending on how thick you like it), season with salt, lower the heat, and continue simmering, stirring frequently, until the cornmeal is done, 15 to 20 minutes. Keep stirring the soup as you ladle it out, or the cornmeal will tend to settle to the bottom. Garnish each bowl with some freshly sautéed or stir-fried greens, roughly chopped, and a thin shaving or two of Parmesan.

CORN CAKES

Serve corn cakes for breakfast with fresh berries, as an hors d'oeuvre with salmon caviar and crème fraîche, or with grilled or roasted squab and wilted greens.

1½ cups corn flour	1 tablespoon honey
1½ teaspoons baking powder	1 cup milk
½ teaspoon salt	4 tablespoons unsalted butter
2 eggs	2 ears sweet corn

In a bowl, combine the corn flour, baking powder, and salt.

Separate the eggs. In a small saucepan, combine the honey, milk, and butter, and heat gently until the butter is just melted. Cool slightly, then whisk in the egg yolks. Make a well in the dry ingredients and add the egg yolk and milk mixture. Blend to make a smooth batter.

Cut the kernels from the corn cobs and add to the batter. Beat the egg whites until they form soft peaks and fold into the batter. Cook the cakes on a lightly oiled, medium-hot griddle.

Makes eighteen 2-inch cakes.

CORN BREAD

¾ cup all-purpose flour
1½ teaspoons baking powder
1½ tablespoons sugar
1 teaspoon salt
1¼ cup cornmeal

¼ pound unsalted butter, plus
  more for greasing the pan
1 cup milk
1 egg

Preheat the oven to 400°F. Place a 9-inch cast iron skillet in the oven from the start of the preheating.

In a large bowl, thoroughly combine the flour, baking powder, sugar, salt, and cornmeal. Put the butter and milk in a small saucepan and heat until the butter is melted.

Break the egg into another bowl, beat lightly, and whisk in the milk and butter. Make a well in the flour mixture, pour in the liquid ingredients, and stir just until smooth.

Take the skillet out of the oven, put in a lump of butter, and swirl it around to coat the pan. Pour in the batter. Bake for 25 minutes, or until a toothpick or skewer inserted in the corn bread comes out clean.

Serves 4 to 6.

CORN BREAD STUFFING

1 small carrot
½ stalk celery
1 small onion
2 teaspoons butter
1 teaspoon thyme leaves

1 bay leaf
Salt and pepper
3 tablespoons cream
2½ cups Corn Bread, crumbled

The corn bread should be made the day before you plan to make this stuffing to give it time to dry out. If baked the same day, break it into large pieces and let them sit out for a few hours. Crumble the corn bread and put it into a large mixing bowl.

Peel and trim the vegetables and chop into fine dice. Cook them gently in the butter with the thyme and bay leaf, seasoned with salt and pepper. When softened, add them to the bowl of corn bread, add the cream and mix well.

Makes enough stuffing for 1 chicken or duck.

CORN BREAD STUFFING WITH GREENS

1 recipe Corn Bread	*½ pound bacon or pork sausage*
1 small bunch greens (kale,	*1 sprig thyme*
chard, escarole, etc.), about	*A few sage leaves*
½ to ¾ pound	*A few sprigs parsley*
Olive oil	*1 egg*
1 small onion	*¼ cup milk*
2 cloves garlic	*Salt and pepper*

Crumble the corn bread into a large mixing bowl.

Wash and trim the greens, chop roughly, and cook until tender in a little olive oil. Peel and dice the onion. Peel and chop the garlic. Dice the bacon (if using sausage, cut it into chunks) and sauté it in a tablespoon of olive oil. When it has begun to render its fat, add the onion and cook until softened, but not too brown, about 2 to 3 minutes. Add the garlic, stirring quickly to prevent it from burning. Remove from the heat and add to the corn bread. Finely chop the leaves of the thyme and the sage; there should be about ½ teaspoon of each.

Finely chop enough parsley to make about 2 teaspoons. Add the herbs; the cooked greens; the egg, lightly beaten; and the milk to the bowl with the corn bread. Mix well. Add more milk if the mixture looks too dry. Season with salt and pepper.

Makes 4 cups, or enough for 2 medium chickens.

CORN BLINIS

1 ½ teaspoons dry yeast	*2 teaspoons sugar*
3 cups tepid milk	*½ teaspoon salt*
3 eggs	*1½ to 2 cups fresh corn kernels*
2 cups all-purpose flour	*1 tablespoon clarified butter*
2 cups buckwheat flour	

Dissolve the yeast in 1½ cups of the milk. Separate the eggs. Put the yolks into a large bowl. Add half the flour (1 cup each all-purpose and buckwheat), sugar, and salt. Add the milk and yeast to the flour mixture and mix into a smooth batter. Cover and let rise until doubled in bulk, about 1 to 1½ hours.

Add the remaining cup of each flour and the rest of the milk. If the batter is too stiff at this point or after the final rising, thin with a bit more milk. Let it rise again until doubled in bulk, then pass through a strainer to remove any lumps. No more than a half hour before cooking, beat the egg whites, add the fresh corn to the batter, and fold in the beaten whites.

Cook the blinis as you would pancakes, on a hot griddle rubbed with clarified butter. Allow 1 tablespoonful batter per blini. Turn after about 1 minute, when the bubbles that form on the top have started to break, and cook for about 1 minute more.

Makes about 3 dozen 3-inch cakes.

Note: To serve blinis in the classic manner, ladle some melted butter over each one and put a spoonful of crème fraîche and a spoonful of caviar or salmon caviar on top. These are also delicious with a lobster or shellfish sauce or ragout.

CORN SALAD
(MÂCHE OR LAMB'S LETTUCE) 🍂
See Lettuces and Other Salad Greens (page 193)

CUCUMBERS ❧

Season: Summer

Cucumber season starts in the heat of the summer, just when their refreshing flavor and juicy crunchiness are most welcome. This is the time for cucumber and onion sandwiches, salads of cucumbers and cured salmon, and cooling cucumber raita to temper hot Indian curries. Because of their mild flavor and crisp texture, cucumbers are a natural for pickling, too. We get good, local cucumbers from early summer until the first cool days of autumn.

Cucumbers can be roughly divided into three kinds: the small pickling cucumbers, the slicing cucumbers, and the Mediterranean, or Middle Eastern, cucumbers. Pickling cucumbers are no more than a few inches long, with warty or spiny green—or green-and-white—striped skins. Traditional slicing cucumbers are six to ten inches long and have smooth, dark green skins. Pickling and slicing cucumbers are both members of the species *Cucumis sativus.* Mediterranean cucumbers can be very long—up to several feet!—but they are always slender. The skin is often ridged and tends to be lighter green than that of slicing cucumbers. These cucumbers have a milder flavor and more tender skins, and may actually be more closely related to the melons, *C. melo,* than to the other cucumbers.

When buying any of these cucumbers, whether pale or dark green, the important qualities to look for at the market are a very firm texture and a bright, lifelike color. Very shiny skin may be misleading, since most commercial cucumbers have been treated with wax to retard dehydration. Soft, dull-looking, or yellowing fruit is probably too mature and will be filled with hard seeds. In general, the smallest cucumbers in the pile will have the smallest, tenderest seeds.

Fresh cucumbers will keep for several days if refrigerated, but since their high water content is a major part of their charm, don't give them a chance to dehydrate even a little: eat them right away or pickle them.

Cucumbers for pickling need only be washed carefully and then quartered, sliced, or left whole, depending on the recipe. Cucumbers for salads may need to be peeled if they are thick-skinned; otherwise it is a question of personal preference. Don't seed the cucumbers unless the seeds are overdeveloped and hard. However, if a recipe calls for you to seed them before slicing or dicing them, simply cut the cucumbers in half lengthwise and scoop out the seeds with a teaspoon.

Cucumbers dressed in advance or used in a sauce may give up too much water and dilute the flavor of the dish. To forestall this, lightly salt the prepared cucumbers, let them sit in a strainer for ten minutes, wrap them in a clean kitchen towel, and wring out the excess moisture.

Cucumbers grown at home can be trained on trellises, conserving ground space. Mediterranean varieties will produce longer, straighter fruit if the ripening cukes are allowed to hang. Home gardeners in search of unusual varieties may wish to try growing the pale yellow, round Lemon cucumber, or one of the rarer Asian varieties.

SAUTÉED CUCUMBERS

Peel the cucumbers and cut in half lengthwise. Remove the seeds if they are large and dice the cucumber. Sauté gently in butter with a little water, seasoned with salt, until just tender throughout but still intact. Finish with an addition of chives or chervil and, if you like, some peeled, seeded, and diced tomatoes. Serve with delicate-textured poached or baked fish.

CUCUMBER, MANGO, AND RED ONION SALAD

This is a good salad to serve with spicy Mexican food. Peel and thinly slice cucumbers, mango, and sweet red onion—about the same amount of each, but exact proportions do not matter at all. Season to taste with freshly squeezed lime juice and salt, and garnish generously with cilantro leaves.

Cucumber Raita

Serve as a side dish with the Spicy Broccoli Vegetable Sauté (page 52) or to complement the Beet Chutney (page 47) alongside spicy braised chicken or lamb.

2 cucumbers
Salt
2 cups yogurt
1 pinch cayenne

Cut the cucumbers in half lengthwise, scrape out the seeds with a spoon, and cut into small dice or thin slices. Salt them, and fold into the yogurt. Add the cayenne and more salt if needed.

Makes 3 to 4 cups.

Pickled Cucumber and Shallots

3 or 4 small cucumbers or
1 large cucumber
3 shallots
1½ tablespoons coarse salt

White wine vinegar
Pepper
About ½ cup coarsely chopped chervil

Peel 3 or 4 small Japanese cucumbers or 1 English cucumber, and cut in half lengthwise. If the seeds are bitter, remove them with a small spoon. Slice the cucumbers crosswise ⅛ inch thick and put the slices in a bowl.

Peel the shallots and cut them in half lengthwise. Slice as thin as possible and add to the cucumbers. Add the coarse salt and toss with the vegetables so they are all coated with salt. Let them sit for 45 minutes.

Rinse the cucumbers and shallots, drain, and taste for salt. If they are too salty, rinse and drain again. Usually once or twice is sufficient. Add the vinegar and pepper. Keep chilled and toss with the chervil at the last minute, before serving.

Serves 6.

QUICK DILL PICKLES

This is a faster method of making pickles than the traditional long-brined technique.

*3 to 4 pounds small pickling
    cucumbers
3 cups apple cider or white wine
    vinegar
3 cups water
⅓ cup kosher salt*

*2 tablespoons dill seed or
    flowering tops of 4 to 5 dill
    plants
Optional: Fresh grape leaves,
    dried chilies, garlic, fennel,
    peppercorns, mustard seeds,
    coriander seeds, cloves*

Wash the cucumbers thoroughly under cold water. Heat the cider vinegar or white wine vinegar, water, and salt to the boiling point. Pack the cucumbers in sterilized jars with the dill. According to your taste, add to each jar a freshly washed grape leaf (grape leaves contain alum, which helps to make the pickles crisp); a dried hot chili; a clove or two of garlic, peeled (or heat garlic cloves in the brine, then remove before filling the jars); fennel seeds or a fresh sprig; black peppercorns; mustard seed; coriander seeds; and a clove. Fill the jars to within ½ inch of the top with the boiling-hot brine. Put on the lids, tighten the bands, and allow to cool. During the cooling you should hear the characteristic pop the lid makes when the vacuum seal forms. If you intend to store the pickles longer than six months, process in a boiling water bath for 10 minutes after sealing. Store in a cool dark place and wait at least 2 weeks for the pickles to cure before eating.

EGGPLANTS &

Season: Midsummer to early fall

Anyone who has seen the White Egg variety doesn't need to be told why this vegetable is called eggplant. The fruit of this eggplant, a perfectly shaped goose egg with a stemmed green cap at the broad end, fully lives up to its name. Eggplants (*Solanum melongena*) come in many shapes, colors, and sizes. Besides the familiar dark purple, they may be green, white, lavender, or striped with red. The fruit of many of the Asian varieties is slender and elongated. Two of the most common Asian eggplants are the dark purple Japanese and the very long, slender, pale lavender Asian Bride, a Chinese variety.

The plants themselves are beautiful at all stages of development. They are generally compact, with gray-green leaves that enhance the colors of their fruit and their small purple flowers.

Eggplants can be grilled, baked, stuffed and braised, sautéed in olive oil, or breaded and fried. In fact, we don't often fry eggplant at the restaurant, because it is such a sponge for oil and tends to taste heavy and oily as a result. Before adding it to a sauté, we prefer to roast, bake, or grill the eggplant first; this makes it more appealing and digestible. Asian varieties are especially good sliced, grilled, and served as a room temperature salad, seasoned with olive oil, balsamic vinegar, and fresh basil. Globe eggplants are good roasted or grilled whole, their flesh scooped out for soup or eggplant caviar.

All eggplants have an affinity for the strong Mediterranean flavors of garlic, anchovies, olives, roasted peppers, basil, and tomatoes. Eggplant frequently appears on our menus as an hors d'oeuvre in one form or another: in vegetable salads; on antipasto plates; in eggplant tarts. Mainstays of the summer repertory are variations on Richard Olney's recipes for eggplant fans and for eggplant and tomato gratins in *Provence the Beautiful Cookbook*. And eggplant is essential for ratatouille.

Because eggplants originated in tropical Asia, they need a long, hot growing season. Like tomatoes, eggplants won't reach their peak of quality until August and September. At that time, look for fruit that is very shiny and firm. The best eggplants have dense, uniformly firm, sweet flesh with small, tender seeds. Eggplants that are dull and puffy are over-the-hill, and will be bitter and full of unpleasantly hard seeds. In the home garden, pick them when they are no more than two thirds full size.

Eggplants should be used soon after they are picked. Their quality also suffers when they are kept too cold—again because of their tropical origins. They will be fine overnight at room temperature, but if you must keep them longer, don't refrigerate them. Try to find a relatively cool place in the kitchen. The ideal storage temperature is 50°F.

To prepare eggplants for cooking, rinse them briefly in running water and dry with a towel. Trim off the green cap and stem. Since the skin of most varieties is attractive and tender, eggplants shouldn't need peeling. But when they are used in a soup or purée they can be peeled quickly and easily with a sharp, thin-bladed paring knife.

If a recipe calls for eggplants to be cooked whole, you can shorten the cooking time of very large eggplants by cutting them in half and placing them cut side down on the baking pan. Eggplant to be grilled should be sliced ¼ inch thick, brushed lightly with good olive oil, and sprinkled with coarse salt.

If you find yourself with an overripe eggplant, you can draw out some of the excess water and bitterness by salting. Cut the eggplant into cubes or slices and sprinkle liberally with coarse salt. Put the eggplant pieces in a non-corroding strainer or colander and allow them to drain for an hour or so. Then remove the pieces from the strainer, put them in a kitchen towel, and press out the water and excess salt before proceeding with the recipe.

If you have a spot with the necessary warmth and sunshine, eggplants are a welcome addition to an edible landscape. The compact plants, decorated with their flowers and fruit, deserve space in the most visible part of your garden. Remember that they need a warmer spot than tomatoes or peppers, and don't set them out until early summer, when the soil is warm.

EGGPLANT CAVIAR

1 large globe eggplant
Salt and pepper
Olive oil
2 shallots

Balsamic or red wine vinegar
1 clove garlic
¼ cup chopped parsley or
*   cilantro*

Preheat the oven to 375°F.

Peel the eggplant and cut into 1-inch cubes. Put the eggplant in a baking dish, season liberally with salt and pepper, and toss with a generous amount of olive oil. Sprinkle with a few tablespoons water, cover tightly, and bake in the oven for 30 to 40 minutes, until very soft.

While the eggplant is baking, peel and dice the shallots very fine. Let them macerate for about 10 minutes in about 2 tablespoons of the vinegar. Peel and mash the garlic and add it to the shallots and vinegar. When the eggplant is done, add it to the shallot and garlic mixture, mashing with a fork, and let it cool to room temperature.

Stir in the chopped parsley or cilantro (or a combination of both) and adjust the seasoning. Add additional olive oil and vinegar to taste. Serve on grilled bread.

Serves 4.

ROASTED GLOBE EGGPLANT

Eggplant roasted or baked in the oven requires little oil and therefore remains sweet and light-tasting. Take large globe eggplants (or any eggplants, provided they are fresh, glossy, and firm), trim off the stems, and cut the eggplants in half lengthwise. Cut the halves into generous wedges, again lengthwise. Small eggplants should be cut only in half: if the eggplant pieces aren't thick enough, they will dry out before they cook through. Salt the wedges generously and let them stand a few minutes. Meanwhile preheat the oven to 400°F. and oil a baking sheet or a shallow baking pan. Lay the wedges out flat on the pan. Oil the exposed side of the eggplant and bake for 20 to 35 minutes. The eggplant is done when the wedges are soft all over and brown on the underside. Remove them from the pan with a spatula. If the eggplant sticks to the pan, let it cool for a few minutes and it will be easier to detach. Serve the eggplant warm or cool, with an interesting vinaigrette.

EGGPLANT COOKED IN THE COALS

4 small globe eggplants *¼ cup extra-virgin olive oil*
1 small bunch cilantro   *Juice of 2 lemons*
 (about 1 cup cilantro leaves) *Salt and pepper*
3 cloves garlic

Prepare a wood fire and allow it to burn down to a bed of coals that are no longer incandescent but still quite hot.

Wipe the eggplants clean with a cloth. With no other preparation, place them directly onto the bed of coals. Turn the eggplants frequently with tongs. The skin will scorch and crack but will remain more or less attached, protecting the flesh. When the eggplants have cooked through and are quite soft, remove them from the fire. When they are cool enough to handle, remove the skin, leaving the eggplants whole and still attached to their stems.

Finely chop the cilantro leaves, and peel and finely chop the garlic. When the eggplants have cooled to room temperature, toss them carefully in a bowl with the olive oil, cilantro, garlic, lemon juice, and salt and pepper. Allow to stand at room temperature for an hour before serving.

Serves 4.

GRILLED JAPANESE EGGPLANT AND SALSA VERDE

1 cup Salsa Verde (page 174) *Salt and pepper*
6 Japanese eggplants   *1 lemon*
Extra-virgin olive oil

Start a fire under the grill. Make the Salsa Verde.

Cut the eggplants into ¼-inch slices lengthwise. Peel the skin off the first and last slices for easier grilling. Brush with olive oil and sprinkle both sides with salt. The grill should be clean and hot; the embers should be glowing, with no flames, and not too hot. It is easy to make the mistake of grilling eggplant over too hot a fire; if you do, the eggplant will brown too fast on the outside without cooking through. Arrange the eggplant slices on the grill and after about 3 to 4 minutes, when they are not sticking to the grill and have distinct grill marks, turn them over and grill 3 or 4 more minutes. The eggplant is done when the flesh is soft to the touch. If necessary, turn the slices back over, rotating them 90 degrees to make cross-hatched grill marks.

As the slices are done, transfer them onto a warm platter and drizzle the Salsa Verde over them. Finish with a squeeze of lemon and freshly ground black pepper. Serve either hot or at room temperature.

Serves 4 to 6.

EGGPLANT, TOMATO, AND ONION GRATIN

3 large, sweet white onions
3 cloves garlic
2 to 3 tablespoons unsalted butter
2 to 3 tablespoons olive oil

2 or 3 sprigs thyme
1 bay leaf
Salt and pepper
3 medium Japanese eggplants
3 ripe tomatoes

Peel and chop the onions and garlic very fine. Stew them over a medium flame for about 5 minutes, until soft, in half the butter and olive oil, with the leaves of the thyme, the bay leaf, and salt and pepper.

Slice the eggplants into ¼-inch-thick rounds. Slice the tomatoes slightly thicker.

Preheat the oven to 400°F. Butter a shallow gratin dish.

Remove the bay leaf from the onions and spread them over the bottom of the dish. Cover with overlapping rows of alternate tomato and eggplant slices. Each slice should cover two thirds of the preceding one. Season with salt and pepper, drizzle with olive oil, cover, and cook in the oven until the eggplant is soft enough to be cut with a spoon, about 45 minutes. Uncover for the last 15 minutes or earlier if the tomatoes are giving up too much liquid. Brush or spoon the juices over the top occasionally to prevent the top layer from drying out. This gratin should be moist but not watery. Serve with grilled or roasted lamb.

Serves 6 to 8.

PENNE WITH EGGPLANT AND TOMATO

Dry ricotta salata cheese is often a key ingredient in vegetable pastas at the restaurant. It is a salty, dry, aged sheep's milk cheese that has a tangy sharp taste. It is not hard like Parmesan or pecorino; it crumbles easily and softens as it warms, blending well with the noodles and vegetables.

2 large globe eggplants
Olive oil
1 onion
2 cloves garlic
1 handful basil leaves
1 handful parsley leaves

1 pound penne pasta
Sherry vinegar
2 cups tomato sauce
Red pepper flakes
½ pound ricotta salata cheese

Preheat the oven to 400°F.

Cut the eggplants in cubes about ¾-inch square, toss them lightly in olive oil, and spread them out in a single layer on a sheet pan. Roast in the oven for 25 minutes or so, until the eggplant is brown and tender.

Put a large pot of water on to boil for the pasta. Peel and thinly slice the onion. Peel and finely chop the garlic and the herbs, separately. Put the pasta on to cook, al dente.

Heat a large sauté pan and sauté the onions in olive oil until just caramelized. Add the garlic, cook for a moment more, and then deglaze with a splash of sherry vinegar. Add the eggplant, tomato sauce, a pinch of red pepper flakes, and the chopped basil. Heat the sauce to simmering, drain the pasta, add it to the pan, and toss gently. Serve with a generous garnish of the chopped parsley and ricotta crumbled over the top.

Serves 4 to 6.

BAKED STUFFED EGGPLANT

Use small and pretty eggplants. Cut them in half and scoop out about half the pulp. Make a stuffing by chopping the pulp and combining it with pitted black olives, chopped garlic, salt-packed anchovy fillets, capers, parsley, and marjoram. Mix in bread crumbs soaked in milk and squeezed dry. Mound the stuffing in the eggplants and put them in an earthenware gratin dish, drizzle generously with olive oil, and bake, loosely covered, in a preheated 350°F. oven for an hour.

EGGPLANT AND TOMATO PIZZA

Grill ¼-inch slices of eggplant (see page 134), or oven-roast them, brushed with oil and seasoned with salt and pepper. Roll out or shape a disk of pizza dough and brush with olive oil mixed with garlic chopped very fine. Make an even layer of thin red onion slices, place a few thin round slices of fresh mozzarella on the onions, and arrange the grilled eggplant slices and large slices of tomato on top, in a single layer. Keep the layers light or the crust will be soggy. Season with salt and pepper, drizzle with olive oil, and bake in a preheated 450° to 500°F. oven for 4 to 10 minutes, until the crust is crisp and golden brown. Scatter basil leaves over the pizza and serve.

Note: For a pizza dough recipe and complete instructions for baking pizzas, see *Chez Panisse Pasta, Pizza, and Calzone* by Alice Waters, Patricia Curtan, and Martine Labro.

ENDIVE
See Chicories (page 101)

ESCAROLE
See Chicories (page 101)

FAVA BEANS ❦

Season: Early spring to early summer

The fava bean, *Vicia faba,* was *the* bean of Europe before contact with the New World. It resembles such shell beans as butter beans and lima beans, but it belongs to a separate branch of the pea family. Fava beans are still a staple of the Mediterranean diet. While fresh fava beans have been quite rare in United States markets until recently, dried brown fava beans have been available in many Italian and Middle Eastern grocery stores. We haven't experimented much with dried fava beans at Chez Panisse, although they are used in several Mediterranean cuisines—soaked, boiled until tender, and made into salads or purées. (One recipe worth trying is to soak the beans overnight or even longer, until they are almost completely rehydrated; drain and instead of boiling them, fry them in olive oil until they are crisp, and serve, salted, as an appetizer, with lemon wedges on the side.)

The fava beans we prize are the fresh beans of early spring to early summer. The bright green, sweet and tender beans form inside five- to seven-inch-long paler green, slightly hairy pods, a half dozen or so to the pod. Shelling fava beans has become a springtime ritual at the restaurant. Big baskets of them are brought out to keep all hands busy during long meetings, menu discussions, and even job interviews.

Many farmers and gardeners plant fava beans as green manure, because they are nitrogen-fixing, and like other kinds of peas and beans, they enrich soil fertility if they are plowed back into the soil before they start to produce beans. Many local growers plant fava beans not just as a cover crop but for harvest as well, because, like garden peas, they grow well in the cool, damp weather of a typical northern California winter. The pods form and mature as the weather warms up in the early spring.

In colder parts of the country, fava beans are planted in early spring, to be harvested before the heat of midsummer.

We use the small, clear green fava beans of the early season in the same ways we use fresh peas: cooked quickly as part of a vegetable ragout, in a puréed soup, or with potatoes and fresh cream. They also are one of the finest accompaniments to the first salmon of early May. Shelled, parboiled, and peeled of their slightly bitter, pale green skins, they take only a few minutes to cook. As the season progresses, the maturing fava beans lose some of their sweetness and tenderness, and become harder and starchier, requiring longer cooking. These are the favas we use mashed into a paste and seasoned with garlic, rosemary, and olive oil, as a purée to spread on croutons or as a stuffing for ravioli. The tender growing tips of the fava bean plants can also be eaten, sautéed in olive oil with other tender spring greens or by themselves.

The pods of the early favas are pale green and rather smooth, giving little indication of the small beans inside, which are tender enough to eat raw. As the pods mature, they lengthen, turn yellowish-green, and look quite lumpy, revealing very clearly the presence of the larger, harder, but still green, beans within. In any case, the freshest fava beans at the market will have firm, bright-looking pods. Avoid any pods with wrinkly skin or blackened ends. Split one open and check inside. The soft inner lining of the pod should feel moist, and the beans should be tightly and smoothly enclosed in their skins. Peel a bean and taste it for sweetness and tenderness. The differences between varieties of favas have more to do with size and number of beans per pod, cold hardiness, and heat tolerance than with their cooking qualities, which depend mostly on their stage of maturity: the older the beans, the yellower, starchier, and coarser; after a certain point, better to let them mature and dry out completely on the vine than cook them fresh.

Fava beans require a two-step preparation for cooking. They must first be shucked from their pods, and then the beans themselves should be peeled. The skin has a bitterness that grows more and more pronounced and unpleasant as the favas mature. We almost always peel them. However, the very smallest beans can be good, shelled at the table, and eaten raw and unpeeled, with a little coarse salt and fine olive oil. In many parts of Italy this is a typical appetizer in the spring.

Shucking the beans may be a little easier if you first snap off the stem and pull away the tough string on the side of the pod. In any case, use your thumbs to break open the pod and strip out the beans from inside. To skin them, drop them first into boiling water for one minute, to tenderize and loosen the skins. Drain and plunge them into ice cold water to stop further cooking. When they are cool, drain them again. Use your thumbnail to break open the skin, and squeeze the bean between the thumb and forefinger of your other hand; the two-lobed, bright green kidney-shaped bean inside will pop right out.

Fava beans do require a fairly large allotment of garden space to pro duce a usable quantity of beans. But the plants and flowers are so handsome, and their contribution to soil fertility so useful, that it is well worth making room for a few plants. The Seeds of Change catalog lists several varieties of fava beans to suit different growing conditions.

It should be mentioned that some people of Mediterranean extraction (and some Asians and Africans, too) may be susceptible to a disease called favism, a serious and potentially fatal toxic reaction to the consumption or inhalation of a substance in fava beans called vicine, which causes a kind of anemia in those who are genetically predisposed to it. Eating undercooked fava beans or being exposed to the pollen of flowering bean plants could conceivably pose a health risk. Therefore, consider your genealogy and be alert for allergic symptoms if you grow fava bean plants or eat a lot of undercooked favas. However, the risk of disease from occasionally eating fresh fava beans, peeled and cooked, is apparently quite small.

Raw Fava Beans with Salami, Prosciutto, and Pecorino

For this hors d'oeuvre use the very first, very smallest, tenderest fava beans. The best are those which, when shelled, reveal beans whose skins are still thin and bright green; they can be eaten unpeeled. As the beans mature, the skin thickens and turns an opaque, very pale green, becoming more and more acrid; however, young beans that have formed an opaque skin are still quite delicious raw if one peels the skin away. And what a nice way to spend a warm early summer evening—shelling fava beans from their pods, dipping them in a little sea salt and olive oil, and eating them with a few slices of salami, prosciutto, and fresh pecorino cheese.

FAVA BEAN RAGOUT

Fava beans cooked this way are often served in a simple pasta dish as well, frequently with the addition of peas and a garnish of crumbled ricotta salata cheese.

3 to 4 pounds young fava beans	*Olive oil*
1 large clove garlic	*Salt and pepper*
1 small sprig rosemary	*½ lemon*

Shell the fava beans and discard the pods.

Bring a pot of water to a boil, add the favas, and simmer for 1 minute. Drain and cool them immediately in cold water. Pierce the outer skin with a thumbnail and squeeze each bean out of its skin with thumb and forefinger. Peel and chop the garlic very fine. Strip the rosemary leaves off the sprig and chop very fine.

Put the fava beans in a saucepan with a mixture of half water and half olive oil, enough to barely cover them. Add the garlic and rosemary, and season with salt and pepper. Bring to a simmer, cover, and cook until the beans are tender, about 5 minutes, more or less, depending on the beans. Finish with a squeeze of lemon juice and another grind or two of pepper, and serve. This is great with Potato Gnocchi (page 247).

Serves 4 to 6.

FAVA BEAN PURÉE

3 pounds mid-season fava beans	*¼ bay leaf*
½ to ¾ cup extra-virgin olive oil	*1 small sprig rosemary*
Salt and pepper	*1 sprig thyme*
2 cloves garlic	*½ lemon*

Put a large pot of water on to boil. Shell the fava beans; discard the pods. Parboil the shelled beans for 1 minute. Drain them and immediately plunge them in ice-cold water for a few minutes to cool. Drain them again and remove their pale green skins, piercing the outer skin of each bean with your thumbnail and popping out the bright green bean inside with a pinch of your other thumb and forefinger.

Warm about ½ cup of the olive oil in a shallow, nonreactive sauté pan. Add the beans and salt lightly. Add the garlic, peeled and chopped very fine; the herbs; and a splash of water. Cook the beans at a slow simmer, stirring and tasting frequently, for about 30 minutes, until they are completely soft and pale green and easily mashed into a purée. Add another splash of water from time to time to prevent the beans from drying out and sticking to the pan.

When the beans are done, remove and discard the herbs, and mash the beans into a paste with a wooden spoon—or pass them through a sieve or a food mill or purée with a food processor. Taste for seasoning and add more olive oil and a few drops of lemon juice to taste. If the purée is at all dry and tight, add still more olive oil. Don't be stingy with the oil; good olive oil is as important to the flavor of the purée as the beans. Serve warm or at room temperature, by itself or spread on grilled bread.

Makes about 3 cups.

Green Risotto with Fava Bean Purée, Peas, and Asparagus

½ pound young fava beans
Olive oil
Salt and pepper
¾ pound fresh green peas
4 spears asparagus
1 medium onion
7 to 8 cups chicken stock

4½ tablespoons unsalted butter
2 cups Arborio rice
⅓ cup dry white wine
¼ cup grated Reggiano Parmesan cheese, plus extra for garnish

Shell the fava beans and discard the pods. Bring a pot of water to a boil, add the favas, and simmer for 1 minute. Drain them and cool them immediately in cold water. Pierce the outer skin of the beans with your thumbnail and pop out each bean with the thumb and forefinger of your other hand. Put the beans in a pot with a little olive oil, a little salt, and water to just about cover, and cook slowly, until they are soft enough to purée but haven't lost their color, about 15 to 20 minutes. If necessary, add water as they are cooking to keep them from sticking. Drain them and pass them through a food mill.

Shell the peas. Cut the asparagus on the diagonal into thin slices. Peel and chop the onion into small dice.

Heat the stock and keep at a low simmer. In another, heavy-bottomed saucepan, heat 3 tablespoons of the butter, add the onion, and cook over medium heat until it is translucent, about 5 minutes. Add the rice and a pinch of salt and cook over low heat for about 3 minutes, stirring often, until the rice has turned slightly translucent. Turn up the heat and pour in the white wine. When the wine has been absorbed, add just enough hot stock to cover the rice, stir well, and reduce the heat.

Keep the rice at a gentle simmer and keep adding stock, a ladle or two at a time, letting each addition be almost completely absorbed by the rice before adding the next. After about 10 minutes, the grains of rice will have softened somewhat but will still be hard in the center. Stir in the peas and asparagus. Continue to ladle in more stock, stirring before and after every addition. After 5 minutes, add the rest of the butter, the cheese, and the fava purée. Stir well. Add more stock if needed: the risotto should have a saucy consistency. Adjust the seasoning. Serve in warm bowls, garnished with more of the Parmesan.

Serves 6 to 8.

CHILLED FAVA BEAN SOUP

2 pounds fava beans	*Salt and pepper*
1 medium onion	*1 quart light chicken stock*
2 cloves garlic	*Rosemary oil for garnish*
½ cup extra-virgin olive oil	*(see page 318)*

Shell the beans, parboil for about 1 minute, cool, and then pop the beans out of their skins.

Peel and dice the onion. Peel and thinly slice the garlic. Sauté the onion in the olive oil until quite soft, 10 to 15 minutes. Add the garlic, cook for 2 minutes more, and season well with salt. Add the fava beans, cook for 2 more minutes, and then add just enough stock to cover the beans. Chill the remaining stock. Cook the fava beans until tender. Purée in a blender until smooth, adding the extra cooled stock until you reach a consistency you like. Cool the soup quickly in an ice bath. Season to taste. Serve in chilled bowls, garnished with a thread of olive oil infused with fresh rosemary.

Serves 6 to 8.

Artichoke Hearts with Fava Beans

6 medium artichokes   *¼ cup extra-virgin olive oil*
2½ pounds fava beans   *Olive oil for frying*
A few sprigs summer savory

Purple artichokes or the wild thorny types are the tastiest for this recipe. Cut off their stems and peel and cut away the outer leaves of the artichokes until their tender, inner green leaves are exposed; then cut off the tops at the "line of tenderness"—that is, where the leaves change from yellow-green to dark green. Clean the choke out with a spoon, preserving the shape of the artichoke. Gently press the artichoke on the counter top, stem side up, taking care to not press too hard or the leaves will break off. (At this point, the leaves will not really flatten; this step just loosens them up.)

Shell the fava beans and parboil them for 1 minute in boiling water; cool, and pop them out of their skins. In a heavy-bottomed pot, cook the fava beans with the savory in the extra-virgin olive oil over medium heat, salted, until tender but still bright green, about 8 minutes. Keep them warm while you fry the artichokes.

Heat 3 inches of olive oil in a heavy deep-sided sauté pan and deep-fry the artichokes over medium heat, gently pressing the leaves flat as they soften. The artichokes will turn a golden brown. They are done when the heart is soft and the leaves a bit crispy. Take care not to let them brown too fiercely. When done, drain them on paper towels and season liberally with salt. Arrange them on a serving platter and spoon some of the favas into each artichoke.

Serves 6.

FENNEL ❧

Season: Spring, early summer, fall

Visitors are sometimes surprised to find fennel growing wild in profusion around the Bay Area, its five- to six-foot-tall celery-like stalks covered with feathery leaves topped with umbels of yellow flowers; but considering the similarities between our climate and that of fennel's native Mediterranean, it makes sense that fennel, once introduced to California (perhaps by the Spanish, over two hundred years ago), would make itself right at home. By the turn of the twentieth century, it even had a local nickname: old ladies' chewing tobacco. Its strong characteristic anise flavor seems to suit other local ingredients, especially fish. We add the feathery leaves and tiny yellow flowers of wild fennel to marinades for fish and to numerous salads, sauces, and soups, and we use them as a garnish, too.

Cultivated fennel is similar to wild fennel except that the bases of its leaf stalks are swollen and form a pale white, compact, succulent bulb. This is the common Florentine fennel found in the market. We use it all the time. The bulbs are sliced and served raw in salads in various combinations with other vegetables; parboiled for pastas; caramelized and served as a side dish; braised whole; and cooked in vegetable broths, court-bouillons, and fish stocks.

Our local wild fennel first appears in the spring, usually in late March, after the rains have subsided and the days are warming up a little. The new leaves are best at this time, when they start emerging from among last year's dried-out, brittle stems. (Fennel is a biennial that blooms in its second season.) These prolific plants continue to produce foliage all through the summer, until they begin to dry out completely at the approach of fall. Sometimes they will keep producing new foliage well into the fall if the plants have been severely cut back during the growing season. Bulb fennel is planted in late February or early March and matures in the summer. Early-season fennel tends to be better; as the season progresses, the bulbs are a little less juicy and the leaves get tough.

The fennel to buy at the market is that with firm, globular, undamaged bulbs that are quite firm and not shrunken or dried out in any way. Some bruising is inevitable and acceptable, since the coarser, outer layers are peeled away when the bulbs are prepared for cooking. Heads that appear slightly flattened are usually less agreeable when eaten raw; they are tougher than the more rounded ones and require longer cooking. However, the flavor is more intense and anise-like than that of the globular varieties.

To prepare fennel, peel away the outermost, coarser leaves, exposing the almost perfectly white, unblemished hearts; usually this means one or two layers. If there are any stalks attached, cut them off flat across the top of the bulb and discard them; reserve their leaves if you wish. Now the bulbs can be halved, cored, and sliced, crosswise or lengthwise, according to the preparation. For braising, fennel is split in half, cored, and browned first; if the bulbs are small enough, they are braised whole, browned or unbrowned. Sliced fennel that is not to be served immediately can be kept immersed in acidulated cold water to prevent discoloring, or it can simply be sprinkled with lemon juice and kept in a bowl tightly covered with plastic wrap. Fennel leaves are stripped from their stalks and chopped fine. The tiny yellow flowers can be pulled off their stems and either chopped or pounded.

As mentioned above, wild fennel grows so well here that it can be hard to eradicate from a garden. If you plant fennel, use purchased seed, because it will produce less aggressive plants, with good flavor. Sow them in place in the early spring, in a sunny location with good drainage. The leaves can be harvested from about the time you begin to thin out the plants. Bulbs should be cut when the base has swollen but is still young and tender. Cut the whole plant unless you are growing fennel specifically for the seed; you will want to remove the plants to prevent them from reseeding. Collect wild fennel from roadsides and vacant lots rather than planting it in the garden, where it will be both very prolific and very competitive.

BRAISED FLORENCE FENNEL

Cut the leafy tops and stem ends off several fennel bulbs and peel away any bruised outer layers. Chop fine a few sprigs of the leaves and reserve. Cut the bulbs in half lengthwise through their cores, and cut each half into 2 or 3 equal wedges.

Put the fennel wedges in a saucepan with a good inch of water, a liberal dousing of extra-virgin olive oil, a generous sprinkling of freshly ground fennel seed, and the chopped reserved fennel leaves; season with salt. Cover and cook over moderate heat for about 20 minutes, shaking occasionally, until the fennel wedges are soft and can be pierced through easily with a knife but are still intact. Add a little more water during cooking, if needed, to maintain a small amount of liquid in the bottom of the pan. The olive oil and water should emulsify into a flavorful, thick broth.

Squeeze in some lemon juice to balance the olive oil. Adjust the seasoning. Serve the fennel with a little of the lemony broth.

GRILLED FENNEL

Prepare a bed of coals for grilling.

Cut off the leafy tops and stem ends of several fennel bulbs, reserving some of the feathery leaves, and peel away any bruised outer layers. Cut the bulbs in half lengthwise through their cores, and cut each half into 2 or 3 equal wedges. Chop the leaves fine and put in a small bowl with a few tablespoons of extra-virgin olive oil, a squeeze of lemon, and a little finely chopped anchovy, if you wish.

Put the wedges into a saucepan and cover with water. Add salt and cook over moderate heat for about 20 minutes, covered, shaking the pan occasionally, until the fennel is tender and easily pierced with a knife but still intact. Remove from the heat.

When the fennel is cool enough to handle, thread the wedges on long skewers, brush them with olive oil and the chopped fennel leaves, and season with a little salt and pepper. Grill the brochettes over a moderate fire until nicely browned, turning frequently. Brush again with more olive oil and fennel leaves and serve at once.

FENNEL GRATIN

6 small fennel bulbs	3 sprigs thyme
3 medium leeks	1½ cups heavy cream
4 tablespoons unsalted butter	1 cup Vegetable Stock (page 321)
Salt and pepper	or chicken stock
3 sprigs parsley	

Remove the tough outer layers of the fennel bulbs, split the bulbs lengthwise, and cut them crosswise into ¼-inch-thick slices.

Peel off the outer layer of the leeks, and trim off the root ends and the dark green tops. Split the leeks lengthwise and cut the leek halves crosswise into ¼-inch slices. Plunge the slices into a big bowl of cold water to rinse off any sand. Lift the leeks out of the water, leaving the dirt to sink to the bottom of the bowl.

Melt 1 tablespoon of the butter in a large sauté pan over medium heat. Add half the fennel slices and cook until they are soft, about 5 minutes. Season with salt and pepper and transfer to a large bowl. Cook the rest of the fennel until soft with another tablespoon of the butter and add to the bowl. Then cook the leeks the same way, in two batches with the rest of the butter, and transfer them to the bowl.

Preheat the oven to 375°F.

Pick the leaves off the parsley and thyme sprigs and chop them. Toss the herbs together in the bowl with the fennel and leeks. Taste, and add more salt and pepper if necessary. Put the vegetables into a shallow ovenproof dish and pour over just enough of the cream and the vegetable or chicken stock to barely cover them. Bake the gratin in the oven for 45 minutes to 1 hour, checking every 15 minutes or so to make sure the cream is still covering the vegetables. If the top of the gratin appears to be drying out, push the vegetables down with the back of a spoon, drizzling a little more cream over the top. The cream will bubble up around the vegetables, and the top will brown nicely. Serve hot.

Serves 6.

FENNEL-INFUSED BROTH WITH HALIBUT

The immature soft green seeds from wild fennel plants give this dish its characteristic flavor, deeper and stronger than that of the cultivated bulb fennel.

3 bulbs cultivated fennel	*4 tablespoons fresh wild or dried*
1 quart fish broth	*fennel seed*
Salt and pepper	*Extra-virgin olive oil*
	2 pounds halibut filets

Preheat the oven to 375°F.

Cut off the fennel stalks from the bulbs, reserving a big handful of the nicest, most tender feathery leaves. Trim any bruised or tough parts from the bulbs. Cut each bulb in 8 wedges. Lay the pieces in a shallow, heat-proof casserole and pour in enough fish broth to cover them half way. Season with salt and pepper, cover, and bake in the oven until they are completely cooked through, about 35 minutes.

While the fennel is braising, prepare the fennel paste. If you are using wild fennel tops, pick the seeds from the fennel flowers. In a mortar, pound the seeds with a pinch of salt, adding the leaves slowly, continuing to pound and grind, until seeds and fronds are reduced to a paste. Cover with the olive oil.

When the fennel bulbs are done, remove them from the casserole onto a dish. Cover loosely and put them back in the turned-off oven with the door ajar. Arrange the halibut slices in the braising liquid left in the casserole. Add more fish broth until the pieces of fish are three-quarters submerged. Put the casserole over medium heat and bring to a slow boil. Simmer gently, covered, until the fish is just cooked, about 4 minutes. Put the halibut into 6 warmed bowls, turn up the heat under the casserole, and whisk the fennel paste into the poaching liquid. Add 4 pieces of fennel and a ladle of broth to each bowl, and serve.

Serves 6.

Note: For a thorough discussion of fish broth, and a recipe, see *Chez Panisse Cooking,* by Paul Bertolli with Alice Waters.

Shaved Fennel, Artichoke, and Parmesan Salad

The method of preparing this salad—paper-thin shavings of vegetables, usually raw, tossed together and lightly dressed just before serving—has become a regular theme on the restaurant's menus. The variations are extensive (peppers, celery, and radishes are often added) and always fresh and satisfying.

2 large artichokes
2 lemons
2 large fennel bulbs
¼ cup extra-virgin olive oil
1 to 2 tablespoons white truffle oil

Salt and pepper
1 piece Reggiano Parmesan cheese (about 3 ounces)
About ½ cup Italian parsley leaves

Pare the artichokes down to their hearts and scoop out the chokes with a spoon, dropping them into water acidulated with the juice of 1 of the lemons.

Cut off the feathery tops of the fennel at the base of their stalks and remove the outer layer of the bulbs. Slice the bulbs very thin with a mandolin or a very sharp knife. Remove the artichoke hearts from the water and slice them very thin the same way.

Assemble the salad in layers on a large platter or on individual salad plates. First make a layer of the fennel slices. Squeeze lemon juice evenly over the fennel and drizzle with about one third of the olive oil and white truffle oil. Sprinkle with salt and pepper. Then make a layer of the artichoke hearts, also sliced very thin. Squeeze more lemon juice over them, drizzle evenly with another third of the oils, and season with salt and pepper. Cut thin shavings of the Parmesan with a cheese slicer or a vegetable peeler and arrange them on top of the artichoke slices. Scatter the parsley leaves over the cheese, season with salt and pepper, squeeze more lemon juice over, and drizzle evenly with the rest of the oils. Serve immediately.

Serves 6.

Note: Slices of very fresh, raw cêpes (porcini, or *Boletus edulis*) are superb in this salad. Another autumnal variation on this salad theme is to dress the shavings of fennel with lemon and olive oil and top with shavings of fuyu persimmon accented with a few drops of balsamic vinegar.

FENNEL À LA GRECQUE

Many vegetables can be prepared this way: try small carrots, peeled and halved; artichoke hearts; cardoons; cauliflower, broken into flowerets; spring onions or pearl onions. Use the same poaching liquid, but cook the vegetables in separate batches and keep the liquid at a low simmer.

2 cups olive oil	*1 lemon*
2 cups white wine vinegar	*24 peppercorns*
¾ cup white wine	*4 bay leaves*
12 cloves garlic	*2 tablespoons fennel seed*
1 medium onion	*4 small bulbs fennel*

In a large pot, bring the olive oil, vinegar, and white wine to a gentle simmer.

Peel the garlic. Peel and slice the onion thin. Slice the lemon crosswise into ¼-inch slices and add to the pot along with the onion, garlic, peppercorns, bay leaves, and fennel seed. Simmer for about 15 minutes.

Cut off the feathery tops and stalks from the fennel bulbs and remove any tough outer layers. Cut the bulbs into eighths. Add them to the simmering liquid and cook until they are tender but still slightly crunchy. Remove them from the pot and let them cool. When both the fennel and the liquid have cooled down, return the fennel to the liquid and refrigerate. This is best if it sits 24 hours before serving.

Serves 4 to 6.

FENNEL PASTA WITH ANCHOVIES

Pick the tenderest feathery leaves from the center of the lower stalks of fennel bulbs and parboil them for about 30 seconds. Drain, cool, and chop them fine.

In a mortar, mash peeled garlic cloves and salt-packed anchovy fillets into a paste, and thin out with some olive oil. (Vary the proportions of garlic, anchovy, and fennel to suit your own taste.) Put some dried linguine or fedelini on to cook in rapidly boiling salted water. Warm the garlic, anchovy, and oil mixture in a large pan, add the chopped fennel leaves, and when the pasta is done, drain and toss it together with the sauce in the pan, a few grinds of the peppermill, and a squeeze of lemon.

FENNEL STEWED WITH WILD FENNEL

2 large fennel bulbs
¼ cup extra-virgin olive oil
1 handful wild fennel leaves
    and flowers

1 tablespoon fennel seed
1 pinch red pepper flakes
1 teaspoon salt
1 tablespoon lemon juice

Clean and trim the fennel bulbs and cut into eighths. Put them in a sauce-pan with the olive oil and ¾ cup water and stew them over medium heat for 5 minutes, covered. Chop fine the wild fennel leaves and flowers, grind the fennel seed, and add to the stew with the red pepper and salt. Stir, raise the heat slightly, and cook until the liquid has nearly evaporated and the fennel is cooked through and soft, about 10 more minutes. Remove the pan from the heat and toss the fennel with the lemon juice.

Serves 4.

WILD FENNEL VINAIGRETTE

This is an aromatic vinaigrette for mixed greens or grilled fish. The Meyer lemon is a variety of lemon crossed with orange, milder and sweeter than the common Eureka lemon. If you use Eureka lemons, cut the quantity in half.

½ cup chopped young, green
    wild fennel leaves
1 Meyer lemon
1 or 2 cloves garlic
4 shallots

1 cup extra-virgin olive oil
1 teaspoon ground fennel seed
Scant teaspoon salt
Optional: 1 or 2 salt-packed
    anchovies

Chop the delicate fennel leaves. Cut 6 thin slices from the Meyer lemon. Seed the lemon slices and chop fine, rind and all. Squeeze the juice from the remaining part of the lemon, measure out 1 tablespoon, and set aside.

Peel and chop the garlic fine. Slice the shallots thin and warm in the olive oil: the oil should be warm, but not hot to the touch; add the shallots and steep for 5 minutes. While the oil is still warm, add the fennel leaves, fennel seed, chopped lemon, and garlic, and let the mixture sit in a warm spot for 30 minutes. Add the lemon juice and salt just before

serving. If using anchovies, add them—cleaned, rinsed, and chopped—
at the end, with the lemon juice, and taste before adding salt.

Serves 4.

CARAMELIZED FENNEL

2 large fennel bulbs
¼ cup olive oil
Salt and pepper

Trim the fennel bulbs, removing any tough outer layers. Cut the bulbs
in half vertically, cut out the cores, and cut the bulbs into ⅛-inch-thick
slices.

Heat a large sauté pan over medium heat, add the olive oil, and when
the oil is hot, add the sliced fennel. (If necessary, cook the fennel in two
batches; the fennel should brown, not steam.) Cook, tossing or stirring
occasionally, for 8 to 10 minutes, until the fennel is caramelized and tender. Season with salt and pepper. Drain off any excess oil and serve.
(This holds well and can easily be reheated; no additional oil is necessary.) Serve with fish and with grilled meats and poultry, or use for a
pizza topping.

Serves 4.

GARLIC 🦢

Season: Spring, summer, fall

Garlic is so important at Chez Panisse that for the past twenty years we
have had an annual garlic festival on Bastille Day, when virtually every
dish is strongly flavored by *Allium sativum*, the stinking rose of the
kitchen. Throughout the rest of the year it remains indispensable.

Garlic is grown in California in enormous quantities. It is generally
planted here in October, to be harvested and dried about nine months
later, at the beginning of summer. Green garlic, or young, immature
garlic, is garlic harvested in May, when its flavor is very delicate and
sweet. It is not harvested commercially on a large scale, but it is brought
to market locally from a few small farms.

Green garlic looks very much like leeks—lots of green stalk with a
slightly bulbous white or rose-streaked root end. The heads with their
individual cloves are just beginning to form among many onion-like
layers. Successive harvests over six to eight weeks show the garlic maturing into full-size heads with fully formed, firm, juicy cloves. Young
garlic has a very aromatic, mild, long flavor. It blends beautifully with
other vegetables and makes excellent purées, soufflés, puddings, soups,
and sauces and fillings for pasta. It is especially good in broths, soups,
poaching liquids, and stews. A few green stalks in the cavity of a roasting bird will perfume the flesh.

Probably the most common and familiar varieties of garlic are the
uniformly sized white kind grown on a huge scale around Gilroy, California; the variety grown in Mexico that is commonly known as Spanish *roja*; and the large, and to some excessively mild, elephant garlic,
which actually belongs to the same species as leeks, *A. ampeloprasum*.
But there are a great many more heirloom varieties worth trying, if you

have the opportunity. A local garlic aficionado recently supplied us with Purple Tip, Burgundy, Creole Red, Chet's Italian Red, Inchelium red, Lorz Italian Red, Simonetti, and Russian Red Toch—and all were noticeably different in flavor. Skin color ranges from white, to white and rose-colored, to almost entirely rose or deep purple. Flavor also varies according to where garlic is grown; as a general rule, the farther north, the harsher the flavor.

Mature heads of garlic are at their freshest and tastiest from mid-June until fall. Look for heads that are very tight, hard, and firm. Summer is the season when garlic can be used generously, even excessively. It is the time to roast whole heads slowly with thyme and olive oil until the cloves melt into a purée. It is also the time to use garlic liberally raw—in aïoli, on croutons, in salads and salsas.

Garlic begins to change in the late fall—about the time it would begin to sprout and root if it were left in the ground in its natural state. A green sprout—the germ—begins to form in the center of each clove, and the cloves begin to shrink and dry. As the winter progresses the juicy sweetness of flavor is replaced by a slightly bitter and aggressively pungent taste. This quality can be minimized by cutting each clove in half vertically and prising out the green sprout before chopping and cooking. Be sure to remove any brown spots as well, and discard cloves that are discolored and spotted all over. Winter is not the best time for raw garlic or for preparations where it is intended to impart the primary flavor.

It is always a welcome relief when the first crop of red garlic from Mexico appears in the market in May, about the time the local green garlic harvest begins and the annual cycle repeats itself.

Garlic should be stored in a cool, dry place where air can circulate around it. Green garlic should be refrigerated, like leeks.

Once cut into, garlic, like onions and shallots, starts to lose juices and volatile compounds to the air. As it oxidizes, its flavor changes rapidly, and in fifteen to twenty minutes the garlic starts to taste bitter and acrid. It is best to chop garlic shortly before cooking it, although you can slow down the oxidation by covering it with some olive oil. Because it is so sensitive to oxidation it does not keep well in sauces over time. The flavor of an aïoli refrigerated for a day will never match that of one freshly made.

A quick and simple way to make a small amount of raw garlic purée (for a vinaigrette, for example) is to hold a fork with its tines resting on a plate or on the bottom of a bowl, and to rub a peeled clove of garlic rapidly back and forth against the points of the tines.

Although some people have a taste for browned garlic, in most recipes garlic should not be cooked so that it colors and smells burnt. Instead it should cook gently. Chopped or sliced and used as a terminal addition to such dishes as fried potatoes or squid, it should be added only in the last thirty to sixty seconds of cooking, not long enough to brown.

Garlic can be grown successfully in a home garden. A single clove will produce a new plant. It is usually planted in the fall in temperate climes, as late as November. It grows slowly through the winter and takes off when the weather starts warming up. In colder regions, it is planted in late winter and early spring. Garlic can be harvested at any stage, from the early leek-like stalks of spring to mature heads in summer. Successive planting will provide a ready source of tender young garlic. The flowers are interesting. When their blooms begin to open, the heads have usually matured.

WHOLE ROASTED GARLIC

Use garlic in season that has not begun to sprout. Select good-looking, firm heads (allow one per person). Peel just the outer skin from the upper half of each head; arrange the heads, root end down, in an ovenproof dish just large enough to hold them snugly in a single layer. Add enough stock or water to reach about ¼ inch up the sides of the dish, drizzle the heads with olive oil, and sprinkle with salt. Cover tightly with foil, and roast in a preheated 375°F. oven for about 20 minutes. Check them to make sure that there is still liquid in the bottom of the dish. They should be fairly soft at this point; if not, re-cover and roast a little more. Add a little more olive oil and let them continue to roast, uncovered, for 5 to 10 minutes.

Serve with grilled bread and mild goat cheese, if you like. It is best served right away. The diners pull apart the cloves and squeeze out the purée within. Roasted garlic can also be squeezed into sauces or passed through a food mill and added to sauces, soups, soufflés, or purées of other vegetables.

Garlic Croutons

Good bread moistened with olive oil and enlivened with garlic is almost always on the Chez Panisse menus in one form or another—at the bottom of a soup plate to thicken a savory fish stew; underneath a roast chicken to catch the mingling juices of the bird and a garlicky salad vinaigrette; as a base for the first really ripe tomatoes of summer; and garnished and served as appetizers, with the intense flavors of seasonal ingredients.

Good bread is the first essential. At the restaurant the bread we use most often is the country-style levain bread baked in the wood-burning ovens of the Acme Bread Company. It comes in large, crusty round loaves, with a full flavor that develops from the slow rising of a starter cultured from the wild yeasts found on the skins of wine grapes. We slice the bread, brush it with flavorful olive oil, and either bake it or toast it on the grill; then while it is still warm, it is rubbed with raw garlic. Occasionally, if a particularly fine olive oil is to be used, the bread is toasted first and then drizzled with oil and rubbed with garlic.

Here are some suggestions for hors d'oeuvre or antipasto croutons: tomatoes and basil, salt-packed anchovy fillets, eggplant caviar, grilled squid and aïoli, grilled vegetables and salsa verde, brandade, tapenade, prosciutto, fava bean purée, roasted peppers, goat cheese and herbs, fresh-cured sardines, grilled or sautéed wild mushrooms.

Aïgo Bouido

In Provençal dialect, *aïgo bouido* means boiled water. This soup is nothing more than a lightly flavored garlic broth, but when made well it is an exquisite introduction to a dinner.

Smash 3 garlic cloves in their skins and boil for 15 minutes in 1 quart of water with salt to taste, a sage leaf or bay leaf, 5 cracked black peppercorns, and a few drops of spicy olive oil. Serve as is or over a slice of toasted bread. This broth can be made richer by putting an egg yolk in the soup bowl and pouring the broth over it, by using chicken stock, or by adding more herbs, such as thyme and parsley; this is fine if you are a little under the weather and need a light supper, but the broth is meant to be pure and simple.

Roasted Garlic and Potato Purée

4 heads garlic	*Salt and pepper*
Extra-virgin olive oil	*¼ pound unsalted butter,*
1 pound russet potatoes	*melted*
1 pound Yellow Finn potatoes	*½ cup milk, warmed*

Preheat the oven to 375°F.

Break apart the heads of garlic into single cloves. Leave them un-peeled and crowd them into a baking dish. Drizzle generously with the olive oil, add ¼ inch of water, and roast for 30 to 45 minutes. The garlic is done when a clove squeezed between thumb and forefinger expresses a soft purée. Do not overcook, or the garlic will dry out and burn, re-sulting in a very unpleasant taste. Extract the purée by squeezing the cloves by hand or passing them through a food mill.

Peel the potatoes and cut them into big chunks. Boil in salted water until they start falling apart. Drain them in a colander and put it in the oven for 5 minutes, to dry out the potatoes a little. Pass the potatoes through a food mill and whisk in the melted butter, the garlic purée, and enough of the warm milk to obtain the right consistency. Season with salt and pepper and finish with a little bit of spicy, fruity olive oil.

Serves 6 to 8.

Stewed Garlic

3 heads garlic
1 cup chicken stock
2 tablespoons unsalted butter
2 or 3 sprigs thyme

Choose very good, early-season garlic. Remove the loose outer skin and break the heads into individual cloves, but do not peel them. Put the cloves in a saucepan with the chicken stock, butter, and thyme; simmer, covered, for 15 minutes. Remove the lid and simmer another 30 min-utes, until the liquid is reduced to a saucy consistency. Pass through a food mill or press the garlic through a sieve with a rubber spatula, di-rectly into a sauce or the pan juices from roast chicken or pork.

Serves 4.

AïOLI

The aïoli is the classic of the Provençal kitchen. It is a very rustic, simple peasant dish that usually includes boiled salt cod, potatoes and carrots, hard-cooked eggs, and often snails, stewed octopus, or squid, all served with the garlic and olive oil paste called aïoli that gives its name to the dish. Every cook in Provence has her own version of the true aïoli. They range from an emulsion of raw garlic, salt, and olive oil (never to be attempted on a stormy day!) to a classic mayonnaise that is simply flavored with garlic.

Aïoli is one of the mainstays of the menus at the restaurant. It sometimes appears in its grand form with the many vegetable and fish components for special-event dinners and Domaine Tempier extravaganzas, but is more typically present on hors d'oeuvre plates as a sauce for deep-fried fish and vegetables, grilled squid, salt cod and oven-roasted potatoes, or green bean and tomato salads. It is a natural complement to many kinds of seafood, either stirred into a spicy fish stew or served with fish and shellfish hot from the grill or cold in a salad.

Here are two recipes: the rugged, intense aïoli Provençal and a vegetable aïoli perhaps more suited to modern tables. Anything in between is fine too.

AïOLI PROVENÇAL

1 small head garlic
½ teaspoon coarse salt
1 egg yolk
2 cups of the best French olive oil

Peel the garlic (about 12 cloves). When choosing the garlic, make sure it has small, juicy cloves and hasn't started germinating. Later in the year, if you cannot find garlic without a green sprouting germ, be sure to cut each clove in two and remove the germ: it is bitter and hard to digest. Chop the garlic coarsely, put it in a mortar with the salt, and work to an even paste. Add the egg yolk and build up very slowly with oil as you would for a classic mayonnaise, using the pestle or a wooden spatula. If you are a purist, you can skip the egg yolk, but make sure it's sunny outside and hope for the best. Or replace it with some bread crumbs soaked in water and squeezed dry. This will give you a strong aïoli, better eaten for lunch and followed by a long siesta.

Serve with salt cod (soaked in the refrigerator for 24 hours in three or four changes of water and simmered until soft in unsalted water flavored with thyme, bay leaves, black peppercorns, and garlic); boiled potatoes and carrots; hard-cooked eggs; and cooked snails, all served together in a large dish, with the aïoli in its mortar.

Serves 6 to 8.

VEGETABLE AÏOLI

This aïoli is a milder garlic mayonnaise, to be served with a variety of spring and summer vegetables (new potatoes roasted with olive oil, garlic, and thyme; parboiled spring carrots; parboiled green and yellow wax beans; strips of bell peppers, either raw or roasted and peeled; spring artichokes, quartered and stewed in olive oil, water, and white wine, with thyme and bay leaves; grilled leeks, etc.) and perhaps a few other elements, such as hard-cooked eggs with black pepper and anchovy fillets, fresh tuna confit in olive oil, niçoise olives, cherry tomatoes, grilled squid. Use your imagination, and make the dish plentiful, generous, and colorful. It is perfect for a summer day's lunch, accompanied by a juicy basil and tomato salad, or served buffet style for a party.

4 cloves garlic	2½ cups oil (light olive oil,
Salt and pepper	extra-virgin olive oil, peanut
2 egg yolks at room temperature	oil, or a combination)
1 lemon	

In a mortar, mash the garlic with a pinch of salt into a smooth paste (the salt helps break down the fiber). Set aside half the paste, and to the other half add the yolks and the juice of half the lemon. Start whisking in the oil slowly, drop by drop at first, until it begins to thicken; then gradually increase the flow. If the mayonnaise becomes too thick to whisk easily, thin it with a few drops of water. Add more garlic, lemon, and salt to taste, but let the mayonnaise rest for an hour in a cool place before making a final decision. (If the aïoli will not be served for another hour or more, set the bowl over ice to keep it cool, or refrigerate it.)

The olive oil or combination of oils that you use is purely a matter of personal taste. Combine your oils to obtain a soft, fruity flavor. If you use extra-virgin olive oil alone, make sure it is not too strong or spicy; otherwise it will overpower your aïoli.

Serves 4 to 6.

ROUILLE

Rouille is the French word for rust as well as for this spicy, rust-colored mayonnaise. It is a frequent enrichment to Provençal-style fish soups.

1 red bell pepper	*½ teaspoon powdered saffron*
1 serrano pepper	*1 egg yolk*
Optional: 1 very fresh fish liver,	*1 to 1½ cups olive oil*
poached (see Note)	*Salt and pepper*
2 cloves garlic	*Red wine vinegar*

Ideally, grill the red bell pepper on a hot grill over wood coals until it is charred; otherwise roast it in the oven, under a broiler, or over a gas flame. Let it cool on a dish in a plastic bag; then cut out the stem and core, scrape away the seeds, and slip off the skin, saving only the pepper flesh and its juices. Remove and discard the stem, core, and half the seeds of the serrano pepper.

In a mortar and pestle, pound to a smooth paste the fish liver, if available; the garlic cloves, peeled; the saffron; and the red bell pepper and the serrano pepper. Incorporate the egg yolk and continue pounding as you pour the olive oil slowly into the paste, forming an emulsion. Season with salt and pepper and the vinegar and thin with a little warm water. Allow the rouille to rest at least 30 minutes before serving, to allow the flavors to amalgamate and ripen.

Note: If you ask ahead of time, your fishmonger may be able to provide you with a fresh fish liver. Anglerfish livers are particularly good in this recipe.

For another version of rouille—more authentic, but less suave—pound the garlic, saffron, peppers, and fish liver to a paste in a mortar; omit the egg and add instead 2 or 3 crustless slices of bread, soaked and squeezed dry; and keep pounding while gradually incorporating the olive oil. Season as above.

GREEN GARLIC SOUP

1 pound green garlic
   (about 8 to 10 plants)
½ pound potatoes
   (Yellow Finn, Yukon Gold, or
   some other tasty variety)

2 medium onions
¼ pound unsalted butter
Salt
2 quarts chicken stock

To clean and prepare the garlic, trim away the root end and peel away any tough or dirty outer leaves. Cut away the tough upper portion of the green leaf; unless very tough, the lower couple of inches of greens are fine to use. Cut the clean garlic into thin rounds or half-circles. Peel the potatoes and cut into ½-inch cubes. Peel and chop the onions into small dice. Melt the butter in a heavy-bottomed pot, add the onion, and cook slowly until translucent and tender. Salt, and add the garlic and potatoes. Cook these together for 5 minutes, then pour in the stock and bring to a boil. Lower the heat to a simmer and cook the soup until the potatoes are tender. Check the seasoning. This soup can be served rustic and chunky, or puréed—either way is delicious.
   Serves 6.

GREEN GARLIC AND POTATO RAVIOLI

The filling is also a delectable purée served on its own. Any leftover filling or purée is also quite good formed into little potato patties—or croquettes—and browned in butter. The ravioli can be served *in brodo* (floating in a little good broth), garnished with spring vegetables: asparagus tips, peas, fava beans, or wild mushrooms.

24 young green garlic plants
Salt and pepper
Extra-virgin olive oil
2 large russet potatoes
6 medium Yellow Finn or
   Yukon Gold potatoes

1 small bunch parsley
A few branches marjoram
5 sheets fresh pasta, rolled out
   to 6 by 24 inches (about 1
   pound, or a 2-egg recipe)

Wash the garlic and trim off the root ends and most of the dark green tops. (Save the tops for stock or soup.) Trim the white parts, slice them very thin, and stew in a small saucepan, seasoned with salt and a splash of olive oil, with just enough water to barely cover. Cook until very soft and set aside to cool.

Peel and cut the potatoes into uniform chunks. Boil in salted water until very soft. Drain the potatoes and pass with the green garlic through a food mill. Taste for salt, and add a small pinch of black pepper. Chop enough of the parsley fine to make about 3 tablespoons, and enough marjoram leaves to make about 2 tablespoons. Add to the garlic and potatoes with olive oil to taste, about ½ cup.

To use as ravioli filling, stuff and cook the pasta following the instructions for Squash Ravioli with Fried Sage (page 280), using about 1 heaping tablespoon of filling for each of the ravioli.

Makes about 4 cups purée, or about 30 ravioli.

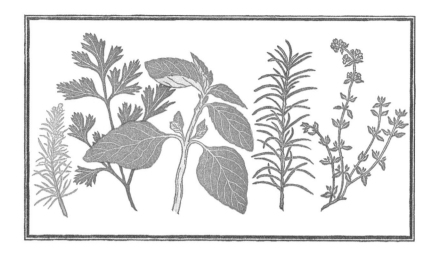

HERBS &

Fresh herbs are absolutely necessary to the cooking we do at Chez Panisse. It is almost impossible to imagine cooking without them, so important are their flavors—whether assertively dominating a dish or quietly supporting and deepening other flavors. Fortunately, fresh herbs are not as uncommon now in food markets as they once were. Even if you have no garden, it is not difficult to grow a few herbs in pots, and the rewards in the kitchen are great.

Some dried herbs—thyme, oregano, marjoram, and bay leaves—are useful for certain preparations. The best dried herbs are those that are picked fresh when they are beginning to flower, are freshly dried, and are used within a few months. Generally speaking, however, dried herbs cannot be substituted for the fresh herbs in the recipes in this book.

BASIL

Basil is a sun-loving, annual herb used all summer long in our kitchens, when tubs full of herbs line the walk-in shelves, fresh every day from the gardens. Basil is an integral part of the Mediterranean tradition that is so much a part of our style of cooking: in pesto or *pistou*, in pastas, on pizzas, on tomato salads.

The culinary basil we use is the Mediterranean *Ocimum basilicum*, sweet basil, from a number of different varieties, both small- and large-leaved. The green-leaved varieties have the finest flavor, especially the large, crinkly-leaved Genovese and the tiny-leaved Piccolo or Piccolo Fino, which makes very good pesto. There are larger "lettuce-leaved" varieties and a number of purple-leaved ones, too, all of which can be quite pretty but are generally not so tasty. We sometimes use purple basil leaves as a terminal garnish, but more for their beauty than for their flavor.

Other basils are the anise-scented Thai basil; cinnamon- and clove-scented basils (this last is a separate species, *O. sanctum*); and lemon basil (*O. basilicum citriodorum*). These all have uses in traditions other than the ones we usually explore, especially in the cuisines of Asia. We have found lemon basil to be interesting in some Asian-style soups and fish and shellfish dishes.

Basil is fragile. It wilts soon after being picked, and dies in cold weather. It has no interest as a dried herb, since it loses all its perfume. Enjoy it fresh. Cut it with a sharp knife or tear the leaves only just before using, to minimize wilting and discoloration.

CHERVIL

Chervil is one of the *fines herbes* of classic French cooking (the others are chives, tarragon, and parsley), and it is an indispensable part of the Provençal mixed green salad known as *mesclun*. It is an annual umbel-lifer, like coriander or dill, which looks like a miniature flat-leaf parsley and grows rapidly, close to shady ground.

The leaves have a delicious anise-like flavor, like a subtle blend of parsley and tarragon. It is wonderful in salads, and added at the last minute to soups and fish dishes. Try it in sauces and with vegetables where a fresh green perfume is wanted, but where basil or tarragon would be too strong. The very pretty, delicate sprigs of chervil make an appealing garnish.

It is never easy to find in the market: its young leaves are too delicate for it to be easily commercialized. The best way to assure a steady supply is to grow some. It does extremely well in cool shade and fog.

Cilantro or Coriander

Fresh coriander, *Coriandrum sativum*—usually called cilantro, some-times Chinese parsley—is rarely if ever used in the Mediterranean-style cooking we claim as the source of most of our inspiration. But when-ever we make something in an Asian or Mexican vein, out come the fresh, strongly-flavored leaves of this rapid-growing annual. Added at the last minute, cilantro gives a clean, fresh edge to a dish, especially in combination with fresh ginger and garlic. Its aroma is particularly rav-ishing when the plants are flowering, although usually it is the young leaves that are harvested. Coriander seed is often used as a pickling spice and in marinades and court-bouillons.

Fennel

Fennel is discussed more fully on page 147. It is listed here as well to re-mind you that its leaves and seeds are used as an herb because of their intensely aromatic, strong licorice flavor. The wild fennel that grows hereabouts is an untamed invader that grows six feet tall and more. Its flavor is more aggressive than that of the cultivated bulb varieties, which makes it superior in marinades and in such fish stews as bouillabaisse. The seeds can be gathered, dried, and stored.

Marjoram

Marjoram, *Origanum majorana*, is a perennial of the mint family that thrives in our area. It is very closely related to oregano and is often con-fused with it, or even misnamed. However, it is not interchangeable with oregano in the kitchen. Oregano has a strong and aggressive flavor, and we find we do not use it much in the restaurant kitchen. Marjoram, on the other hand, has a much sweeter, milder flavor, which goes well with fresh goat cheese, for example. Every day marjoram flavors both the goat cheese and prosciutto filling for the calzones baked in the pizza oven and the marinade for little fresh round goat cheeses that are then coated in bread crumbs and baked. Marjoram is also used to flavor veg-etable pastas and ragouts, particularly those with summer squash. It delicately perfumes fresh tomato sauces (where fresh oregano would be disagreeably pungent) and it can be good in tomato salads with onions and olives. Many cooks use it routinely with eggs, which we do not often cook on their own at the restaurant, but we do add it to soufflés, frittatas, and gratins.

PARSLEY

The overwhelming majority of the parsley consumed by the guests of Chez Panisse is the flat-leaf Italian parsley, *Petroselinum crispum* var. *neapolitanum*, rather than the curly-leaved parsley, *P. crispum* var. *crispum*. We prefer Italian parsley for its stronger, sweeter flavor, but curly parsley can make a very effective parsley salad with a garlicky vinaigrette and toasted bread crumbs or grated Parmesan—the cheese and crumbs lodge themselves in the folds of the leaves. Curly parsley also makes a delightful garnish when it is deep-fried for a few seconds, salted, and tossed on a plate with vegetable fritters or little fried shrimp. Both kinds are biennials with handsome yellow-green flowering umbels, and both are easily grown. The second year they will grow back from established roots, but if you keep reseeding, you can dig up the roots after the plants have flowered and gone to seed and use the roots instead of parsley stems in bouquets garnis; they will give a very fine flavor to stock.

The leaves and sprigs of parsley are not just a visual garnish: like nearly all the embellishments we make to a dish immediately before serving, parsley serves a gustatory function. It adds a fresh, clean taste that provides a lift to long-cooked flavors. Because of their stronger presence, sometimes whole leaves are used instead of chopped parsley in a vegetable dish, or in a salad or pasta.

The two classic chopped parsley garnishes are the French *persillade*—the mixture of finely chopped parsley and garlic—and the Italian *gremolata*—the same mixture plus chopped lemon zest. The proportion of garlic to parsley in a persillade depends on how much garlic the preparation it will be added to can support. A persillade added for the last few seconds to a dish of sautéeing potatoes or squid will release an explosion of parsley and garlic aroma. A gremolata is very good with all kinds of dishes—certainly with grilled chicken or fish and in its traditional role as a garnish to slowly braised veal shanks or lamb shoulder.

ROSEMARY

Rosemary, *Rosmarinus officinalis*, is another perennial herb that is a common ornamental plant in our region. There are both creeping, trailing varieties that cascade handsomely over concrete and stone retaining walls and more upright, bushy varieties. Rosemary is usually grown from plants, and once established is quite self-sufficient, requiring only sun and a little water. Untended rosemary plants can become quite sprawling and ungainly.

Because of the very strong flavor of the essential oils in its leaves, rosemary is used sparingly in most European cuisines, although least so in some Italian cooking. It can easily dominate a dish. We find that it can harmonize well with onions and potatoes, and especially with fava beans and dried beans. Whole branches are tossed into marinades for pork and lamb, and the sturdy straight branches of the upright variety can be used as skewers for grilled meat, fish, or poultry. And branches can be burned in a charcoal or wood fire to perfume the smoke of a grill.

Fresh noodles flavored with rosemary are a frequent variation on the pasta theme at Chez Panisse. Chopped fresh rosemary leaves are added to the pasta dough for noodles that get tossed with young fava beans; with caramelized onions or a quick sauté of spring onions; and with wilted greens of many kinds. This is the sort of pasta dish we serve as a first course or with a main course of roast meat or fowl, when the noodles can be enriched by the roasting juices.

SAGE

Another family of decorative perennials, the salvias, includes common garden sage, *Salvia officinalis*, another essential Mediterranean herb. Like most salvias, sage flourishes in sun and in relatively dry soil. It has beautiful blue-purple flowers. If the seed pods are removed after sage blooms in the spring, and if it is cut back in the fall, it will do fine. It should be used judiciously in the kitchen: its strong flavor can easily be overpowering. It goes well with rich and sweet winter squashes, and is a classic ingredient in chicken or veal saltimbocca—a dish in which a thin fillet of breast is pan-fried with a thin slice of prosciutto and a sage leaf, and a quick deglazing sauce is made with marsala and stock. Another interesting use for sage leaves is to make a garnish of whole leaves fried very briefly in hot olive oil. The leaves turn very crisp, and their flavor is tamed, becoming mild and light.

Savory

There are two kinds: the annual, *Satureja hortensis*, or summer savory, and the perennial, *S. montana*, or winter savory. We use them both. The leaves are a little tough, especially the smaller, drier leaves of winter savory, and not tender enough to be used without being chopped. Both savories are good bean herbs, enhancing the flavors of fava beans, black-eyed peas, lima beans, and flageolets. Winter savory has a much more subtle and complex flavor. We have learned to appreciate more of its qualities thanks to the example of Lulu Peyraud (see *Lulu's Provençal Table*, by Richard Olney). She uses it as her principal herb flavoring, along with lots of garlic, in tomato sauce, in meat stews, with grilled and baked fish, and in vegetable gratins.

Thyme

Common, or English, thyme, *Thymus vulgaris*, is the herb used most in the Chez Panisse kitchen. It is nearly always in bouquets garnis, and its sprigs flavor all sorts of basic preparations. We don't know of a cook who has ever tired of the pleasing aroma of a mirepoix of carrot, onion, and celery gently stewing in butter, with bay leaf and thyme. Mild but insinuating, thyme blends with almost everything in the kitchen, bringing depth and concord to whatever it flavors.

Like rosemary, lavender, marjoram, and many others, thyme is a perennial member of the mint family, one of the labiate herbs (so called for their distinctive lip-shaped flowers). It is much more often cooked slowly with a dish than added to it at the last minute, although when flowering it is especially sweet and can be used as a garnish for pastas and ragouts. Chop it fine with other herbs (savory, rosemary, marjoram, and chives) and use it with your best olive oil to marinate small fresh goat cheeses—then spread oil, herbs, and cheese together on good crusty bread.

The year-round availability of fresh thyme in markets makes the use of dried thyme unnecessary, unless you prefer its greater intensity when flavoring certain stews or pâtés.

Because of its intense citrus-oil aroma and flavor, lemon thyme is rarely used in savory preparations at the restaurant. However, it makes a beautiful tisane. We always offer a fresh herbal infusion on the menu; usually mint, lemon verbena, or lemon thyme, either singly or in combination.

PESTO

Purists agree that the very best way to make pesto is to pound it by hand in a mortar. If you have the time and tools to do so, you will be rewarded with the pleasure of the process and the authentic taste of the resulting crude paste. However, it is impractical to make large quantities by hand. We compromise by using a machine to purée the basil leaves minimally, and add them to garlic and nuts ground in the mortar.

2 or 3 cloves garlic
¼ cup pine nuts (or walnuts)
2 cups basil leaves
½ cup extra-virgin olive oil

½ cup grated Reggiano Parmesan cheese
Salt and pepper

Peel and slice the garlic. Pound it with the nuts in a mortar to make a paste. Add the basil leaves by small handfuls, continuing to pound and grind in the mortar. Add oil as needed with the leaves as you work the paste. When all the leaves are ground to a somewhat smooth texture (part of the charm is the uneven consistency), stir in the remaining oil and the cheese, and season to taste. The pesto is best used the same day but will keep in the refrigerator for a few days with a thin layer of olive oil on top, tightly covered.

Another way to make a quick pesto when you have a quantity of fresh leaves to use up is to roughly purée the leaves and nuts in a blender or food processor with enough oil to facilitate the process. Then stir in the cheese, more oil, and seasoning to taste. This can then be stored in the refrigerator, tightly covered, until ready for use. Before using, add fresh garlic, pounded in the mortar, or chop garlic fine and cook it briefly in a little olive oil before adding the pesto and boiled pasta, for example.

Makes about 2 cups.

Salsa Verde

A versatile sauce for fish and shellfish, antipasto vegetable salads, and grilled chicken.

½ cup chopped chervil
¼ cup chopped chives
¼ cup chopped parsley
Optional: 2 teaspoons chopped tarragon
1 tablespoon rinsed and chopped capers
1 shallot, finely chopped

Zest of 1 lemon, finely chopped
1 cup extra-virgin olive oil
Salt
Optional: 2 salt-packed anchovy fillets
Optional: Lemon juice or wine vinegar

Combine the chopped herbs, capers, shallot, and lemon zest with the oil, and add salt to taste. For a more savory salsa, add the anchovy (rinsed and chopped). For a sharper, more acid version, add lemon juice or vinegar, but do so at the last minute or the acid will turn the color of the herbs from bright to dull green. For a thinner sauce, add more oil.

Makes about 2½ cups.

Salsa Rustica

2 shallots
2 to 3 tablespoons red wine vinegar
2 tablespoons capers
3 salt-packed anchovies

3 hard-cooked eggs
1 cup chopped Italian parsley
¼ cup chopped thyme
1 cup olive oil
Salt and pepper

Dice the shallots very fine, cover them with the red wine vinegar in a small bowl, and let them macerate for about 20 minutes.

Rinse the capers and soak them in water for 5 minutes. Drain and chop coarsely. Rinse the anchovies well, remove their fins and backbones, and chop the fillets fine. Chop the eggs.

Combine the herbs, anchovies, and the shallots and vinegar with enough olive oil so that the mixture has a saucy consistency. Season with salt and pepper and more vinegar, if necessary. Gently stir in the chopped egg so as not to break up the yolk too much. Spoon over grilled vegetables or over grilled meat or fish.

Makes about 2 cups.

Parsley and Toasted Almond Salsa

1 shallot	*1 cup finely chopped Italian*
2 to 3 tablespoons red wine	*parsley*
vinegar	*2 tablespoons chopped chervil*
Salt	*¾ cup olive oil*
1½ tablespoons capers	*½ cup toasted almonds*
2 salt-packed anchovies	

Dice the shallot fine and cover with the red wine vinegar. Add a good pinch of salt and let macerate for 20 minutes.

Meanwhile, rinse the capers and soak them for 5 minutes. Drain and chop coarsely. Rinse the anchovies, remove their fins and backbones, and chop the fillets. Mix together the chopped herbs, capers, anchovies, and the shallots and vinegar. Add enough olive oil to reach a saucy consistency. Chop the almonds very fine and add to the salsa. Serve drizzled over the Snap Pea, Asparagus, and Turnip Ragout (page 232) or with seared tuna, grilled polenta, or grilled vegetables.

Makes about 1½ cups.

Parsley Salad

Pluck the leaves from a large bunch of Italian parsley. Wash them and spin them dry in a salad spinner. Just before serving, drizzle with a small amount of olive oil, enough to coat the leaves; add a squeeze of lemon juice; and grate over a generous amount of Parmesan. Toss and season with salt and pepper. If you wish, garnish with a few thin curls of Parmesan shaved from the block of cheese with a cheese slicer or a swivel-bladed vegetable peeler.

KALE 🦌

Season: Late fall and winter

Most varieties of kale (and collard greens too) belong to the same species of the mustard family as cabbage, broccoli, and brussels sprouts: *Brassica oleracea.* (Russian and Siberian kale belong to a separate species, *Brassica napus.*) Kale originated in the eastern Mediterranean, like most of the other brassicas, and the leaves of kale have a bright, sweet-spicy flavor similar to that of cabbage. Where kale puts its relatives to shame is in its leaf shapes and colors. The leaves of different varieties of kale can be serrated, crinkled, or even deeply cut and feathery, and they come in many combinations of blue-green, white, purple, and yellow.

Ornamental, or flowering, kale is an important landscape accent in many parts of the world. The foot-wide rosettes are not flowers at all but the brilliantly colored leaves of the plant; the leaves of flowering kale can be eaten when very young. Even the kales grown for food are beautiful.

Laciniato, an heirloom Italian variety, has very dark blue-green, narrow leaves up to a foot long, with an attractive crinkly texture. Some growers call this variety dinosaur kale, because of its prehistoric appearance. The leaves of Red Russian kale are deeply toothed and splotched with red and purple, and have red midribs. A local organic grower, Full Belly Farm, has recently been bringing to the farmer's market what they call Carinata kale, which has broad oval leaves the size of those of collards, but in a brilliant reddish purple.

All these kales are in season at a welcome time, late fall and winter, when the abundance of other vegetables is waning. They develop their best flavor and color only after a period of cold weather, and can take a considerable degree of frost. At their best, kales have a strikingly distinctive flavor, rich and almost sweet, and what some people describe as minerally or earthy.

The first, tender leaves of kale are best cooked quickly, sautéed in a little olive oil and seasoned with garlic. Later in the season, the larger, more substantial leaves are favored by long cooking, and seasoned with onions, or cream and lemon, as well as garlic.

At any stage of its development, you will recognize the best kale in the market by its bright color and the absence of wilting or bruising on the leaves. Kale for long cooking should have thick leaves with a lot of body to them.

Don't try to store kale for very long after it is harvested. It should be kept in a plastic bag in the refrigerator for no more than a few days. All kale should be rinsed and drained shortly before cooking. When preparing kale for quick cooking, remove the stems and cut out the tough midrib of any large leaves. Tender stems can be left on kale that will be cooked a long time. Once prepared for cooking, kale can be returned to the refrigerator in a plastic bag for several hours before use.

Because of its bright colors and undemanding growth habits, kale is an attractive vegetable to grow. Consider landscape uses for kale outside the kitchen garden as well. But while choice eating varieties of kale may make good landscape plants, the ornamental varieties rarely make good eating.

KALE AND POTATO SOUP

A Portuguese recipe, called *caldo verde* (green broth) in Portugal, where cabbage is often substituted for the kale.

1 bunch kale (about 1 pound)	*1 teaspoon salt*
2 pounds boiling potatoes	*Optional: 1 garlic sausage*
2 quarts water	*Extra-virgin olive oil*

Remove the stems from the kale, wash the leaves, and cut them into a chiffonade. You should have about 6 to 8 cups.

Peel the potatoes and chop them up very fine (Yellow Finns are good for this—or use some other flavorful boiling potato). Bring the water to a boil with the salt. Add the chopped potatoes, return to a boil, and cook for 2 minutes, covered. Add the kale and cook 2 minutes more. Taste for seasoning. If desired, serve with sliced garlic sausage heated briefly in the soup and a splash of the olive oil.

Serves 4 to 6.

Note: The proportion of kale to potatoes in this soup is not terribly important. Nor do you need to chop the potatoes; but if you slice them, they will need to cook a little longer before you can add the kale. You can also pass the soup through a food mill and serve it as a purée; moisten it with chicken stock instead of water; or enrich it with other vegetables. One very good variation is to stew sliced shallots and garlic apart until they are very soft and caramelized, and then purée them with the kale and potatoes.

LONG-STEWED RED KALE

1 slice smoked bacon	*Salt and pepper*
1 onion	*½ cup cream*
1 small carrot	*Grated zest of ½ lemon*
3 cloves garlic	*(about ½ teaspoon)*
2 bunches red kale (about 2 pounds)	

Cut the bacon into small dice and render it over low heat for about 8 minutes. Peel and chop the onion, carrot, and garlic into small dice and add to the bacon with a splash of water. Cover and stew the vegetables until they are soft and the onion is translucent, about 10 minutes.

Wash, stem, and coarsely chop the kale (or a combination of kale and mustard greens, or other winter greens). Add the kale to the vegetables along with some salt and cook uncovered over moderately high heat; the greens will give off a lot of water. Keep cooking until the liquid is almost evaporated, about 10 to 15 minutes. Add half the cream and simmer until it has been almost completely absorbed, then add the other half and keep simmering until it, too, is nearly absorbed. Add the lemon zest, taste and correct the seasoning, and serve.

Serves 6.

SAUTÉED KALE WITH GARLIC AND VINEGAR

This is a basic method of cooking greens that works equally well with nearly all the leafy greens. It also makes a simple pasta dish: Put on some pasta to cook while you sauté, and when the noodles are done, toss them together with the greens, moistened with a little more olive oil and a ladle of the pasta cooking water.

2 bunches kale (about 2 pounds)	*2 cloves garlic*
3 tablespoons olive oil	*1 to 2 tablespoons red wine*
Salt	*vinegar*

Strip the kale leaves off their stems and cut away the tough midribs of any large leaves. Chop coarsely and wash in plenty of water. Drain well, but do not spin dry.

Heat a large sauté pan and add the olive oil and enough kale to cover the bottom of the pan. Allow these greens to wilt down before adding more. When all the kale has been added, season with salt, stir in the garlic, and cover the pan. The greens will take anywhere from just a few minutes to 15 minutes to cook, depending on their maturity. When they are tender, remove the lid and allow any excess water to cook away. Turn off the heat and stir in the vinegar.

Serves 4 to 6.

Note: The kale can be served with roast chicken or other meats, or as part of an antipasto platter—in which case, allow the kale to cool, squeeze it dry with your hands, arrange on the platter, and drizzle with very good olive oil.

LEEKS &

Season: Year-round; small leeks, midsummer through late fall

In France, leeks are called "poor man's asparagus," and are prized for their succulence and sweet, delicate flavor. In the United States, leeks can be almost as costly as asparagus, but they are available over a much longer season, generally from late summer until the end of spring.

The leek (*Allium ampeloprasum*) is a member of the garlic and onion family, and is grown for its blanched, white stem. In the market leeks are usually found with their roots and most of their long, straplike leaves still attached. Some varieties (Varna, for example) have quite elongated, pale green stems. Others, such as the heirloom Scotland, have very short, thick shanks. Most varieties you find at the market will have stalks six to eight inches long and an inch or two in diameter.

At the restaurant we use large, mature leeks in many of the same ways we use onions, but the results are different. The flavors of a soup or stock made with leeks will seem more integrated and refined than those of one made with onions alone. The cloying sweetness of some kinds of onions is subdued by adding a few leeks. We routinely add leeks to poultry and vegetable stocks. Leek tarts and leek pizza and focaccia are favorite hors d'oeuvres. We also find that leeks have a special affinity for fish, so we add them to bouillabaisse, stew them with squid and red wine (following Richard Olney's inspired recipe in *Simple French Food*), and use them as a bed for braised sea bass. Leeks add a rich, round flavor when braised with chicken or beef too. And cut into julienne and deep-fried, leeks make a crispy topping for grilled or steamed fish.

At some times of the year small, finger-size leeks are available at the market. These are perfect either steamed or brushed with olive oil and grilled, and served warm or at room temperature, as part of an aïoli

181

plate, or with salsa verde or a mustard vinaigrette and sieved egg, as a salad.

Because leeks have a growing season of three or four months, they are most abundant in the fall. In many parts of the country, mature leeks can be left in the ground and harvested throughout the winter and into the spring. Smaller leeks first come to market in midsummer. They are usually common until late fall.

Leeks in the market should have firm, white stalks and stiff, dark, green or blue-green leaves. Any roots still attached should be firm and white. Leeks for grilling or steaming whole should be finger size or slightly smaller. When you pick them up, they should be nice and stiff, not limp.

Leeks keep best if they are not trimmed until just before use. Meanwhile bundle them in a damp towel and keep them in a plastic bag in the refrigerator. Smaller leeks should be used in a day or two, but larger ones will keep well for four or five days.

Small leeks to be cooked whole should have their roots trimmed off just at the base of the stem. Be careful not to cut off the basal plate, or the leeks may fall apart during cooking. Trim the tops, leaving several inches of the tender green leaves on the stem, and pull off one outer layer of leaves. Then make a lengthwise cut, starting two inches from the base and continuing through the tops. Hold the prepared leeks under a stream of cold running water and rinse out any dirt or sand that may be trapped between the layers.

Larger leeks that will be sliced, diced, or julienned should have their roots removed by cutting just above the basal plate. Cut off almost all of the green leaves and pull off one or two of the outer layers. Cut the stalk in half or in quarters, as the recipe suggests, and cut up the leeks. The cut leeks should then be washed thoroughly by rinsing them in a large bowl of cold water. Swish the pieces around in the bowl for a minute or two until no traces of dirt or sand are left clinging to them. Let the bowl of leeks stand undisturbed for a few minutes to allow the dirt to settle, and then carefully scoop the leeks out of the bowl with a skimmer or strainer. Don't pour the leeks into the strainer, or the dirt will come right out of the bowl and be trapped by the leeks. Leeks to be deep-fried benefit from soaking overnight in clean, cold water.

Because leeks require a long growing season, home gardeners should start with transplants, either your own or ones purchased from a nursery, and put them out in the spring. To achieve a nicely blanched stalk, bury the seedling up to the base of the first leaf joint, and hill the soil up

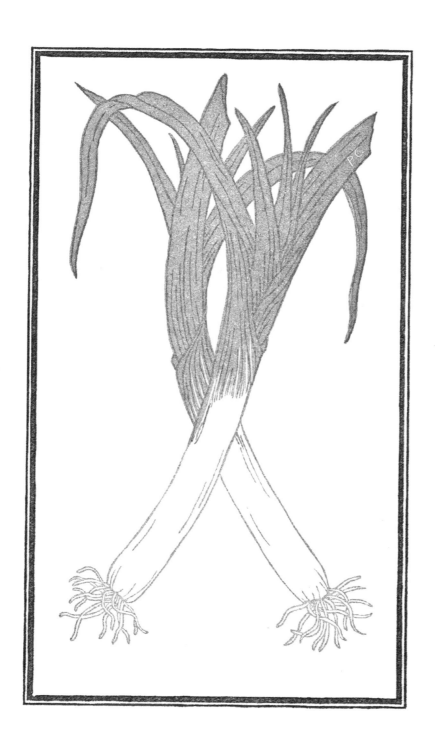

around the plants as they grow. Since leeks are very hardy and are not bothered by most insect pests, they should be welcome in any garden. The Seeds of Change catalog lists many varied types for the home gardener to try.

LEEK TART

3 pounds leeks	½ recipe Galette Dough
3 tablespoons unsalted butter	(page 320)
1½ tablespoons water	1 tablespoon flour
8 sprigs thyme	1 egg, beaten
Salt and pepper	

Trim off the roots and the green tops from the leeks. Slice the white parts in half lengthwise, and then cut them crosswise into ¼-inch slices. Rinse well in lots of cold water to remove all sand and dirt.

Heat a large sauté pan and add the butter and water. When the butter has melted, add the leeks and thyme, and season with salt and pepper. Stir well and cook, covered, over medium heat until the leeks are completely tender—about 10 minutes. Shake the pan occasionally to prevent sticking and add more water if the pan is going dry before the leeks are done.

Preheat the oven to 400°F.

Roll out the pastry dough into a 12-inch circle and place it on a baking sheet. Sprinkle the pastry with the flour and spread the leeks evenly over the dough to within 1 inch of the edge. Fold the uncovered dough up and over the leeks, making a crude shell around the edge, and brush it with the egg. Bake on the lowest shelf of the oven until the crust is nicely browned, about 20 to 30 minutes. If the top should brown before the bottom, cover with a sheet of aluminum foil and continue to bake until the bottom has browned.

Makes one 10-inch tart.

Note: For a more intensely flavored version of this tart, combine flaked cooked salt cod or Potato and Salt Cod Purée (see page 249) with the leeks. Moisten with a little cream and garnish the tart with pitted black olives just before baking.

GRILLED LEEKS AND GREEN GARLIC MIMOSA

24 small leeks
  (½-inch diameter)
24 green garlic plants
  (see page 157)
Salt and pepper
2 large eggs
2 shallots

¼ cup white wine vinegar or
  sherry vinegar
1 teaspoon Dijon mustard
¾ cup extra-virgin olive oil
4 salt-packed anchovies
Italian parsley

Thoroughly clean the leeks and green garlic. Cut off their roots and coarse green tops and peel off their outermost layers. Cut the leeks almost in two with a lengthwise cut starting 2 inches above the base, submerge the leeks and garlic in water, and agitate to remove any clinging dirt. Cook separately in well-salted boiling water until just tender, about 4 minutes, and drain.

Bring a pot of water to a boil, put the eggs in a sieve, and immerse them in the boiling water for 9 to 10 minutes. Remove the eggs from the water and cool under running water or in a bowl of ice water. The yolk should be just set. Peel the eggs.

Build a fire for grilling the leeks and garlic.

Prepare a vinaigrette: Peel the shallots and dice them very fine. Cover with the vinegar and macerate for 20 minutes. Add the mustard and whisk in the olive oil. Season with salt and pepper. Rinse and fillet the anchovies. Chop a handful of Italian parsley leaves.

Brush the leeks and garlic with olive oil, and salt them. Grill over low to medium heat, turning frequently, until they are lightly browned on all sides, about 10 minutes.

Arrange the leeks and garlic on a platter. Drizzle the dressing generously over them, arrange the anchovies on top, pass the eggs through a medium sieve over the platter, and sprinkle with the chopped parsley.

Serves 6.

Note: Grilled leeks can be added to an antipasto plate or served on toasted croutons spread with stewed garlic, and topped with anchovy fillets.

LEEK SOUP

10 medium leeks
Olive oil
Salt and pepper
8 cups chicken stock
1 stalk celery
A few sprigs thyme
1 bay leaf

1 small branch rosemary
2 cloves garlic
Champagne vinegar or white
    wine vinegar
A few sprigs parsley
Optional: 8 slices country-style
    bread

Prepare the leeks: Cut off their roots and most of their coarse, outer green leaves and peel off an outside layer or two. Quarter the stalks and chop into ¼-inch dice. Wash the diced leek thoroughly in a large basin of cold water, and after the dirt has settled, carefully scoop the leeks out of the water with a sieve or strainer and let them drain.

Heat 4 tablespoons of olive oil in a heavy-bottomed stockpot, add the leeks, and cook over medium-high heat until just tender, about 5 minutes. It is important not to overcook them. They should not lose either their bright green color or a very slight crunch to their texture. Salt them to taste and add the chicken stock and a bouquet garni made up of the celery, thyme, bay leaf, and rosemary. Bring to a very low simmer. Add the garlic, crushed, peeled, and thinly sliced, and simmer for about 20 minutes. Season to taste with about 1 tablespoon Champagne vinegar or white wine vinegar, and more salt, if necessary. Serve hot, garnished with a little chopped parsley and a few grinds of the peppermill, and if you wish, with grilled or toasted slices of bread.

Serves 8.

OVEN-BRAISED LEEKS WITH CREAM

Cut off the roots and tough green tops of the leeks and remove their outer layer of skin. Slice the leeks almost in half with a vertical cut starting an inch or so above the root end, rotate the leek 90 degrees, and make a second cut. Rinse them and soak them in cold water, working free any dirt. Tie the leeks into a bundle and parboil them in well-salted boiling water until tender throughout. Remove the bundle, cut off the string, and drain and cool at room temperature.

Arrange the leeks in a buttered baking dish. Cover with a mixture of one part stock to three parts heavy cream. Dot with unsalted butter, and season with salt and black pepper. You can also add a branch of thyme or some fresh chopped thyme leaves. Bake at 375°F. for about 30 to 40 minutes, until the liquid has reduced enough so that it coats instead of covering the leeks. Serve warm.

Note: A lighter way of cooking leeks with cream is to braise them until tender in a covered saucepan on top of the stove with butter and water. Then add enough cream to barely cover the leeks, and simmer, uncovered, until the cream has reduced and coats the leeks.

Baby Leek Salad with Mustard Vinaigrette

This salad is often served as part of an antipasto plate with thin slices of prosciutto.

24 very small leeks	*4 tablespoons light olive oil*
2 shallots	*(or peanut oil)*
4 tablespoons Dijon mustard	*Parsley*
2 tablespoons red wine vinegar	*1 hard-cooked egg*
Salt and pepper	

Trim off the roots and the dark green tops of the leeks. Split them lengthwise through the greens and partway through the white part with a sharp knife. Rinse them and soak in cold water to loosen any residual dirt. Remove the leeks from the water and tie into a bundle with some string—they will stay together and be easier to remove from the pot. Cook the leeks in a large pot of salted boiling water until tender, about 8 minutes. Drain well and squeeze lightly in a towel to remove excess water.

Prepare a vinaigrette: Peel and dice the shallots very fine and put them in a bowl with the mustard, vinegar, salt, and pepper. Let sit for 5 minutes and whisk in the olive oil. Toss the leeks in the vinaigrette and arrange on a platter. Chop about 1 tablespoon of parsley and sprinkle over the leeks and push the egg through a sieve over the salad.

Serves 4.

GRILLED LEEKS AND STEWED GARLIC ON TOAST

The garlic in this recipe is simmered in three changes of water to make a very mildly flavored garlic purée, so that the flavor of the smoky, sweet grilled leeks is in bold relief.

1½ pounds young leeks
(½-inch diameter)
About ½ cup extra-virgin
olive oil
2 heads very fresh garlic

Optional: 5 or 6 salt-packed
anchovies
8 thin slices country-style bread
Salt and pepper

Cut off the small roots of the leeks without cutting into the white flesh. Trim off the green tops an inch or so above the point at which they start to branch out from the main stem. Cut the leeks almost in two with a lengthwise cut starting about 2 inches above the base. Wash them thoroughly and cook them in salted boiling water for 6 or 7 minutes; a knife point should easily pierce the stalks. Drain the leeks and arrange them in a single layer on a platter. When they have cooled to room temperature, lightly toss them with some of the olive oil.

Start a wood or charcoal fire for grilling.

Break the heads of garlic into cloves and peel them. Cover with water in a small saucepan and simmer for 5 minutes. Drain off the water and repeat with fresh water. Drain again and simmer in a third change of water, until the cloves are very soft but not falling apart. Drain and purée the garlic with 1 tablespoon of the olive oil. If you want to garnish the leeks with anchovies, rinse and fillet them now and cut them into thin strips.

Grill the leeks over a medium-hot fire, turning occasionally to brown them evenly. When they are done, set them aside in a warm spot. Lightly oil the bread and toast on the grill. Smear the toasted slices liberally on one side with the garlic purée and place the toasts on a large platter. Split the leeks lengthwise and arrange them on the toast. Garnish with the strips of anchovy. Drizzle lightly with a little more of the olive oil, sprinkle with salt, and grind a little pepper over the top.

Serves 4.

LENTILS 🌰

Season: Year-round

The small, lens-shaped seeds known as lentils, *Lens culinaris*, are another of the pulses—edible, ripe, dried seeds of the legume family, like navy beans or split peas. Not all legumes are pulses, because some legumes are inedible, but all pulses are legumes. Like other pulses, lentils are rich in protein and carbohydrates, as well as rich in flavor. At Chez Panisse we are most familiar with the tiny, dark green lentils so prized in France, the *lentilles de Puy*, and the more common large brown lentils. In fact, most lentils have a brown or green seed coat. However, our friend Niloufer Ichaporia, an authority on the Parsee cuisine of her native Bombay, has introduced us to the brightly colored lentils from India, which have had their seed coats removed to reveal their brilliant red and orange colors. These lentils tend to break up as they cook, and are most often puréed in soups or Indian dals.

We use green lentils as an hors d'oeuvre, cooked and cooled to room temperature, and dressed with olive oil, vinegar, goat cheese, and a mirepoix of aromatic vegetables. In the winter, we like to make lentil soup, and we sometimes serve lentils, whole or puréed, as an accompaniment to grilled pork or sausages.

Tiny green French lentils can be found in specialty grocery stores in 250- or 500-gram packages, and brown lentils are available in the bulk foods sections of many supermarkets. To find yellow, orange, or red lentils, try an Indian grocery or a health food store.

Lentils do not need to be soaked before cooking, but they should be picked through to find and discard any pebbles or clumps of grit. Rinse the lentils in cold water just before cooking to remove any traces of sand.

Lentils should be cooked in barely simmering water or stock. Because they absorb a great deal of liquid while cooking, it is best to start with at least two cups of water or stock for every cup of lentils. Carefully monitor the amount of liquid during cooking, adding more if necessary to prevent scorching. An onion half, a bay leaf, and a few sprigs of thyme may be added to enhance the flavor of the lentils. Wait until the lentils have softened before adding salt; salting earlier toughens their skins.

Tiny green lentils should be fully cooked in about twenty to forty minutes, depending on their age and dryness, but larger brown lentils may take as long as an hour and a half. In any event, they should be simmered until completely tender. Lentils to be used as a salad should be drained after cooking. A little vinegar added at this point will help keep them from getting too soft.

MEDITERRANEAN LENTIL SOUP

1 onion
1 carrot
2 tablespoons olive oil
Salt and pepper
1 cup brown lentils
½ cup red lentils
1 small bunch parsley
  (about 3 ounces)

½ head garlic
½ small fresh chili pepper
2 quarts water
½ teaspoon cumin seed
1 teaspoon fennel seed
Lemon juice or red wine vinegar
Extra-virgin olive oil

Peel the onion and carrot and cut into small dice. Sauté them in the olive oil in a soup pot over medium heat, seasoned with salt and pepper, and cook until they are tender. Meanwhile, carefully pick through the lentils, removing any small stones or debris. Rinse the lentils thoroughly in cold water.

Pick the parsley leaves from the stems and save the leaves to be chopped for garnishing the finished soup. Wrap the parsley stems, the garlic, and the chili in a cheesecloth sack, and add it to the soup pot. Add the lentils and the water. Bring to a boil and simmer until the red lentils have broken up and the brown lentils are very soft, 45 minutes to 1 hour.

While the soup is cooking, toast the cumin and fennel seeds in a skillet over high heat for a minute or two, until their aroma is released. Pound them in a mortar. Chop the parsley leaves.

When the soup is done, take out the cheesecloth sack and squeeze any broth back into the soup. Add the ground spices and taste for seasoning, adding salt and pepper, if necessary, and a dash of lemon juice or red wine vinegar. Serve garnished with a dribble of extra-virgin olive oil and a sprinkling of the chopped parsley.

Serves 6 to 8.

Note: Another very good flavor with lentils is sorrel. Instead of adding the chili and spices to the soup, 10 minutes before the soup is done, add a large handful of sorrel leaves cut into a chiffonade. Finish the soup with olive oil, chopped parsley, and some small fried croutons.

Green Lentil Salad

½ pound small green lentils
1 small leek
1 small onion
1 small carrot
2 cloves garlic
2 cloves
Bouquet garni: thyme, parsley,
*   bay leaf*

Optional: one 3-ounce piece
*   smoked bacon*
Salt and pepper
2 shallots
2 tablespoons sherry vinegar
4 tablespoons olive oil
1 small bunch chives

Rinse the lentils and remove any pebbles. Trim and wash the leek thoroughly. Peel the onion, carrot, and garlic. Push the cloves into the onion.

Put the lentils in a saucepan with the leek, onion, carrot, garlic, the bouquet garni, and the bacon. Cover with cold water. Bring to a boil and simmer for 10 to 15 minutes. Let stand for 5 minutes. The cooking liquid should be almost completely absorbed. Remove the bacon and dice it. Remove and discard the bouquet garni, onion, leek, carrot, and garlic. (If you wish, you can save the carrot, dice it, and add it to the salad for more color.) Lightly salt the lentils.

Peel and finely chop the shallots and mix in a bowl with the vinegar. Add the lentils, bacon, olive oil, and pepper, and toss together. Correct the seasoning. Chop the chives and sprinkle over the salad.

This salad is best if not refrigerated. Serve warm or at room temperature with slices of prosciutto or cured duck breast and a green salad, or as part of an antipasto plate with a variety of other salads. This is also good with fresh goat cheese crumbled into the salad.

Serves 4.

Lentil Sauté

Cook lentils as for the Green Lentil Salad, above (in water with aromatic vegetables). In olive oil, sauté a little finely chopped mirepoix of carrot, onion, and celery (along with the bacon from the lentils, diced), until the vegetables have softened. Add the lentils and a few finely chopped garlic cloves, and toss and cook briefly. Taste and adjust the seasoning, adding a splash of red wine or sherry vinegar just before serving. Serve with sausages or roast poultry, especially pheasant or guinea hen.

LETTUCES AND OTHER SALAD GREENS 🌿

From the first day the restaurant opened, one of our most cherished goals at Chez Panisse has been to offer our guests a plain garden salad composed of nothing more than a few kinds of tasty leafy lettuces and other greens, picked fresh, washed, dried, and tossed with a simple oil-and-vinegar dressing. Twenty years ago this seemed almost impossible: virtually the only commercially available salad greens consisted of a few kinds of heading lettuces—either crispy iceberg types; the cylindrical heads of romaine; or a few butterhead, or Bibb, kinds.

The salad we were dreaming of was another thing altogether: a salad of small, wild-tasting leaves like the *mesclun* in salads in the south of France. *Mesclun* is a Provençal word that means "mixed." Traditionally, mesclun was picked wild—a mixture of the shoots and leaves of the tender edible plants that start poking up on the hillsides after the rains in winter and early spring. Nowadays it is mostly cultivated from mixed seed. By the late seventies, we could approximate the classic mesclun combination (dandelion greens, two or three different kinds of lettuces, rocket, garden cress, and chervil) with greens grown for us by several local gardeners who had begun to sow mixtures of seeds imported from France. By the late eighties, farmers nearby had begun to plant and market several kinds of pricey salad mixes, some of which stray rather far from our ideal of a balanced combination of salad flavors and textures. Often they include leaves that are too tough and strong to enjoy raw, such as curly kale and chard, or they are overloaded with hot, peppery mustard greens. Authentic mesclun-type mixtures of greens should include the sweet young leaves of various lettuces; perhaps a little refreshing bitter curly endive; the stronger, peppery flavors of dandelion greens or rocket; and the grassy, spicy notes of herbs such as chervil.

The lettuces are all cultivars of *Lactuca sativa*. Of the familiar head lettuces, we do not use the crispheads, because they tend to taste bland, especially after you have tried the more fragile varieties. We do serve various kinds of romaine, especially when they have been harvested relatively small; there are red- and bronze-leaved varieties as well as the familiar pale green. We also use some of the butterhead lettuces in salads. However, most of the lettuces we serve are the salad bowl, or loose-leaf types, also known as cutting or gathering lettuces. These lettuces grow without forming tight heads; when their leaves are cut off they obligingly resprout. They can be sown densely, and will yield several crops of delicious leaves. There are dozens of varieties of loose-leaf lettuces; we are especially fond of the variously colored oak-leaved types.

Of the many salad greens we use that are not lettuces, the chicories, spinach, and watercress and garden cress are discussed elsewhere, in their own sections. Dandelion greens (*Taraxacum officinale*) are rather bitter, but can be quite good when contrasted with something sweet. The plant known botanically as *Eruca sativa* is more commonly known as arugula or roquette than by its old English name of rocket. We use the relatively mild spring cuttings of rocket in salads; stronger, more peppery rocket is sometimes cooked (see the recipe for Pasta with Potatoes, Rocket, and Rosemary on page 246).

Valerianella locusta, another wonderful salad plant that is making a comeback, used to be called lamb's lettuce or corn salad (the leaves are said to resemble lambs' tongues, and it grows amidst the corn). We usually call it mâche, its French name, on the menu, to avoid confusion (when we called it corn salad, customers expected a salad made of sweet corn kernels). Mâche is a lovely and hardy little plant with rosettes of dark green leaves on short stems. It has a flavor all its own that makes it distinctive as a salad by itself, simply dressed. Because its leaves have more body than tender lettuces, it combines well with fruits and vegetables in composed salads. Hereabouts it is grown winter and summer, but in Europe it is usually a cold weather salad.

The various salad greens seem to fall naturally into certain seasons of the year. In the early spring, we satisfy our salad cravings with tender sprouting rocket and chervil and the oak-leaf and other "cut-and-come-again" lettuces. Later on in the year, when they have had the longer time they need to develop, the romaine lettuces come to market. In the early summer we also get the best dandelion greens and spinach. On the other hand, the fall and winter are the best times of year for the sturdier, more bitter chicories.

Lettuces must be handled gently and lovingly. Wash them in the sink or in a large basin filled with plenty of cold water, which can perk them up considerably in hot weather. Lift them out of the water, drain them, and dry in small batches in a salad spinner. Refrigerate the clean leaves layered between towels in an airtight container or a plastic bag. If you need to break a head lettuce into leaves or trim away imperfections, instead of tearing the lettuce with your hands, use a knife; this will limit bruising and wilting. Mâche can be a particularly difficult salad green to wash if you leave the leaf rosettes attached together, which makes the prettiest presentation: inevitably there is sand lodged at the base of the stems, and you must wash and rewash, agitating the little clusters of leaves underwater.

SALADS AND DRESSINGS

We often serve salad greens, undressed, as a bed for an entrée or a savory dish; the seasoned juices of the meat or fish are all the dressing one could wish for. Some salads, notably romaine, can stand up to a creamy, highly flavored dressing made with mayonnaise, or with mashed avocado and cream (see Green Goddess Dressing, page 19), or with egg yolk and anchovies and grated cheese (as in a Caesar salad). Served all alone, very fresh young greens with a variety of clean wild flavors can be excellent with nothing but a little olive oil, salt, and pepper.

Most salads we serve with a vinaigrette. Specific recipes for shallot vinaigrettes are scattered throughout this book, but they are all made the same way: finely diced shallots are macerated in vinegar with a little salt for twenty minutes to an hour (this tempers the raw shallot flavor); then a few grinds of the peppermill, and extra-virgin olive oil is whisked in—usually in a ratio of three parts oil to one of vinegar. However, this is just a starting point; the specifics will vary, depending on what is being dressed. A little smashed garlic is desirable for some salads. Avoid overdressing your salads; they should sparkle with a light coating of oil and vinegar, nothing more.

196

It is useful to have different wine vinegars on hand. We use red wine vinegar (some we make ourselves), balsamic vinegar, Champagne and white wine vinegars, and sherry vinegar. As with every other ingredient, quality varies: cheap wine vinegars are sometimes made from very bad wine, and taste like it. If you drink wine, save the remains of any good bottles for your own vinegar (see Paul Bertolli's instructions for home-made vinegar in *Chez Panisse Cooking*).

Real balsamic vinegar, highly concentrated and aged, is rare and a great luxury. The widely distributed brands are considerably less expensive and are useful, although they are perhaps better when combined with other red wine vinegar, since they are sweet and forceful by themselves. Red wine and balsamic vinegars go well with all kinds of salad greens, tomatoes, green beans and shell beans, and grilled foods. Champagne and other white wine vinegars have a natural affinity for fish and shellfish and for certain vegetables, such as fennel, leeks, potatoes, avocados, and artichokes. In some cases, lemon juice or another citrus juice either augments or replaces the vinegar. Sherry vinegar is well suited to the autumnal salads made with fall fruits and nuts. Few, if any, of the commercial vinegars flavored with garlic or with various herbs are worth buying.

There is no real substitute for extra-virgin olive oil from a good producer. The finest, fruitiest first-pressing olive oils taste their best when in salads because their flavor is so clearly appreciated in contrast with the clean flavors of greens. Olive oil labeled "extra-virgin" must be extracted from the olive, without heat, by pressure alone. It must contain less than 1 percent acidity. "Virgin" olive oil must contain less than 4 percent. Olive oil labeled "pure" usually designates highly processed olive oil, sometimes with some virgin olive oil blended back in.

It is a good idea to have two or three kinds of olive oil in your kitchen: a general-purpose virgin olive oil that is mild, not spicy, and rather light in color, to use for cooking and as a base; and a more expensive, extra-virgin olive oil, deeper in color and with a stronger and fruitier flavor, to use in salad dressings and for finishing touches.

Like wine, good olive oil varies with its "vintage," and we have frequent blind tastings at the restaurant to decide on what brands to keep on hand. We generally prefer Italian and Spanish extra-virgin olive oils, because Italy and Spain produce the greatest quantity and selection of olive oil for export, but there are also good French oils. A few Californians have begun to experiment with the production of high-quality olive oils using traditional, artisanal techniques.

Commercially flavored oils, like flavored vinegars, are usually disappointing, but made at home they can be quite good (see Flavored Oils, page 318). Some very good quality white truffle oil from Italy has made its way to our markets. Although expensive, the oil is quite delicious, and only a few drops are needed to flavor a dish.

We also occasionally use walnut and hazelnut oils in salads. Nut oils are intensely nutty in flavor, and go beautifully with certain bitter greens, such as curly endive, and with fall fruits such as persimmons, apples, and figs. They do not keep well and can become rancid in a short time. Store them in the refrigerator once the can or bottle has been opened and use it up within a month or two. As an alternative to purchasing nut oil, try making a vinaigrette infused with freshly toasted and chopped nuts.

Chez Panisse salads are sometimes strewn with whole flowers and flower petals: violets, violas, calendulas, rose petals, nasturtiums, and herb flowers (especially borage). The garden salads we serve daily in the café always contain Garlic Croutons (page 160). Croutons are also served on the side of many salads—spread with either duck or pigeon liver pâté, with Fava Bean Purée (page 142) or Fresh Shell Bean Purée (page 35), with Potato and Salt Cod Purée (page 249) or Tapenade (page 317), or topped with fresh-cured sardines or anchovies (page 256). Pickled onions and pickled cherries appear in green salads on occasion, as do such fresh fruits as pears, apples, and persimmons in the fall. Pine nuts, almonds, and walnuts are often toasted and tossed in with the greens. Crumbled Roquefort cheese finishes some salads; thin planings of Parmesan are scattered on others.

MARJORAM &
See Herbs (page 169)

MUSHROOMS &

Season: Year-round

Wild mushrooms are one of the last truly foraged, wild foods available to most cooks. Almost all of the other plants we use have long been domesticated and bred to emphasize qualities we find desirable. Wild mushrooms, on the other hand—with their woodsy, earthy, complex flavors and aromas, and their rich, primeval colors and forms—bring to our kitchens a reminder that all the places we inhabit were once wildernesses.

North America is rich in mushrooms. In some mild climates like ours, edible wild mushrooms can be found nearly year-round. Even in the Rockies and the cold winter areas of the Midwest, wild mushrooms spring up in abundance in late spring and early summer. Because we have the good fortune to have so many wild mushrooms available to us and because their flavors are so much more interesting than those of the cultivated varieties, we seldom serve cultivated mushrooms.

A few poisonous wild mushrooms are similar in appearance to edible mushrooms. Therefore, don't eat any wild mushroom unless you are absolutely sure of its origin and safety. Wild mushrooms gathered by professional mushroom hunters and displayed for sale in established produce markets can be assumed to be safe to eat. To gather your own, first learn more about the edible mushrooms in your area. There are mycological societies in many cities that will be happy to provide more information. Many organize educational hunts for beginners and offer identification services to their members.

Of all the edible fungi, the most celebrated are undoubtedly the black truffle and the white truffle, found only in France and Italy. Because they grow underground, they are undetectable without the help of trained dogs or pigs; and because of shrinking habitats, overharvesting, and causes unknown, they are now rarer than ever. Consequently, they are staggeringly expensive: a pound of black truffles can cost over five hundred dollars, and a pound of white truffles over a thousand.

This oddball luxury has been gathered for centuries, and it has inspired a literature of hyperbolic appreciation, in which much is made of the truffle's alleged aphrodisiac properties. Skeptics are encouraged to take a deep whiff of a good, fresh specimen.

At Chez Panisse, we succumb to our weakness for fresh truffles only for very special occasions during the winter, when they are in season. Black truffles need a little cooking, and can flavor sauces, stuffings, salads, roasts—almost anything, in fact. The Italian white truffles are served raw, often grated paper thin over plates of pasta. (The Italians also export a white-truffle-infused oil, with a powerful and authentic white truffle aroma. It is expensive, but used only a few drops at a time, a little bottle goes a long way.) Every few years someone announces a breakthrough in truffle research, and we are told that soon affordable truffles will be growing in American oak groves, artificially inoculated with European truffle spores! Then nothing more is heard.

If you are willing to spend the money, buy only very firm, very sound truffles; they will smell strange, but in a wonderful way, with no hints of moldy or off aromas.

Also a luxury, but a considerably more affordable one, is the delicious *Boletus edulis* mushroom. This is the same wild mushroom as the French *cèpe* and the Italian *porcino*, and it is found throughout North America. In California and Oregon there are two seasons, one after the first warm rains in the middle to late fall, the other in late spring, when the weather is warming up, but the ground is still moist. *Boletus edulis* looks like a giant meaty version of the cultivated white agaricus mushroom, with a very fat and swollen stem and a reddish or orange-brown cap that may reach six inches across; but instead of spore-bearing gills under the cap, it has a dense, spongy layer of tiny pale yellow or greenish tubes. There are many other edible boletes, but none so good as *B. edulis*.

When very fresh and healthy specimens are available, we feature cèpes in uncomplicated preparations: sliced and baked in parchment;

sliced and grilled, seasoned with lemon juice and fine olive oil; sliced paper thin and served raw in a layered salad with equally thin slices of fennel, Parmesan cheese, and, sometimes, white truffle. Dried *B. edulis* mushrooms are also prized in the kitchen. They infuse a deep, earthy flavor into stocks, consommés, and *brodo* for ravioli, and into sauces such as a creamy béchamel for a lasagne made with a combination of fresh and dried wild mushrooms. They also make an incomparable risotto.

Still more widespread are the chanterelles. They spring up in North American woods throughout the summer and fall, whenever there is sufficient moisture. In California, the season lasts into early winter. The most familiar is the golden chanterelle, *Cantharellus cibarius*, with its golden yellow or pale orange flattened and undulating cap. The caps may be anywhere from one to six inches across; on their gracefully tapering undersides there are blunt veinlike ridges that blend into the cream-colored stems. Sometimes our mushroom hunters offer us white chanterelles, *C. subalbidus*, pale ivory versions of the more common golden chanterelle. We use chanterelles sautéed with garlic, herbs, and cream, and tossed with delicate fresh pasta; and we bake them in gratins in the wood oven. We sauté them, add a handful of persillade, and mix them into corn bread stuffing.

The wild mushrooms called variously black trumpets, horns of plenty, or trumpets of death, *Craterellus fallax* and *C. cornucopioides*, are closely related to chanterelles, but are smaller, have thinner flesh, a dark gray or blackish brown color, and a more distinct trumpet shape. They are found all over North America. Despite their funereal colors and somber aspect, they are delicious; in France they are sometimes called "truffles of the poor."

The morel mushroom is inextricably associated with spring. In the Midwest there are famous springtime morel festivals. The morels we serve are gathered in northern California and the Pacific Northwest, from middle to late spring. Their earthy, nutty flavor goes perfectly with all the spring vegetables: asparagus, peas, new onions, potatoes, green garlic. There are several species; all of them are hollow, with elongated, conical caps irregularly honeycombed on the outside with deep pits and ridges. The black morels (*Morchella conica*, *M. elata*, *M. angusticeps*, etc.) have broad whitish stems and caps that generally have dark ridges and lighter pits; they are often found in great numbers where there has been a forest fire. The common, or yellow, morel, *M. esculenta*, has a more oval-shaped yellow-brown cap, and is found under hardwoods, in old orchards, along roadsides, even in gardens.

Throughout their season, we eat these and other wild mushrooms sautéed and incorporated into gratins and in vegetable stews; in sauces for roast meat; and garnishing croutons accompanying salads and appetizers.

Cèpes and chanterelles can be eaten raw by most people, but you may want to try a little bit first if you are not sure of your own tolerance level: some people find chanterelles unpleasantly bitter uncooked. Morels and most other edible wild mushrooms should always be cooked completely before eating.

At the market look for wild mushrooms that appear fresh and alive and that smell good. Unfortunately, too often the specimens that reach produce markets are entirely too old: either desiccated and shriveled, or darkened, waterlogged, and moldy. Look for healthy ones that feel firm and heavy for their size. As a rule, smaller and less mature mushrooms are better. Cut into the stems of boletes and morels to check for worms, especially during warm weather.

Mushrooms can be stored in the refrigerator for several days, as long as there is good air circulation around them. Put them in a paper bag with a few small holes punched in it. Do not store them in a plastic bag or wrapped in plastic: They will sweat and rot quickly.

To prepare mushrooms for cooking, trim away any darkened or discolored areas with a knife, and pare off the ends of the stems and any dirt that may be clinging tightly. Use as little water as possible to clean them. A soft-bristled brush can usually clean most of the dirt off most mushrooms. If the mushrooms are a little damp, use a clean towel to wipe them clean. Morels, however, may need to be soaked and rinsed if they have lots of sand embedded in their pitted caps. Then drain them and let them dry on towels before cooking. The dark green tubes under the caps of mature boletes are often bitter, and are easily removed with a sharp paring knife. Big boletes are sometimes wormy; cut into the stems and caps to check, and discard or use for stock any that have more than a few tiny holes.

SAUTÉED CHANTERELLES ON TOAST

1 pound chanterelles
2 shallots
½ clove garlic
Parsley
1 tablespoon unsalted butter

Salt and pepper
¼ cup heavy cream or
  crème fraîche
4 slices bread

Gently clean the mushrooms with a brush or a paring knife to remove dirt and small leaves. If the chanterelles are large, slice them; otherwise leave them whole. Peel the shallots and garlic and chop very fine. Chop about 1 tablespoon of parsley.

Heat the butter in a sauté pan, add the cleaned chanterelles, season with salt and pepper, and cook over high heat for 3 minutes. Add the shallots and garlic and cook for another minute. Pour in the cream, reduce the heat, and simmer for 5 minutes, until the mushrooms are coated with a silky cream reduction.

Meanwhile, toast the slices of bread and put them on a platter. When the mushrooms are ready pour them over the toast. Sprinkle with the chopped parsley and serve as an appetizer.

Serves 4.

CHANTERELLES FROM THE WOOD OVEN

Clean the chanterelles with a mushroom brush or a small knife, removing any dirt, debris, or dark spots from them. Quarter or halve large specimens; leave small ones whole. Toss the mushrooms lightly with extra-virgin olive oil, salt and pepper, a few sprigs of thyme or savory, and a splash of dry white wine. Put them in a shallow baking dish and cover with very thin slices of butter. Cover and bake for 20 minutes in a wood-burning oven. Uncover and bake 20 minutes longer, turning twice during the cooking. The mushrooms should be soft, tender, and wonderfully smoky, and the liquid should have nearly evaporated. Serve hot with grilled meats or vegetables, or cool in a winter vegetable salad.

Note: Although the wood smoke does impart a particularly savory quality to chanterelles, this method produces delicious results in standard gas or electric ovens as well.

Chanterelle Pasta

This is a general method that works well with all the fresh wild mushrooms. The dish can also be served as a gratin: After combining the pasta with the mushroom sauce, put it in a gratin dish, top with toasted bread crumbs, and bake in a hot oven, as in the Wild Mushroom Pasta Gratin recipe (page 207).

1 ounce dried porcini
¾ cup heavy cream
1½ cups chicken stock or
    Mushroom and Herb Broth
    (see page 210)
1 pound chanterelles (or horns
    of plenty, hedgehogs, etc.)
3 or 4 sprigs thyme
2 cloves garlic

1 leek
4 tablespoons unsalted butter
Salt and pepper
1 pound fresh pasta
Reggiano Parmesan cheese
¼ cup chopped parsley
Optional: Toasted Bread
    Crumbs (page 319)

Put the dried porcini in a saucepan with the cream and chicken stock or the broth and heat gently for 30 minutes or so to infuse the mixture with mushroom flavor. Remove the porcini from the cream with a slotted spoon or strainer, and strain the cream through cheesecloth or a fine sieve to remove any sand.

Clean and slice the chanterelles. Chop the thyme leaves and peel and chop the garlic. Clean and chop the leek and sauté in 1 tablespoon of the butter until soft and translucent. Remove from the pan and reserve.

Put a pot of water on for the pasta.

Sauté the mushrooms in the rest of the butter, seasoned with salt, pepper, and the chopped thyme. When nearly cooked through, add the garlic and cook 1 minute more.

Pour the strained cream and stock over the mushrooms, add the leeks, and simmer gently while the pasta is cooking. When the noodles are done, add them to the mushrooms. Taste and correct the seasoning. Serve garnished with grated Parmesan, the parsley, and, if you like, a scattering of Toasted Bread Crumbs.

Serves 4 to 6.

Sautéed Fresh Morels

5 ounces morels	*2 tablespoons unsalted butter*
2 large shallots	*Salt and pepper*
1 small clove garlic	*Lemon juice*
1 tablespoon olive oil	*2 tablespoons chopped parsley*

Clean the mushrooms with a brush or paring knife, removing any dirt or debris. If they appear to be sandy, wash briefly in water and drain. Depending on their size, halve or quarter the morels.

Peel and finely chop the shallots and garlic. Heat the olive oil and half the butter in a sauté pan. Add the shallots and garlic and cook over low heat for 2 or 3 minutes, until the shallots look translucent. Add the morels and about ½ cup water, and season lightly with salt and pepper. Cover and simmer about 4 minutes. Uncover, add the remaining butter, raise the heat slightly, and cook about 3 minutes more, until the morels are soft and tender and the liquid has almost completely evaporated.

Turn off the heat, squeeze a few drops of lemon juice over the mushrooms, adjust the seasoning, and toss in the chopped parsley. Serve immediately, on toast as an appetizer or as a side dish.

Serves 4.

Potato, Morel, and Onion Fricassee

1½ pounds Yellow Finn or russet potatoes	½ pound morels
Salt and pepper	2 tablespoons unsalted butter
1 small onion	¼ to ½ cup clarified butter
	¼ cup chopped parsley

Peel the potatoes, cut them into big chunks, and boil in salted water until they are very soft and the edges have started breaking down. Be careful not to overcook them, lest they fall apart completely. Drain and set aside to dry. Slice the onion very thin.

Cut the morels in half lengthwise and wash quickly in plenty of water. Drain and sauté in the butter over a high flame. They will release some water. Turn the flame down to medium, let the mushrooms reabsorb their juices, and continue cooking until they are completely dry.

Fry the potatoes in a large skillet in ⅛ inch of the clarified butter over medium heat. When the potatoes have started to turn golden brown, add the sliced onions. When the potatoes are crispy and the onions start caramelizing, drain off any excess butter, add the morels and the chopped parsley, and season with salt and pepper. Toss together and serve.

Serves 6.

Note: You can vary this dish by replacing the morels with cèpes, or by using green garlic instead of onion. (Green garlic should be added at the end of the cooking, just before the mushrooms.)

Wild Mushrooms Baked in Parchment

This delicate method of cooking wild mushrooms captures their singular flavors and aromas. Put a baking sheet in the oven and preheat it to 450°F. Enclose sliced mushrooms—a single variety or a combination—in a parchment paper package: Fold a length of paper in half, open the fold, and place the mushrooms on the top half of the sheet. Flavor the mushrooms with whatever you like, keeping in mind that they cook very quickly and that a simple treatment is best. Season with salt and pepper and perhaps a little shallot or fresh herbs, and moisten with a little butter or olive oil and a squeeze of lemon. Fold the bottom half of the paper up over the mushrooms. Beginning at one corner, make small overlapping folds around to the other corner; then twist tightly to seal the package closed.

Put the parchment packages on the baking sheet in the oven and bake for 5 minutes or so. The packages will puff up from the steam trapped inside. Serve immediately so that each diner will have the pleasure of opening a package and inhaling the escaping aromas.

WILD MUSHROOM PASTA GRATIN

1 ounce dried porcini	½ pound fresh wild mushrooms
3 tablespoons unsalted butter	(chanterelles, cèpes,
1 tablespoon all-purpose flour	hedgehogs, etc.)
1½ cups reduced chicken stock	1 or 2 cloves garlic, finely chopped
1 cup heavy cream	2 tablespoons chopped parsley
Salt and pepper	1 pound fettuccine
Nutmeg	Reggiano Parmesan cheese

Put the porcini in a bowl and cover with boiling water.

While the porcini soak, make a thin béchamel sauce: Melt 1 table-spoon of the butter in a heavy-bottomed saucepan. Stir in the flour and cook gently for a few minutes. Warm the chicken stock and cream and whisk into the flour and butter. Season lightly with salt and pepper and a scraping of nutmeg. Add 2 to 3 tablespoons of the porcini soaking liquid to the sauce, being careful not to disturb any sand that has settled to the bottom of the bowl. (The strength of the mushroom liquor will vary; add it to taste.) Simmer the sauce for 30 minutes or so.

Clean the fresh wild mushrooms and slice thin. Lift the porcini out of their liquor, chop them, and sauté with the other mushrooms in the rest of the butter. Season with salt and pepper, and when the mushrooms are nearly cooked, add the garlic and the parsley. Add the sauce to the mushrooms and taste. If needed, strain in more mushroom liquor.

Preheat the oven to 425°F.

Cook the pasta and add it to the mushroom sauce; taste and correct the seasoning. Put the pasta in a buttered gratin dish or in individual dishes and top with grated Parmesan. Bake for about 15 minutes, until the top is crusty and golden.

Serves 4 to 6.

WILD MUSHROOM AND GREENS RAVIOLI

1 onion
1 head escarole
   (about ½ pound)
4 cups loosely packed rocket
4 or 5 sprigs thyme
½ cup parsley leaves
6 ounces chanterelles
6 ounces horn of plenty
   mushrooms
4 ounces brown cultivated
   mushrooms

Extra-virgin olive oil
1 recipe Mushroom and Herb
   Broth (page 210)
Salt and pepper
¼ cup dry bread crumbs,
   if needed
Juice of ½ lemon
5 sheets fresh pasta, rolled out
   to 6 by 24 inches (about 1
   pound, or a 2-egg recipe)

Peel and finely dice the onion. Wash and roughly chop the escarole and rocket. Chop the thyme and parsley fine. Set aside half the chopped herbs for the filling and half to garnish the finished ravioli.

Clean the mushrooms: Trim away any discolored and soft spots from the chanterelles, scraping away any dirt and debris with the tip of a small knife. Slice the chanterelles. Pull apart the horns of plenty lengthwise (they should tear into strips naturally), running your finger down the inside to dislodge any dirt. If they feel gritty, rinse them rapidly in a bowl of cold water. Trim the tough stems from the brown mushrooms, brush off any dirt, and slice.

Heat a large sauté pan over medium heat, add enough of the olive oil to make a thin film on the bottom of the pan, and add the sliced chanterelles. Sauté briskly. If the mushrooms give off a lot of juice, pour it off and add to the Herb and Mushroom Broth. Continue cooking until the chanterelles are golden brown. Remove from the pan to a large bowl.

Deglaze the pan with some of the broth, pouring the deglazing liquid back into the broth. (Do not deglaze the pan if there are any burned spots: the deglazing liquid will be bitter.) Use the same pan to sauté the sliced field mushrooms, starting again with the olive oil. When they have browned some, add them to the chanterelles and deglaze the pan again, returning the liquid to the broth.

Finally cook the horns of plenty, but use more gentle heat. Cook them only until their brown-gray color has turned black. Do not try to brown them or make them crisp: they have an unpleasant flavor when overcooked. If they give off a lot of juice, do not add it to the broth: it has an unappetizing gray color. Add half the horns of plenty to the bowl and set aside the other half for the garnish.

Using the same pan, cook the diced onion in more of the olive oil until translucent but not browned. Add the onion to the bowl with the mushrooms. Cook the escarole in the sauté pan in a little of the olive oil over high heat, just long enough to wilt the leaves but not so much that they lose their bright green color. Transfer to a colander. Cook the rocket the same way and add it to the colander. Press down on the greens in the colander to extract as much liquid as possible, and then chop them together very fine.

Chop the cooked mushrooms very fine and put them back in the bowl, adding the chopped greens and half the chopped herbs. Season to taste with salt and pepper. If the mixture seems too juicy, add enough bread crumbs to absorb the excess moisture. Add a few drops of lemon juice to brighten the flavors, and taste again for seasoning.

Stuff the ravioli, following the instructions for Squash Ravioli with Fried Sage (page 280) and using about 1 tablespoon filling for each of the ravioli.

Cook the ravioli in a large pot of simmering salted water. Drop the ravioli gently into the pot and simmer for 3 to 5 minutes. Check for doneness by tearing off a little piece and eating it. While they are cooking, heat a few ladlefuls of the broth in a large sauté pan. Add a generous splash of fruity extra-virgin olive oil and boil vigorously to reduce and thicken just a bit. Taste for seasoning and adjust, adding a little lemon juice if you like.

Scoop the ravioli out of the water when they are done and add to the reduced broth. Let them reheat in the broth and become well coated with the sauce. Serve them on a warm platter, with the sauce poured over, garnished with the reserved horns of plenty and sprinkled with the rest of the chopped parsley and thyme.

Serves 6 (about 30 ravioli).

MUSHROOM AND HERB BROTH

This is a good recipe to use for any leftover wild mushroom stems and trimmings. Just add them to the vegetables along with the dried porcini.

2 onions	*2 or 3 sage leaves*
1 leek	*4 or 5 sprigs thyme*
1 small carrot	*8 sprigs parsley*
2 stalks celery	*1 ounce dried porcini*
1 tablespoon olive oil	*mushrooms*

Peel and chop the onions. Trim, wash, and chop the leek. Peel and roughly chop the carrot. Wash and chop the celery. Heat the olive oil in a medium nonreactive saucepan, add the onion, and cook until it caramelizes and turns a rich brown color.

Add the remaining vegetables, the herbs, and the mushrooms to the saucepan, and cook over medium heat, stirring occasionally, until the vegetables have softened. Add enough water to cover the vegetables by about 2 inches. Bring to a boil over high heat. Reduce the heat and simmer for about 45 minutes. Strain the broth through a fine sieve and discard the vegetables, herbs, and mushrooms.

Makes about 1 quart.

GRILLED CÈPES

This is also a fine way to cook the meaty caps of cultivated portobello mushrooms.

Trim some very fresh cèpes, cutting away any dirt or pine needles embedded at the base, and brush or wipe the caps and stems clean. Cut them into ¼-inch-thick slices. Brush them with the olive oil and season with salt and pepper on both sides. Chop some parsley leaves and shallot, and mix them together.

Grill the cèpes over a low fire for about 4 minutes on each side. They should be golden brown and softened through. Arrange the mushrooms on a warm platter. Squeeze lemon juice over them, sprinkle with the parsley and shallot mixture, drizzle generously with olive oil, and serve. Or omit the parsley and shallot and serve the grilled cèpes on a bed of rocket leaves.

ROASTED WILD MUSHROOM SALAD WITH PARMESAN

This is a good recipe to use for less-than-perfect mushrooms that are very dirty or slightly over-the-hill, because you can wash them in water, if necessary, and simply roast them a little longer. Roasting the mushrooms enhances their flavor.

½ pound wild mushrooms
Salt and pepper
Extra-virgin olive oil
½ cup white wine
2 sprigs thyme
Optional: 2 to 4 tablespoons
  poultry roasting juices

1 small shallot
1 tablespoon balsamic vinegar
1 tablespoon sherry vinegar
¼ pound mixed lettuces
Reggiano Parmesan cheese

Preheat the oven to 375°F.

Clean the mushrooms and cut them into ½-inch wedges or chunks. Put them in a baking dish, season with salt and pepper, pour the olive oil and white wine over them, and add the thyme and the optional juices. Cover and bake for 30 to 40 minutes.

While the mushrooms are baking, peel and dice the shallot very fine and put it in a salad bowl to macerate with the vinegars and a pinch of salt. When the mushrooms are done, uncover them; a good deal of juice will have been rendered. Pour it off into a small saucepan and reduce to a syrupy ¼ cup.

Turn up the oven to 425°F., return the mushrooms to the oven, uncovered, and roast them until they have browned slightly. (Do not over-brown cèpes; they get bitter.) Pour about half of the reduced mushroom juice, well seasoned, over the mushrooms, and reserve the rest to drizzle over the finished salad.

Wash and dry the lettuces. Whisk olive oil to taste into the vinegars and shallots and adjust the seasoning. Toss the lettuces in the vinaigrette and arrange on plates. Dress the mushrooms with the vinaigrette left in the bowl and scatter over the lettuces. Drizzle the rest of the reduced mushroom juices over the salad, and arrange some shavings of the Parmesan on top.

Serves 4.

WILD MUSHROOM AND POTATO GRATIN

*½ pound chanterelles (or a
    combination of chanterelles
    and other wild or cultivated
    mushrooms)*
4 tablespoons unsalted butter

Salt and pepper
*12 medium Yellow Finn or
    Yukon Gold potatoes*
1 pint heavy cream

Preheat the oven to 375°F.

Gently clean the chanterelles with a mushroom brush or a paring knife. Cut the mushrooms into thick slices and sauté them in the butter over medium-high heat until they absorb their liquid and begin to get crisp. Season lightly with salt and pepper.

Peel and dice the potatoes and cook in boiling salted water until they are fully cooked but not mushy. Carefully scoop them out of the water onto a sheet pan to cool.

Butter a 9 by 12-inch baking dish and layer the potatoes alternately with the cooked chanterelles, seasoning the potatoes with salt and pepper. Cover with the cream. Bake for about 20 minutes, or until the cream is bubbling and the top of the gratin is golden brown.

Serves 6 to 8.

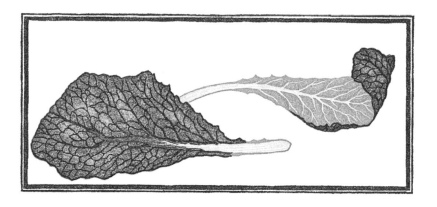

MUSTARD GREENS 🍃

Season: Year-round

The many pungent, peppery mustard plants sold as mustard greens are varieties of yet another member of the cabbage family: *Brassica juncea*. They were all originally developed in Asia, from whence they have spread worldwide. For a long time now, mustard greens have been an important part of the repertory of Southern American cooking.

There is a bewildering variety of mustard greens: broad-, narrow-, jagged-, and curly-leaved; green, red, purple, and variegated in color; bulky and fat-stemmed like chard, and forming bunched heads like cabbages. In China, many are grown to be pickled, and some are grown for their roots. But in our kitchens, we usually use fresh red mustard greens and cook them in the same ways we cook kale, chard, and broccoli raab—often just wilted, alone or combined with other greens, and then wrapped in prosciutto and served as an antipasto; or dressed and served alongside grills, braises, and stews. Or we use little red mustard leaves in salads, sometimes with garden cress, as described below. When very small, the leaves all taste quite mild, and many little mustard leaves find their way into commercial salad mixes with lettuces and other greens, such as rocket. Their strength varies among the varieties, but in general, the larger the green, the stronger the flavor. Cooked mustard greens lend themselves equally well to the Southern seasonings of onion and smoked bacon and to an Asian treatment with sesame oil and soy sauce.

Mustard greens are in our markets all year, although the small, delicate ones are best in the spring. They can be harsh-tasting in the summer if they are allowed to grow too big or they have started to go to seed. Selecting mustard greens in the market is easy: just pick the liveliest, crispest, healthiest-looking leaves. Prepare them the same way you would any other greens: wash and pick over them, stripping them off their stems (if the stems are tough) and chopping them roughly, or not, as you choose.

Mustard greens are undemanding and quick-growing. In frost-free areas like ours, they can be sown outdoors year-round, and they are not particularly susceptible to insect damage. Perhaps pests are discouraged by the peppery flavor.

WILTED MUSTARD GREENS AND PROSCIUTTO

*2 bunches mustard greens (or
   chard, escarole, or young kale)
¼ cup olive oil
6 cloves garlic, finely chopped
Red pepper flakes*

*Red wine vinegar
Salt and pepper
12 thin slices prosciutto
   (about ¼ pound)*

Remove the stems from the mustard greens, wash the leaves, and drain them. Heat the olive oil in a large sauté pan and add the garlic. Let it sizzle for an instant and then add the greens. Cook, covered, for about 5 minutes, until the greens are tender. Let them cool, season with a pinch of red pepper flakes, the vinegar, salt and pepper, and more olive oil, if necessary, to moisten them. Chop the mixture coarsely.

Lay the prosciutto slices out on a flat surface and cut them in half. Place a small ball of the greens on each piece of prosciutto and roll the greens up inside. Or instead of making little rolls, serve the greens on the center of a platter surrounded by the prosciutto. Serve as an hors d'oeuvre or as part of an antipasto plate with a mesclun salad, fennel marinated with lemon, Pickled Spring Onions (page 219), and the Moroccan Carrot Salad (page 76).

Serves 4 to 6.

WILTED RED MUSTARD

Small young leaves of red mustard—their bright green, toothed leaves edged with deep purple—are very good raw as a salad green. Their spicy flavor makes a fine complement to composed salads that include lamb, winter vegetables, or tuna. Tender mustard most frequently appears on the menu as a leafy garnish to an entrée serving of grilled meat or poultry. When the meat is placed directly on a bed of greens, the heat, juices, and added sauce combine to gently wilt the leaves and release their flavor without diminishing the hot freshness that is their prime quality.

Leaves that are too large to be used in just this way can be very briefly wilted in olive oil with a little shallot or garlic, with or without a splash of vinegar. One wonderful combination is to serve wilted greens with roast pork loin, fried apples, and corn bread.

ONIONS 🍃

Season: Spring through fall

Imagine cooking without onions. Most dishes from the savory side of the Chez Panisse kitchen contain at least a suggestion of onions. Onions are basic to all stocks and broths, most soups, and the essential mire-poix—the diced aromatic trio of onion, carrot, and celery. Both shallots and onions are representatives of the same species of the lily family, *Allium cepa*, but because shallots are generally used differently than are onions, they are treated separately in this book.

Onion season at the restaurant runs year-round. In late winter, as we use up the last of the dry storage onions, the earliest spring onions appear. Some, not even bulbing yet, look like big, fat scallions. Others, such as Crystal Wax and Purplette, are miniature versions of beautiful white or red bulbing onions. These onions add a freshness and sparkle missing from the more mature storage onions. They are a treat brushed lightly with olive oil and grilled until tender and brown. If their season lasts, they can be combined with the first of the English peas.

Later in the spring come the large and sweet white, yellow, and purple bulbing onions, just pulled from the earth, with their green tops still attached. This is also the time for the elongated purple torpedo onions. These onions are delicious sliced and eaten raw in salads and sandwiches. But they are sometimes so sweet that they need to be tempered with the addition of leeks or shallots.

As spring turns to summer, these sweet types appear cloaked in their dry, papery skins, suitable for storage. Walla Walla, in Washington, and Vidalia, in Georgia, have become well known for their sweet onions maturing in early summer. These should be used immediately after purchase, since they do not store well. This is the time of year to make onion tarts and pizzas, and crisp sweet deep-fried onion rings.

Midsummer brings the greatest abundance and variety of onions. At this time farmers bring to market scallions, many kinds of fresh and dry bulbing onions, and both fresh and dry pearl onions. This is also a time of peak production in the big onion growing areas of Texas, New York, and California.

Since onions require cool, damp weather at the beginning of their growing season, the end of summer often means the end of the onion harvest. Throughout fall and early winter we use the firmer, dry-skinned onions coming out of storage.

The green tops of fresh onions tell a lot about their quality. When considering scallions and other fresh onions at the market, look for tops that are dark green and stiff. Avoid onions with tops that droop or that have started to decay. Any roots at the base of the onions should be fresh and white, not withered. The best dry onions will have thin necks and papery skins that crackle. Don't buy any that smell moldy or that feel soft, especially at the neck.

Fresh onions should be stored loosely wrapped in plastic in the refrigerator and used quickly. However, moisture is the enemy of dry onions. These should be stored in a cool, dry area with good air circulation. They should be stored in their own space, because they can pick up moisture from other vegetables, such as potatoes, and begin to deteriorate. Super sweet onions like Vidalias and Walla Wallas should also be stored in a cool, dry place, but in any event should not be kept for more than a week or so before use.

Fresh onions are very easy to prepare for cooking. Simply cut off the roots and the green tops and peel off one or two thin outer layers of the bulb. You can do this with your fingers or with the help of a paring knife. To peel large, dry onions, first cut off the root and stem ends. If you are not making whole round slices, peeling is easier if you cut the onion in half longitudinally. Tiny dry onions should be parboiled for a minute first, and then eased out of their skins with your fingers or a small knife.

All the members of the onion family begin to oxidize when cut. The juices trapped between their cell walls start mixing together and forming new compounds in contact with the air, among them the irritants that make you cry. It is therefore preferable to slice or dice onions with a very sharp knife, rather than chopping them roughly. The longer that sliced or chopped raw onions sit around, the more they oxidize and develop off flavors, so plan on cooking them right away. (It is for this reason that when we make vinaigrettes, we dice shallots and immediately cover them with vinegar; and when we have to chop garlic in advance, it tastes much better if it is covered with oil until it gets used.) Onions for salads can be sliced and kept submerged in ice water for several hours before serving. This is also a way to tame a too-hot onion that you want to eat raw.

Onions are easy to grow in loamy soil that has had lots of organic matter added before planting. Bulbing onions are very sensitive to day length, so be sure to ask for advice from experienced gardeners when choosing varieties that are adapted to your area and to the time of year they will be planted.

SPRING ONION SANDWICHES

Onion sandwiches were an old favorite of James Beard's. These are best made in May when onions are very sweet. Trim the crusts off thin slices of good white bread. Spread two slices of bread with mayonnaise, on one side. Slice fresh onion very thinly and make a layer of onion slices on one slice of bread. Top that with the other slice of bread. Dip the four side edges of the sandwich into thin mayonnaise and then into chopped parsley.

PICKLED SPRING ONIONS

Trim the stems and roots off small, round spring onions. Peel away their outer skins, cut them in half, and simmer them, covered, in a mixture of 5 parts water to 1 part white wine vinegar, with some coriander seed, some peppercorns and allspice berries, 2 or 3 cloves, and a bouquet of thyme. When the onions can be pierced through easily with a small knife, turn off the heat, set the pot aside, and allow the onions to cool in their own liquid. Serve or cover and refrigerate.

GRILLED SPRING ONIONS

Trim off the root end of white or red spring onions and trim off an inch or two of the green leafy ends, making the onions all the same length and removing any less than perfect leaves. Peel away the outermost layer from the onions if it seems tough or damaged in any way. If the onions are small enough—the bulbs the size of your thumb, the stems not much thicker than pencils—simply drizzle them with a little olive oil and season with salt and pepper before grilling; if they are larger, parboil them in salted water until they are cooked through, drain on towels, and then oil and season them.

Grill the onions side by side over a moderate fire, turning them every 3 or 4 minutes so that they brown evenly as they cook. Small spring onions grilled raw will take 12 to 14 minutes; parboiled larger ones take only 5 or 6 minutes. When the onions are done, arrange them on a warm platter, drizzle a little extra-virgin olive oil over them, and sprinkle with a little lemon juice or, if you have it, a few drops of very good old balsamic vinegar.

Note: Mature onions are also tasty grilled. Cut thick slices; keeping them intact, brush with olive oil, season with salt and pepper, and grill 5 to 10 minutes on each side.

BAKED SPICY ONION SLICES

Onions cooked this way can be served warm or cold, as a side dish, or by themselves. Sweet juicy yellow onions are best for this recipe. Peel them, slice them ¼ inch thick, season well with salt, and place them on a well-oiled baking sheet. Brush the exposed sides of the onions with olive oil and bake them in a preheated 375°F. oven for about 30 minutes, or until the onions are soft, and browned on their undersides. When the onions are cooked, place them carefully in a shallow dish, keeping the slices intact. Pour over them a vinaigrette made with 1 part sherry vinegar, 4 parts extra-virgin olive oil, salt, and a pinch of ground cayenne or hot pepper flakes. Let the onions marinate in the vinaigrette for about 20 minutes. Serve them cool, or warm them gently in the oven.

Sweet red onions are also good baked this way. Peel, slice, season, and brush red onion slices with oil as above, then sprinkle some good balsamic vinegar over them. As they bake, the vinegar helps them caramelize. Either serve them warm right off the tray or dress them in a shallow dish with olive oil and a little more balsamic vinegar and marinate them a while first.

ONION CONFIT

Onion confit is delicious in a pasta with wilted greens (of all kinds) and chicken stock. It can be served as an hors d'oeuvre on a crouton, form part of a savory tart with other vegetables (potatoes, grilled chicories and anchovy, cabbage), or serve as a condiment with grilled or roasted fish and fowl.

4 large onions	*2 cups red wine*
4 tablespoons unsalted butter	*¼ cup red wine vinegar*
Salt and pepper	*¼ cup sherry vinegar*
1 tablespoon sugar	*Optional: Cassis*
3 or 4 sprigs fresh thyme	

Peel and slice the onions very thin. Brown the butter in a large heavy-bottomed pot and add the onions. Season with salt and pepper. Cover and cook for 5 minutes or so, until the onions begin to soften. Stir in the sugar and cook, covered, a few more minutes, to allow the sugar to caramelize slightly. Add the thyme, the red wine, the vinegars, and cassis, if you wish. Simmer, uncovered, for 1 to 1½ hours, until the liquid is cooked down to a syrup.

Makes about 2 cups.

DEEP-FRIED ONION RINGS

Peel and slice sweet onions ⅛ to ¼ inch thick. Separate the rings and soak them in a mixture of half buttermilk and half milk for at least 1 hour. In a deep-fryer or a deep pot, heat peanut oil to 365°F. Drain the onions and toss them in flour, shake them in a sieve to remove excess flour, and fry in small batches until golden brown. Drain, salt, and serve.

Onion Panade

6 medium yellow onions	12 large, thin slices country-style
2 cloves garlic	bread
¼ cup olive oil	A few sprigs thyme or a few
4 tablespoons unsalted butter	sage leaves
½ cup red wine	½ cup grated Reggiano
1½ quarts rich chicken or	Parmesan cheese
beef stock	Salt and pepper
	¼ cup grated Gruyère cheese

Peel the onions, cut them in half, and slice very thin. Peel the garlic and slice it thin. Put the olive oil and butter in a heavy-bottomed pan over medium heat, add the onions and garlic, and cook until they are golden brown, about 35 minutes. Scrape the bottom of the pan occasionally with a wooden spoon to incorporate browned bits that may be sticking to the bottom. Pour in the red wine to deglaze the pan while the onions are still in it, stirring to remove all the browned onion from the bottom of the pan.

Divide the onion mixture in half. Put one half in a pot with the chicken or beef stock, bring to a simmer, and put on the back of the stove, off the heat. Leave the other half of the onion mixture in the pan.

Preheat the oven to 375°F.

Toast the bread and brush lightly with olive oil. Chop about 1 tablespoon of thyme leaves or sage leaves. In a 3-inch-deep gratin dish, make a single layer of bread slices, breaking them up into pieces about 2 inches square as you go. Spread half of the caramelized onion mixture left in the pan over the toast, sprinkle with some of the herb leaves and some of the grated Parmesan, and lightly season with salt and pepper. Follow with another layer of broken toast; another layer of onions, using those remaining in the pan; more of the Parmesan; and salt and pepper. Make a final layer of broken toast on the top. Ladle in the chicken and onion stock until the liquid rises just to the top layer of toast. Sprinkle the top of the panade with a mixture of the Gruyère and the remaining Parmesan, and sprinkle with the rest of the herbs.

Cover the baking dish tightly with foil and bake for 45 minutes in the middle of the oven. Uncover the panade and bake for another 30 minutes, until the top is well browned and crisp. Serve scoops of the panade in soup bowls moistened with ladlefuls of the broth.

Serves 8.

PICKLED RED ONIONS

2 large red onions
½ cup red wine vinegar
3 tablespoons sugar
½ cup water

Peel the onions and cut them in half lengthwise. Slice them very thin—
as close to paper-thin as possible. Put them in a heat-proof container.
Put the vinegar, sugar, and water in a small saucepan and bring to a boil.
Add the boiling hot brine to the onions and leave to cool at room temperature. Drain just before serving.

PISSALADIÈRE

Onions stewed slowly for an hour or more with herbs in olive oil are the
base for the Provençal tart called *pissaladière*. The onions provide a very
sweet contrast to the salty olives and anchovies that garnish the tart.

3 large yellow onions   *Salt*
3 cloves garlic   *5 or 6 salt-packed anchovies*
3 to 4 tablespoons olive oil   *Prebaked 9-inch tart shell*
1 bay leaf   *1 small handful niçoise olives*
6 sprigs thyme

Peel the onions and garlic and slice them very thin.

Pour in enough olive oil to coat the bottom of a heavy pan; add the
onions, garlic, and herbs. Salt, cover, and stew over medium heat for
1 hour or more, stirring frequently, until the onions are completely soft
and reduced to about one third of their original volume. They should
turn a pale golden color, but not brown. Meanwhile, rinse and fillet the
anchovies. Strain the onion mixture, reserving the liquid.

Preheat the oven to 350°F.

Spread the onion mixture over the prebaked tart shell and garnish
with the anchovy fillets and the niçoise olives. Put the tart in the oven
for 10 minutes to allow the anchovy and olives to bake into the onions.
Just before serving drizzle the tart with the reserved onion liquid.

Serves 6.

PIZZA WITH ROASTED ONIONS, EGG, ANCHOVY, AND WALNUTS

2 medium yellow onions
Extra-virgin olive oil
Salt and pepper
Champagne vinegar or
*   white wine vinegar*
2 sprigs thyme

2 large eggs
½ cup shelled walnuts
5 salt-packed anchovies
Pizza dough for 1 pizza
½ cup grated mozzarella cheese

Preheat the oven to 350°F.

Peel the onions, cut them into medium dice, and toss with enough of the olive oil to coat them lightly. Season with a pinch of salt and a few drops of vinegar. Add the leaves of the thyme. Put the onions in a small ovenproof sauté pan, put it in the oven, and roast, stirring occasionally, for about 30 minutes, until the onions are cooked and golden. Remove the onions, put in a pizza stone, and turn up the oven to 450° to 500°F.

Boil the eggs until the yolks are just set (9 or 10 minutes, if the eggs are put into already boiling water). Cool and peel them, and cut into slices.

Spread the walnuts in a sheet pan and toast in the oven for a few minutes, checking and stirring them once or twice.

Rinse and fillet the anchovies.

Roll out the pizza dough 12 to 14 inches in diameter (or shape it by hand) and place it on a floured peel or on the back of a lightly floured sheet pan. Using a pastry brush or your fingers, brush olive oil on the dough, leaving a ½-inch border. Sprinkle the grated cheese on top of the oiled dough and spread the roasted onions over the cheese. Slide the pizza into the oven onto the stone and cook until the crust is crisp and golden brown, 4 to 10 minutes. Garnish the pizza with the egg slices, anchovy fillets, and walnuts; grind a little pepper over, slice, and serve.

Makes one 12-inch pizza.

PARSLEY
See Herbs (page 170)

PARSNIPS ❧

Season: Late fall and winter

The thick, long (up to fifteen inches), ivory-colored root of the parsnip (*Pastinaca sativa*) resembles that of its close relative, the carrot. But don't try to eat a parsnip the way you would a raw carrot: parsnips are practically inedible raw. Only after thorough cooking do they develop a rich, nutty flavor. The choicest variety of parsnip is an heirloom variety —fortunately widely available—called Hollow Crown. Its name refers to the characteristic depression at the top of the root.

Parsnips prove their worth at Chez Panisse during the colder months of the year by adding variety and sweetness to mixtures of roasted vegetables, and by enriching the flavor of root vegetable purées. A simple purée of parsnips and potatoes, for example, is the perfect foil for the rich flavors of duck, pigeon, or game. Parsnips can also deepen and complicate the flavors of stocks; and they can be grilled and deep-fried with great success.

Winter is, in fact, the peak season for parsnips. They require a three- or four-month growing season, and they develop their sweetest and richest flavors only after a frost, prolonged cold weather, or cold storage after harvest. The first parsnips come to market from the northern growing areas of the United States in mid-fall. Because they keep well in the ground or in a root cellar, good-quality parsnips can be found until early spring.

When shopping for parsnips, the most important clues to quality are firmness and a smooth skin. The most efficient yield will come from medium parsnips: very large ones may have cores so woody they have to be cut out and discarded, while small, thin roots can be immature—and after they are peeled, there may be hardly anything left. Also avoid any roots that appear to be damaged or discolored.

ROASTED WINTER VEGETABLES

You will need parsnips, turnips, rutabagas, celery root, fennel bulb—in any combination—and about the same quantity of butternut squash. Trimmed and peeled, the vegetables should be cut into ½-inch cubes—except for baby turnips, which can be left unpeeled and cut in halves or quarters, and fennel, which should be trimmed and sliced into thin wedges.

Toss the vegetables in enough clarified butter to coat them lightly, season with salt and pepper, and spread them out on large baking sheets with 1-inch sides. Roast for 30 to 40 minutes in a preheated 400°F. oven until they are thoroughly cooked and beginning to caramelize nicely, stirring them occasionally with a spatula to make sure they don't stick. (Beware of overroasting: a little browning makes them sweeter, but if you let them get too dark, they will taste bitter.) Serve directly from the oven or set aside and reheat later. Before serving, check the seasoning and sprinkle with your choice of herbs (sage, thyme, winter savory), chopped fine.

PARSNIP CHIPS

Parsnips can be deep-fried like *pommes frites*. Peel and slice the parsnips about ⅛ inch thick or a little less. Fry as you would potatoes, in a deep pot of peanut oil heated to 365°F., until golden brown. Drain on paper towels, salt, and serve immediately.

Another method is to "oven-fry" them. Toss the slices lightly in olive oil or clarified butter, season, and spread them out on a baking sheet. Roast in a preheated 475°F. oven for about 5 minutes, then turn them with a spatula, and cook for another 5 minutes or so, until nicely browned but not too dark.

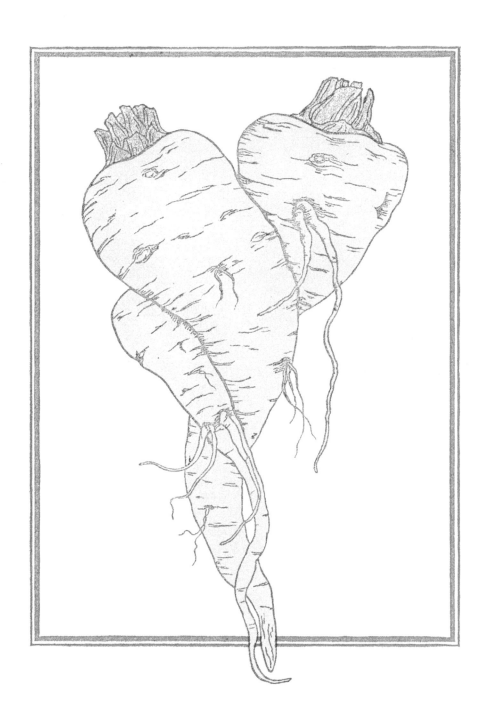

Grilled Parsnips

Trim and peel some crisp, fresh parsnips and cut them lengthwise into about ½-inch-thick slices. Steam or parboil the slices until just tender. Brush them with olive oil, season with salt and pepper, and grill over a medium-hot charcoal fire until lightly browned on both sides. Serve with aïoli or herb sauce and other winter vegetables (fennel, squashes, rutabagas) grilled the same way, or as an accompaniment to roast or grilled meat or poultry.

Parsnip and Potato Purée

Peel and dice about equal quantities of parsnips and potatoes. To control their cooking times, cook each vegetable separately, in boiling salted water. Purée them together and season with salt and pepper. Finish with butter and thin to the desired consistency with warm milk.

PEAS

Season: Spring and early summer

The arrival of freshly picked green peas is one of the events that define high spring at Chez Panisse. The best peas—green, tender, sweet, and plump—can make us forget all the damp, dreary days of winter. Besides the many varieties of the familiar green shelling pea—often called the English pea, for no very good reason—which must be shucked from its tougher pod, and those shelling varieties grown for drying and for animal feed, there are several varieties of peas with edible pods; these are the sugar peas. Among them are the Chinese peas, called snow peas, with their flat light green pods and tiny, immature seeds showing through the skin, and sugar snap peas, a very recent hybrid that looks like a slightly miniaturized version of English peas, with their dark green, full-podded look. The crisp, fleshy pods of sugar snap peas are much sweeter than those of other varieties.

Tiny peas fresh-shucked and sweet are so tender that they really don't need any cooking at all, and they can be thrown raw into a salad. The tender tips or shoots of the growing pea vines can be eaten as well—raw in a salad with other tender young greens or briefly steamed or stir-fried, which enhances their sweet pea flavor. At the restaurant we like to serve them with the first shucked English peas of the season and with tiny fava beans.

The season for green peas is short, confined to the cool, moist conditions of spring and very early summer. The edible pod varieties tolerate more heat and can be found in the market until the hottest days of summer. (In the fog belt of the West Coast, however, fresh peas are available throughout the summer.)

Green peas are unforgiving if they are not rushed from the field to the market. They start losing their natural sugars after harvest, but this can be slowed down if they are cooled immediately. The freshest peas at the market will look shiny and firm, and their pods will squeak when rubbed together. Don't buy peas with pale green or yellow pods, or that look dry or wilted. The best peas will be tiny to medium, tender and sweet, and will fill up their pods well, without looking swollen or crowded. Avoid the largest and heaviest pods; the peas will be tough and starchy. Lightweight pods generally indicate immature, flavorless peas. Pea plants are very sensitive to changes in the weather and will begin producing tough, starchy peas after only a few days of hot, dry weather.

If possible, peas should be kept cool on the way home, and refrigerated immediately. To prepare edible-pod peas, snap off each end, pulling down the side of the pod to remove the strings. They can be left whole or sliced just before cooking. Over-age sugar snap peas with pods too stringy to eat can be shucked and used like English peas.

Pea shoots need only be rinsed and drained, and can be sautéed with a little water still clinging to them. First pick out and discard any shoots that have bruised leaves or large stems. Once cleaned, pea-vine shoots can be refrigerated in a plastic bag for up to a day.

Peas are one of the best crops for the home gardener, since so few commercially available green peas are picked small enough or eaten soon enough after harvest. The vines are attractive for much of the spring, and there are dwarf varieties that don't need trellising. But don't try to grow them if spring weather is inconsistent.

Stir-fried Pea-Vine Shoots

Pea-vine shoots are usually found in the spring at Asian markets. They are tender and sweet and need no elaborate preparation to be delicious. Wash the pea shoots and cook, still wet, in a frying pan with a tablespoon of hot duck fat or oil. Season with salt and keep stirring and tossing over high heat until just tender. It shouldn't take more than a minute. Just before removing from the heat, add a splash of water. The shoots should be bright green and shiny. For a stronger flavor, cook with a peeled, smashed garlic clove, then remove it before serving.

Pea and Pea Green Soup

1 onion
1 carrot
2 tablespoons olive oil
4 cups chicken stock
1 sprig thyme

4 pounds fresh, young peas
Optional: ¼ cup hazelnuts
1 small handful fresh, young
pea-vine shoots

Peel the onion and slice it thin. Peel and dice about a tablespoon of carrot. Stew the onion and carrot in the olive oil over low heat, covered, until soft and translucent. Add the chicken stock and thyme, bring to a boil, and simmer, uncovered, for 15 minutes. Shell the peas while the soup is simmering.

Prepare a large bowl half filled with ice, and a smaller bowl that fits inside it, preferably stainless steel, resting on the ice. Add the peas to the soup, simmer for 5 minutes more, and remove from the heat. Immediately purée the soup in a blender and pour it through a medium strainer into the bowl in the ice bath. Stir the soup slowly until it has cooled to room temperature, then remove from the ice. (Quick cooling keeps the soup from losing its bright green color.)

Heat the oven to 350°F. Toast the hazelnuts for about 10 minutes in the oven and chop finely.

Wilt the pea-vine shoots for several minutes in boiling salted water, drain, and chop coarsely. At serving time, reheat the soup to a simmer, but do not boil. Stir in the chopped pea vine shoots and serve, garnishing each bowl with about a teaspoonful of the chopped hazelnuts.

Serves 6.

Snap Pea, Asparagus, and Turnip Ragout

2 cups snap peas	*1 tablespoon unsalted butter*
3 spring onions	*Salt and pepper*
20 asparagus spears	*1½ teaspoons chopped garlic*
10 baby turnips	*1 cup Vegetable Stock (page 321)*
2 carrots	*or water*
2 tablespoons olive oil	*½ lemon*

Remove the strings from the snap peas. Trim and peel the vegetables. Slice the vegetables so that they are all about the same size—about ¼ inch thick. The asparagus, snap peas, and carrots can be sliced on the diagonal. Parboil the carrots for 1 minute in salted water.

Heat a large sauté pan and add the olive oil and ½ tablespoon of the butter. When the oil is so hot that it shimmers, start adding the vegetables, tossing regularly: the turnips first, then the snap peas, onions, and asparagus, and finally the carrots, cooking each vegetable briefly before adding the next. Add salt and pepper. Taste for doneness and seasoning: the vegetables should be just tender to the tooth. Add the garlic. Continue tossing, and when the scent of garlic hits your nose, remove the vegetables from the pan.

Deglaze the pan with the vegetable stock (or water) and add the remaining butter and a squeeze of lemon juice. Let the sauce reduce by one third and pour it over the vegetables. This ragout is especially good served with Farro (page 321) and drizzled with Parsley and Toasted Almond Salsa (page 175). Or make it spicy by adding ginger and cilantro, and serve with Saffron Rice (page 319).

Serves 4.

Sautéed Sugar Snap Peas

Top and tail the sugar snap peas, pulling off the threadlike strings. Slice on the diagonal into ½-inch-thick pieces. Put into a sauté pan with ¼ inch of water, butter, and a sprinkling of salt. Bring to a boil and reduce the heat to medium. Cook until done, about 3 minutes. The water and butter should be emulsified and coat the snap peas, which should be bright green and just tender. Adjust the seasoning and serve. You can also cook fresh pea shoots with the snap peas.

PEAS WITH SPRING ONIONS, LETTUCE, AND HERBS

Slice thin some delicate spring onions, or leave whole if they are very small. Gently stew the onions and separated tender leaves of lettuce in butter and a little water with a sprig of thyme, until the onions begin to soften. Add shelled sweet peas and cook until just tender. Season and finish with a little butter and some finely chopped chervil and chives.

PEA AND FAVA BEAN RAGOUT

Shell peas, and shell and skin young fava beans in the usual manner (page 140). Gently stew the fava beans in extra-virgin olive oil and add some finely chopped garlic and a chiffonade of basil or mint. Add the peas and cook until the peas are just done.

Serve as a vegetable dish or as a pasta sauce for freshly cooked thin noodles, with some chicken stock or water to make it more saucy. Pesto sauce is also delicious with pasta, peas, and fava beans. (The additions and variations go on and on: artichoke hearts, sugar snap peas, morels, asparagus tips, tender green beans, spring onions, green garlic, prosciutto, new potatoes.)

PEPPERS &

Season: Midsummer through fall

The peppers are warm season vegetables, natives of Central and South America. Most of them belong to one species, *Capsicum annum*, although there are some rare peppers from other species. Peppers can be divided into two main groups, the sweet peppers and the chili peppers. In general sweet peppers are large, with thick, mild-flavored flesh. They may be roughly barrel-shaped, like the bell peppers, or slender and tapering. Chilies, or hot peppers, are usually smaller than sweet peppers, conical in shape and not as meaty, but with much more fire in their taste. Peppers of both types are at their best from midsummer through the fall.

Both types come in many colors. Before they reach full maturity, they can be green, white, brown, or purple. As they mature, green peppers may turn red, yellow, or orange, according to the variety. White peppers shade into ivory, and brown and purple peppers become dark red. Since one plant may have many fruit at different stages of maturity, the color combinations can be striking.

Besides the well-known bell pepper, sweet peppers come in many shapes and sizes. There are the small, round, red cherry peppers. Hungarian Wax and Lipstick peppers are about four inches long, slender and tapering. Corno di Toro peppers do indeed resemble bulls' horns. The very thick-fleshed pimentos are often described as heart-shaped, because of their blunt tops and tapering, pointy ends.

Many sweet bell peppers are sold at the green stage, well before they are ripe. This is a mistake, because green bell peppers have not developed their full, rich flavor, and may in fact be rather bitter. All peppers lose their green color when they are fully ripe. People who say they don't like peppers, or find them hard to digest, are probably talking about green peppers, and may have never tasted a fully ripe pepper of any kind.

But once they have started to color, slightly immature sweet peppers can be delicious. At this stage they can be used raw, since the skins are usually tender, and the flesh rather thin and crisp. At the restaurant we sometimes use peppers at this stage, sliced thin, on pizza or in pastas. As the peppers mature, however, the flesh and skin thicken, and the peppers are best roasted or grilled, and peeled. Some sweet peppers, especially pimentos, should always be peeled.

There are many, many different hot chilies, but most often when we need a spicy pepper we choose jalapeños or serranos. The larger, milder jalapeños measure three inches long and an inch across, while the hotter serranos are generally half that size. Whether in their green or their red state, both of these chilies have a clean, hot flavor that is especially good with sweet vegetables like corn or carrots.

Somewhat less pungent, but richer in flavor, is the poblano chili. These medium, heart-shaped peppers turn from a shiny, almost black green to a dark brick-red when ripe. Green poblanos are becoming widely available. The ripe ones are much harder to find, but worth the effort. We like to mix a few slices of poblano with other sweet peppers to add heat and flavor.

Frequently a grower who specializes in peppers can be found at local farmer's markets. Some bring to market an extraordinary array of chilis of all colors, covering the full range of heat, from mild to "branding iron" hot. Sampling these peppers, both fresh and dried, and talking to their growers is a good way of learning about unfamiliar varieties and their uses.

Whether selecting sweet or hot peppers at the market, the criteria are the same: look for peppers that have a smooth, shiny skin, with no watery spots or wrinkles. Choose peppers that are firm and heavy for their size. And always choose ripe, colored peppers over green ones.

Ripe, mature peppers are best when they are roasted and peeled. The basic aim of any roasting technique is to burn and blister the skin so it can be easily removed. However, this must be done without softening the flesh too much. Whether you use a charcoal fire, the broiler, or an open gas flame, place the peppers as close to the heat as possible, and turn them frequently so that their skins blacken evenly. As the peppers are done, place them in a covered container so that they steam, which

236

further loosens any clinging skin. The skin should then slip off easily when the peppers are cool enough to handle.

Be especially careful when working with chilies. Do not touch your eyes or other sensitive areas while preparing them. The oil from the skins, membranes, and seeds is extremely irritating, and may cause burning and blistering. The interior membranes and seeds are especially spicy, and can be removed before adding chilies to a dish.

Because of the beauty of the plants and their fruit, chilies and sweet peppers are useful as landscape plants as well as in the vegetable garden. Most pepper plants grow no more than two and a half feet tall and are otherwise well behaved. Their dark green leaves make a brilliant contrast with the colorful fruit.

Marinated Roasted Peppers

Roast whole peppers over a very hot wood or charcoal fire (flaming is best), turning frequently to allow the skins to completely blacken and blister. When they are charred, remove them from the grill and let them steam in a container with a tight-fitting lid or on a plate put inside a plastic bag; steaming loosens the skins and makes the peppers easier to peel.

When the peppers are cool enough to handle, peel off their skins. Cut off the stem end and open the peppers up. Remove the core and seeds, flatten out the pepper, and scrape off any remaining flecks of skin with the back of a paring knife. Cut the peppers in strips the size you want, season with salt and pepper, and marinate in a little olive oil with a few garlic cloves and basil leaves. These make delicious appetizers when served on a freshly grilled garlic crouton, with or without anchovy fillets.

Note: Alternatively, you can roast the peppers, lightly oiled, in a hot oven or under a broiler until the skins are browned and blistered; or put the peppers directly over a gas flame on the stove top to blacken the skins.

Roasted Pepper and Tomato Salad
with Brandade Croutons

2 to 3 pounds tomatoes
4 ripe bell peppers
¼ to ½ cup extra-virgin olive oil
Salt and pepper
1 bunch rocket (about ¼ pound)

6 slices country-style bread,
  toasted
1 cup Potato and Salt Cod Purée
  (Brandade)(page 249)

Choose the ripest tomatoes, of as many different colors and sizes as are available, and sweet bell peppers of various colors.

Roast the whole peppers in a preheated 350°F. oven for about 40 minutes, until the flesh is soft. Remove from the oven and put the peppers in a covered container to steam briefly (this makes them easier to peel). When the peppers are cool, peel and seed them and cut them into wide strips.

Cut any cherry tomatoes in half and the large tomatoes in wedges. Mix with the peppers and about ¼ cup of the olive oil. Season with salt and pepper. In another bowl, lightly dress a large handful or two of rocket leaves with the olive oil. Arrange the rocket on a platter, mound the tomato and pepper salad in the center, and garnish with croutons spread with the brandade.

Serves 6.

Pepper and Onion Salad

Seed and slice thin some peppers of different colors and varieties. Slice a small to medium sweet red onion very thin and toss together with the pepper slices, some pitted niçoise olives, and a spoonful of capers rinsed of brine.

Make a vinaigrette with red wine vinegar and good olive oil, and season with chopped garlic and jalapeño pepper and red pepper flakes. Taste and season with salt and pepper. Cut basil leaves into a chiffonade and sprinkle over the salad. This salad should be spicy and robust; taste and adjust the seasoning if necessary.

STUFFED ROASTED RED PEPPERS

4 large sweet red bell peppers
1 bunch scallions
    (about 12 scallions)
Olive oil
12 ounces soft sheep's milk
    cheese
½ cup chopped basil leaves

¼ cup chopped Italian parsley
    leaves
⅓ cup pine nuts, lightly toasted
½ cup Toasted Bread Crumbs
    (page 319)
1 teaspoon chopped garlic
Zest of 2 lemons
Salt and pepper

Roast the peppers over a medium-hot charcoal fire until they have begun to soften and their skins are lightly charred and blistered. At the same time, grill the scallions, brushed with olive oil, until tender, and set them aside for the stuffing. When the peppers are roasted, put them in a covered container to steam briefly.

When the peppers are cool enough to handle, peel them, leaving them whole; carefully cut off the tops, as if you were beginning to carve a pumpkin. Reach in and remove the seeds inside and drain off any excess water.

To make the stuffing, mix together the sheep's milk cheese (at room temperature), ¼ cup of the basil, the parsley, 3 tablespoons of the olive oil, the grilled scallions, the pine nuts, and the bread crumbs. Add half the garlic and half the lemon zest (grated or finely chopped), and let the mixture sit for a minute to let the flavors settle in. The seasoning can be fine-tuned with salt and pepper, and more of the garlic and lemon zest, if desired. Remember that the peppers have a strong flavor, so the stuffing should be very assertive by itself.

Preheat the oven to 250°F.

Fill each pepper with one quarter of the stuffing, place them all on a baking sheet, and put them in the oven for 5 to 10 minutes, just long enough to warm them through. To serve, drizzle a little olive oil over them and garnish with the rest of the chopped basil.

Serves 4.

PIZZA WITH RED AND YELLOW PEPPERS

3 bell peppers—1 red, 1 orange,
   1 yellow
½ small red onion
¼ cup parsley leaves
¼ cup basil leaves
3 tablespoons olive oil

1 teaspoon red wine vinegar
Salt and pepper
2 ounces mozzarella cheese
1 clove garlic
Pizza dough for 1 pizza

Preheat the oven—with a pizza stone in it—to 450° to 500°F.

Slice thin the peppers and onion, and roughly chop the parsley and basil. Toss in a bowl with 2 tablespoons of the olive oil and the vinegar, and season to taste with salt and pepper.

Coarsely grate the cheese. Chop the garlic fine and mix it with the re-maining tablespoon of olive oil.

Roll out a disk of pizza dough 12 to 14 inches in diameter and place it on the back of a lightly floured sheet pan or a pizza peel. Using a pastry brush or your fingers, brush the garlic and oil mixture on the dough, leaving a ½-inch border. Sprinkle the grated cheese on top of the oiled dough. Spread the pepper mixture on top of the cheese. Slide the pizza directly onto the pizza brick and bake for 4 to 6 minutes, or until the dough is crispy and thoroughly cooked. Slice and serve immediately.

Makes one 12-inch pizza.

Note: For another version of pepper pizza, season the pepper mixture with chopped marjoram or oregano, and thyme, and sprinkle the crust with a large pinch of hot pepper flakes. Garnish with chopped parsley before serving.

Another variation is to season a pepper pizza with chopped cilantro and a julienned jalapeño pepper (seeded or not, as your taste dictates), and to garnish it with cilantro leaves and a squeeze of lemon juice.

For the most volcanic pepper pizza of all, use only jalapeños: slice thin about 10 jalapeños into wagon-wheel rounds; macerate them in rice wine vinegar, salt, chopped cilantro, and a little olive oil; bake on a pizza crust, as above; and serve, garnished with cilantro leaves.

Harissa

Harissa is a traditional Moroccan pepper sauce that we serve at Chez Panisse with grilled vegetables, couscous dishes, and tagines.

4 fresh serrano chilies
Olive oil
1 teaspoon cumin seed
2 cloves garlic
1 tablespoon paprika

½ teaspoon cayenne
¼ cup clarified butter
1 tablespoon lemon juice
Salt

Cut the chilies in half, remove the stems, and scoop out the seeds; lightly coat the chilies with olive oil. Roast them on a baking sheet, cut side down, in a very hot oven, until the skins blister and begin to blacken. Cool the roasted chilies in a plastic bag or covered bowl and peel them.

Toast the cumin seed on top of the stove in a very hot sauté pan until they start popping a little and release their aroma. Grind them in a mortar and pestle. Peel the garlic and add it to the mortar with the paprika, cayenne, and chilies. Pound everything into a smooth paste. Slowly work the clarified butter into the purée to make an emulsion. Add the lemon juice, and salt, and more cayenne if you want it to be very spicy.

Makes ½ cup.

Pickled Cherry Peppers

10 to 15 cherry peppers
1 clove garlic
⅛ teaspoon black peppercorns
1 small bunch cilantro
1 bay leaf

1½ cups white wine vinegar
¼ cup balsamic vinegar
1 cup water
1 teaspoon coarse salt
2 teaspoons sugar

Wash and dry the peppers and put them in a nonreactive container. Peel the garlic clove, cut it in half, and add it to the peppers with the peppercorns, the cilantro leaves, and the bay leaf.

Combine the vinegars, water, salt, and sugar in a saucepan. Boil for 1 minute, remove from the heat, and pour over the peppers. Cool completely at room temperature, cover, and refrigerate. The peppers will be ready to eat after 1 week. They will keep up to 2 months, refrigerated.

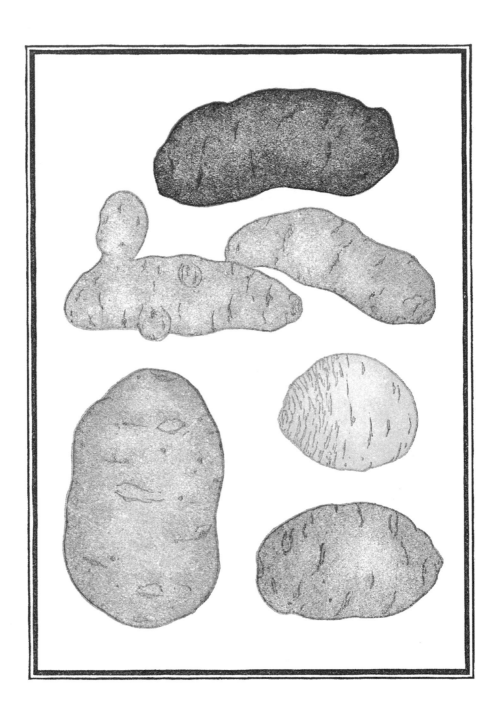

POTATOES ⸙

Season: Midsummer to early winter; new potatoes, early summer

This member of the nightshade family, *Solanum tuberosum,* is grown from coast to coast. (Maine and California are both major producers.) The forebears of many of the varieties now available in this country came from the Andes in what is now Chile, but many recent introductions to the market can be traced to wild potatoes from Peru, Bolivia, and Ecuador. Potato tubers grow in many colors, shapes, and sizes. Their flesh can be white, yellow, blue, pink, or red; their skin can be different colors and textures, both smooth and irregular; they can be shaped like elongated bananas, or be oval, or round; they may be as tiny as marbles or big enough to weigh a pound.

Potatoes form on underground vines started from small pieces of the previous season's crop, called seed potatoes. Because they produce most prolifically when temperatures are around 60°F., potatoes are generally harvested in the fall or spring, although they are harvested in the summer in the cool coastal areas of California.

Strictly speaking, only fragile-skinned, slightly immature potatoes that have just been harvested from potato vines that still have green leaves should be called "new potatoes." At this stage the tubers are thin-skinned and hard. They may look a little unattractive—what potato growers call "skinned" or "feathered"—because of unavoidable damage to their skins during harvesting. However, most potatoes are harvested in a more mature state, shortly after the vines begin to bloom or start to turn color. At this stage the skins are tougher and the flesh is drier than that of new potatoes. These potatoes are then cured in a cool (60°F.), dark place for a few weeks, to allow any damaged areas to heal before being stored at a lower temperature.

243

The rich, earthy flavor of a potato can be completely satisfying by itself, but potatoes also accompany and enhance other foods beautifully. Who could resist a few simply steamed new potatoes with some garlicky mayonnaise; or smooth, buttery mashed Yellow Finns with braised chicken; or steak with *pommes frites*? We cook potato gratins year-round with different varieties in season and in combination with other vegetables. You will find gratin recipes throughout this book.

At Chez Panisse we use genuine new potatoes whenever we can get them from local farmers, but generally from late spring through late fall. New potatoes are best in the simplest preparations, where their delicate flavor and texture can be appreciated. Boiling, steaming, and roasting (in the oven or in the fireplace) suit them best. Because of their tender skins, new potatoes seldom need peeling.

We have found that the specific variety of potato is often of less importance than the conditions under which it was grown or harvested, but for local new potatoes we look for Bintje, Yellow Finn, Désirée, Rose Fir, Ruby Crescent, and German Fingerling potatoes.

Waxier, medium potatoes with dense flesh are usually best for gratins. We like to use Red LaSoda, Désirée, and Pink Blossom, but some russets and Yellow Finns are good too. More mature potatoes are better for making mashed potatoes. Some organically-grown russets have the right starch balance to make perfect mashed potatoes, and mature Yellow Finns are very good as well.

Russets work best for french fries, because with enough soaking and rinsing, they will release most of their starch, unlike many other potatoes. It is the starch in potatoes that absorbs fat, resulting in soggy, greasy fries. Russets, well rinsed and dried, will fry crisp on the outside while remaining dry and fluffy on the inside.

In any event, you will have to experiment to learn the cooking qualities of the potatoes you use, because they come to market from different areas and storage conditions.

Never buy potatoes that have even a hint of green skin. All potatoes exposed to natural or artificial light will develop green skins, which may indicate the presence of solanine, a toxin. This can be peeled away, but it is best to avoid having to do so. Otherwise, look for potatoes that are firm, with no soft or discolored spots. A little soil on the skin is fine and may only mean that the potatoes were not exposed to a potentially damaging washing. New potatoes may look roughed up, but they should be rock hard.

No potatoes should be stored in the refrigerator for long, because the starch will gradually change into sugar, causing an unpleasantly sweet taste. Mature potatoes will keep best around 45°F., and need good air circulation. At home, do not plan on keeping truly new potatoes very long. Even under refrigeration they lose moisture through their thin skins.

Potato vines may take up more space than some other crops, but potatoes are worth growing in the home garden if you are fond of a particular variety or cannot get real new potatoes in the market. We seem to have forgotten what many vegetables really taste like. Perhaps more than that of any other vegetable, the flavor of a freshly harvested new potato from your own garden can be a revelation.

Roasted New Potatoes with Garlic and Thyme

This type of roasting is best for potatoes that have a fine, creamy texture and a moderate moisture content. We have had the most success with new Yellow Finns, German Fingerlings, and Red LaSodas, but most important is that the potatoes be small and firm.

Preheat the oven to 400°F. Scrub the new potatoes well in water and drain them. Choose a shallow baking dish or pan just large enough to hold the potatoes in a single layer. Toss the potatoes in the pan with olive oil; heads of garlic separated into cloves, peeled or not, as you prefer; sprigs of thyme or winter savory; and a splash of water. Season with salt and pepper.

Tightly cover the baking pan with aluminum foil and put in the middle of the oven. After 40 minutes, carefully lift one corner of the foil and check the potatoes for doneness. They should pierce easily with a small knife. If the potatoes are not tender, replace the foil and continue to roast them until they are done. When they are, take them out of the oven and loosen the foil to allow the steam to escape. They can be kept warm for a few minutes before serving.

Note: Potatoes can also be roasted in the fireplace or in the charcoal fire of a grill. Toss the potatoes with the garlic, seasonings, and water, as above, and seal them up tightly inside packets carefully folded out of 3 sheets of aluminum foil layered together, holding potatoes and garlic in a single, evenly thick layer. Roast the packets under coals of a fire that are dusty white all over but still glowing red in the center. Rake out the coals into a layer about 1 inch thick, place the packet on top, and then spread a light dusting of coals over the top.

The time they take to roast will depend on the heat of the embers, but 40 minutes to 1 hour is usually about right. Turn the packet over every 15 minutes or so, replenishing the coals underneath and on top as needed. When they are done, the potatoes will be soft throughout and lightly browned all over.

PASTA WITH POTATOES, ROCKET, AND ROSEMARY

1 pound firm boiling potatoes
About ½ cup extra-virgin
   olive oil
Salt and pepper
2 bunches rocket
   (about ½ pound)

1 small red onion
4 to 6 cloves garlic
1 sprig rosemary
¾ pound penne or other
   tubular pasta
½ lemon

Preheat the oven to 400°F.

Slice the potatoes about ⅓ inch thick and toss them with a small amount of the olive oil, salt, and pepper. Spread them in a single layer in an ovenproof dish or on a baking sheet and roast in the oven until they are golden brown and cooked through, about 15 minutes.

Meanwhile, wash the rocket (older, larger leaves are preferable to tender sprouts), drain, and set aside. Slice the red onion thin. Peel and chop fine the garlic cloves and the rosemary leaves. Put a large pot of salted water on to boil for the pasta.

When the potatoes are done, remove them from the oven and put the pasta on to boil. Heat a sauté pan, add some of the olive oil, and sauté the sliced onion until it is soft and translucent and starting to brown, about 5 minutes. Lower the heat, add the potato slices, the garlic, and the rosemary, and toss together for a minute or two. When the noodles are done, drain them and add to the potatoes and onion along with the rocket. Add a squeeze of lemon juice and toss everything together. Drizzle a little olive oil over and serve.

Serves 4.

Potato Gnocchi

3 large russet potatoes   *1 large egg*
3 tablespoons unsalted butter   *1½ cups all-purpose flour*
3 ounces milk   *Melted butter*
Salt and pepper   *Reggiano Parmesan cheese*
Freshly grated nutmeg

Peel the potatoes and cut them into chunks about 2 inches thick. Bring a large pot of well-salted water to a boil, add the potatoes, and cook until very tender, about 15 minutes. Drain in a colander and allow to dry for 5 minutes. Pass through a ricer or the fine disk of a food mill into a large bowl.

Warm the butter and milk together in a small saucepan over low heat, until the butter is melted. Stir gradually into the potatoes to make a thick mash. Season liberally with salt and pepper and a few grates of nutmeg. Add the egg and stir until completely incorporated. Stir in half the flour and blend thoroughly.

Turn the dough out onto a floured board and work in the remaining flour as you would for bread. It should be quite soft, like soft bread dough, but should not stick to the board; you may need to add a little more flour to achieve the right consistency.

Divide the dough into 4 parts. Roll each part into a long cylinder 1 inch in diameter and place them on a floured pan. Chill for half an hour. Remove from the refrigerator and, one by one, put each cylinder on the floured board and cut crosswise into ¾-inch-thick slices. Finish shaping the gnocchi in the traditional way by pressing on one side of each slice with the tines of a fork. Put all the gnocchi back on the floured pan and refrigerate until you are ready to cook them.

Bring a large pot of well-salted water to a boil. Add the gnocchi, reduce the heat, and simmer for 5 minutes. Drain carefully and sauce with melted butter and grated Parmesan. Or serve with warm pesto sauce, thinned with a little water. In the spring, serve with fresh peas, sage, butter, and Parmesan.

Serves 8.

Potato Gratin

Rub an earthenware gratin dish with smashed peeled garlic and butter. Layer overlapping slices of potato cut ⅛ inch thick. Season with salt, pepper, and thyme leaves. Make another layer of potato slices, and season again. Moisten with cream, cream and chicken stock, or milk to the level of the top layer of potatoes. According to taste, sprinkle the top with grated Parmesan or Gruyère cheese, and distribute thin shavings of butter on top. Bake 45 minutes to 1 hour in a preheated oven at 375°F., until nicely browned.

Many variations are possible: potato and turnip (page 302), potato and celery root (page 89), potato and winter squash (page 276), potato and leek, potato and black truffle, or potato and sweet potato. Try adding a layer of some other delicious thing between the potato layers: sorrel, green garlic or roasted garlic, grilled chicory, sautéed wild mushrooms, caramelized onion, kale or chard, black olives, artichoke hearts.

Warm Potato Salad with Crème Fraîche

This salad was improvised one night to be served with a little rocket salad as an accompaniment to sautéed shad roe wrapped in bacon, but it could go with any number of things or be enjoyed all by itself.

1½ pounds new Bintje potatoes
2 shallots
¾ cup cream
Salt and pepper
½ cup crème fraîche
Sherry vinegar

Boil the potatoes in their skins until tender; drain. When they are cool enough to handle, cut them into ¼-inch slices.

Peel and dice the shallots fine, and put them in a small pan with the cream. Season with salt and pepper and warm gently: the trick here is to slowly soften the shallots without reducing the cream. When the shallots have softened, take them off the heat and stir in the crème fraîche. When you are ready to serve the salad, put the potatoes in the cream mixture, add a splash or two of the sherry vinegar to taste, and warm again gently. Correct the seasoning and serve garnished with freshly ground black pepper.

Serves 6 to 8.

248

FINGERLING POTATO COINS

Ruby Crescent is the variety of fingerling potatoes we use most commonly at the restaurant. These potatoes are an inch or so in diameter, but may be up to 6 inches in length. They are very waxy and don't break down easily, so they don't have to be served immediately—they can be kept warm for a while after they have been cooked.

Slice the potatoes into thin coin-shaped pieces, about ⅛ inch thick. (A small Japanese mandolin makes this job go much faster.) Put the potatoes in a high-sided sauté pan with just enough water to cover, add salt, and boil, covered, for 10 minutes over medium heat. The potatoes should be tender. Lower the heat, add butter, and cook, uncovered, for another 10 minutes; this allows the butter to penetrate the potatoes. Keep warm until serving.

POTATO AND SALT COD PURÉE (BRANDADE)

1 pound salt cod fillet	*2 tablespoons red wine vinegar*
Water or milk	*¼ cup mild olive oil*
½ pound red potatoes	*Salt and pepper*
½ cup half-and-half	*Garlic Croutons (page 160)*
2 cloves garlic	*Italian parsley*

Soak the salt cod in water for 24 to 48 hours, refrigerated, changing the water two or three times, to reconstitute and desalt it. Cook the salt cod in lightly simmering water or milk until soft, about 5 to 10 minutes. Drain, and when it is cool enough to handle, flake the flesh, removing and discarding any skin or bones. Peel and boil the the potatoes until soft, then put through a ricer or a food mill or mash coarsely.

Warm the half-and-half. Peel and chop the garlic very fine. Mash the flaked salt cod with the potatoes and the warm half-and-half, mixing together thoroughly. Season with the vinegar, the olive oil, half the garlic (it is best to start by adding only half the garlic, as the flavor tends to get stronger as it sits; you can always add more after 15 minutes), and salt and pepper. The texture should be almost like mashed potatoes but with a little more body. Serve spread generously on Garlic Croutons, garnished with chopped parsley.

Makes about 4 cups.

WAFFLE POTATOES

Peel large mature russet potatoes and keep them immersed in cold water until you are ready to slice them. To make waffle potatoes, you need a mandolin with a crinkle-cut blade. Adjust the thickness of the slice to about 1/16 inch. After each slice, give the potato a turn so that a crisscross waffled pattern is created. The slices should be of an even thickness, thick enough that they don't break apart, but thin enough so that a perforated waffle pattern is clearly visible. Rinse the slices in a bowl under cold running water until the water runs clear, about 15 minutes. Spin dry in small batches in a salad spinner or pat dry with paper towels.

In a large heavy pot or deep-fryer, heat about 2 quarts of peanut oil to 365°F. Fry the rinsed and dried potatoes in small batches until golden brown, skimming out any broken or burnt bits before frying another batch. Drain the crispy chips on paper towels, salt generously, and keep warm until serving.

YELLOW FINNS FRIED IN DUCK FAT

1 to 2 pounds Yellow Finn or russet potatoes
¾ cup rendered duck fat
Salt and pepper

Peel the potatoes and cut them into ¾-inch cubes. Boil them in salted water until they are completely tender when pierced with a knife, about 12 minutes. Drain and cool.

Over medium heat, warm a nonstick or cast iron sauté pan large enough to accommodate the potatoes in a single layer. When the pan is hot, pour in about ¾ cup rendered duck fat and add the potatoes. Allow them to fry undisturbed over medium heat until they begin to brown. Toss, or turn with a spoon, and continue to cook, stirring often, until they are well browned on all sides. Watch the heat carefully; duck fat can burn easily. (If you wish, you can use a mixture of duck fat and clarified butter.) Season with salt and pepper. If you like, add some finely chopped garlic and parsley during the last minute of cooking.

Drain the potatoes in a sieve. You can hold them in reserve in a warm place for up to 10 minutes before serving.

Serves 4.

STRAW POTATO CAKE

2 large russet potatoes
¼ cup clarified butter
Salt

Peel and rinse the potatoes. Julienne them fine with a mandolin (1/16-inch by 4-inch sticks). Put the julienned potatoes in a bowl of cold water for 30 minutes. Drain and dry the potatoes well by wringing them in a cloth towel.

Put half the clarified butter in a 10-inch nonstick pan over low heat and add the potatoes, packing them down with a spatula, and season with salt. Cook over low to medium heat for 6 to 8 minutes, continuing to pack down the potatoes occasionally, until the bottom has turned golden brown. Make sure that the cake slides around freely in the pan, adding more butter if necessary. When the bottom has browned, carefully flip over the potato cake with two spatulas. (Or slide the potato cake out of the pan onto a plate, invert the pan over the plate, and carefully turn plate and pan over so the cake falls back into the pan.) Lightly pack the potatoes down again with a spatula. Add more of the butter around the edges of the pan and cook for another 5 minutes. When the potato cake is nicely colored on the bottom, slide it out of the pan to drain on paper towels, cut it into 4 wedges, season with a little more salt, and serve immediately.

Serves 4.

PUMPKIN ❧
See Squashes, Winter (page 273)

RADICCHIO ❧
See Chicories (page 101)

RADISHES &

Season: Year-round; best in spring and fall

No meal at Chez Panisse is quite complete without radishes. In one brilliant flash of red and green, they help define where and who we are. Our cool coastal climate allows us to grow and enjoy perfectly crisp, mildly peppery radishes nearly year-round. We ask all our growers for radishes, and when they all show up with baskets brimming, and we find ourselves with several thousand radishes, radishes go on every table, after no more preparation than a quick rinse. Our major supplier of radishes is now the Garden Project, a hugely successful model program that changes lives by teaching organic gardening skills to former inmates of the San Francisco County jail.

Everyone is familiar with round, bright red radishes. But have you tried Easter Egg—round or oval radishes in white, purple, and lavender, as well as red? What about the long thin White Icicle, whose flesh is tender, crisp, and snow white? French Breakfast, one of our favorites, is an elongated radish whose color changes from magenta at the top to white at the tip.

Every fall the Chinos send us Chinese radishes, large round or oval roots, each of which may weigh more than a pound. Cut into one, and the rather plain green and white skin reveals a sweet-fleshed interior with brilliant kaleidoscopic patterns in red, pale green, and white. Each one seems to have a different pattern of color. Daikon radishes, grown everywhere in Japan, can also be found in many markets in the United States. There are many named varieties of these large, white radishes, but the ones most commonly found in this country are a foot or so long and several inches in diameter.

All of these many kinds of radishes belong to a single species of the mustard family: *Raphanus sativus.* The tremendous diversity of size, shape, and color is not surprising, given the huge area of Europe and Asia where they are native, and the thousands of years that radishes have been under cultivation.

Radishes at Chez Panisse are served most often at the very beginning of the meal. They are brought to the table with bread and butter as soon as the guests are seated. A light sprinkling with coarse salt is really all the accompaniment needed. Red radishes add color, spice, and crispness to composed salads with other cool season vegetables, or cut into fine julienne and strewn over lobster or crab salad. Fine-julienned daikon combines beautifully with other root vegetables, such as carrots, beets, celery root, and green onions. A pile of these matchsticks, lightly dressed, is the perfect counterpoint for thin slices of rare, grilled tuna or salmon tartare. Daikon can also be substituted for turnips in raw or quickly cooked preparations.

When radishes grow quickly in cool weather, they are crisp, juicy, and mild. The availability of table radishes peaks in the late spring, but in most parts of the country there is a secondary season in early fall. In California we can get them all year, but a few days of hot weather anywhere will cause radishes to become unpleasantly hot and pithy. The large, Asian varieties are at their best in middle to late fall, although some will keep well into winter.

When selecting table radishes in the market, look for those with fresh, bright green tops. The thin roots at the bottom of the radishes should look healthy and not withered. The radishes themselves should have smooth skins and feel firm. Avoid any that are spongy. Avoid radishes packed in plastic bags without their green leaves. A large number of big leaves, however, is not a sure sign of a good radish. Some varieties, particularly the French Breakfast types, have short tops.

Asian varieties are often sold without their rather considerable tops. Other than asking for a taste, the best indications of good quality are a firm texture and unblemished skin, especially for daikons. The interior color of Chinese radishes can be quite variable, but a pink color in the small root at the bottom of the radish is often an indication of a colorful interior. A few small cracks in the skin are considered by some growers to indicate the best stage of maturity.

Just before serving table radishes, give them a good soaking in cold water to refresh them, and then drain thoroughly. You can pinch off the tiny root at the bottom if you wish. Peel Asian radishes shortly before use; if they have lost some of their sweetness, soak the sliced or julienned flesh in ice water for thirty minutes before serving. Dry in a salad spinner just before serving.

Table radishes are the ideal crop for a kitchen garden. They mature in three to four weeks, and can be planted in the early spring where other crops will be grown in summer, or between rows of plants that will need more room later. In the fall they will give a crop after spent summer vegetables have been taken out. Because they give such quick results, radishes are the perfect crop for impatient children and adults to plant. The Asian varieties should be attempted only if you have gardening space and even temperatures for a period of two or three months. A wonderfully complete discussion of growing and cooking Asian radishes can be found in *Oriental Vegetables*, by Joy Larkcom. Ms. Larkcom describes not only daikon and Chinese radishes, but also how to use radish leaves, radish sprouts, and radish seed pods.

RADISH, FENNEL, AND DANDELION SALAD

2 bunches young dandelion greens	*¾ cup extra-virgin olive oil*
	Salt and pepper
1 Meyer or other variety of lemon	*Optional: white wine vinegar*
	2 bulbs fennel
2 shallots	*1 bunch small red radishes*

Wash and spin dry the dandelion greens; refrigerate. Peel a few strips of zest from the lemon and chop very fine to make about ½ teaspoon. Juice the lemon; there should be about ¼ cup.

Peel and chop the shallots very fine, put them in a salad bowl, cover with the lemon juice and lemon zest, and macerate for about 20 minutes. Whisk in the olive oil and season with salt and pepper. Add a splash of white wine vinegar if you like.

Trim the tops and root ends of the fennel and remove the outer layer and any bruised or damaged parts. Slice it very thin (about ⅛ inch) with a knife or on a mandolin. Wash the radishes, leaving the tops on if they are delicate, and cut the radishes into halves or quarters lengthwise—or trim off the tops and slice the radishes into rounds on a mandolin.

Just before serving, toss all the ingredients with enough of the dressing to just coat them. Adjust the seasoning and serve immediately.

Serves 6.

RADISH SALAD WITH CURED FRESH ANCHOVIES

1 bunch large crisp radishes
4 stalks celery
1 bunch Italian parsley
Salt and pepper
1 or 2 lemons

24 fillets Cured Fresh
  Anchovies (see recipe below)
Optional: Pickled Red Onions
  (page 223)

Wash and trim the radishes and, using a sharp knife or a Japanese mandolin, slice into thin rounds. Trim the celery and remove the strings. Slice the celery crosswise on a long diagonal, as thin as possible. Pick the leaves off the parsley stems. Wash and dry the leaves.

Just before you plan to serve the salad, toss the vegetables and parsley leaves together and arrange on plates. Season lightly with salt and squeeze lemon juice over all. Place 6 anchovy fillets per serving on the vegetables and finish with freshly ground black pepper. Serve with crusty bread and, if you like, pass the Pickled Red Onions at the table.

Serves 4.

CURED FRESH ANCHOVIES

1 pound fresh anchovies
About 2 tablespoons coarse salt
1 lemon
3 or 4 sprigs thyme

2 bay leaves (fresh, if possible)
½ teaspoon black peppercorns
2 cups extra-virgin olive oil

One by one, lay the anchovies on their sides and scrape each fish gently with the back of a paring knife to remove its scales. Rinse each fish in a bowl of cold water to wash off any loose scales. Fillet the anchovies: Lay each one on its side and make a slit just behind the gill cover at an angle parallel to it, cutting down to the spine. With an angular motion, slide the knife along the spine toward the tail, avoiding the abdominal cavity and its contents and removing in one piece the flesh on one side. Turn the fish over and repeat this step. Discard the skeleton.

Rinse the fillets quickly in cold water and drain in a colander. Lay the fillets, flesh side up, side by side in a shallow crock. Salt the flesh well and evenly, so that the entire amount of salt is evenly distributed over all the fillets. (The fillets can be layered in the crock.) Cover the crock with plastic wrap and refrigerate for 24 hours.

Slice the lemon (a Meyer lemon, if available) very thin. Remove the fillets from the crock and discard any liquid that has collected in the bottom. Layer the fillets back into the crock, with the lemon slices, thyme sprigs, bay leaves, and peppercorns evenly dispersed among them. Pour the olive oil over, cover, and refrigerate for 8 days. Do not eat the anchovies before this time has elapsed; they will not be sufficiently cured. (When fully cured, they will have softened and become infused with the aromatics.) The anchovies will keep for 3 to 4 days more under refrigeration but no longer. Serve them slightly cooler than room temperature, on lightly grilled croutons, with a few drops of lemon juice and a grind of pepper.

Makes about 60 fillets.

RADISH AND ANCHOVY OPEN-FACE SANDWICH

Choose a very fresh sweet baguette. Cut it in half lengthwise and spread liberally with unsalted butter. Wash and trim radishes, leaving on their tender leaves. Cut the radishes in half lengthwise and place them on the buttered baguette. Garnish with salt-packed anchovy filets or cured fresh anchovies and ground black pepper.

ROSEMARY
See Herbs (page 171)

SAGE
See Herbs (page 171)

SAVORY
See Herbs (page 172)

SHALLOTS 🍃

Season: Best in summer

Close relatives of the onion, shallots have a flavor that is more intense than that of sweet onions, and at the same time less hot. This means they can be used more readily raw than onions. They do not, as some say, taste like a combination of onion and garlic. Although their flavor complements these other alliums, shallots have a distinctive, piquant character of their own.

The restaurant is seldom without shallots. We use them to flavor most vinaigrettes and compound butters. They are essential to béarnaise sauce, beurre blanc, and red wine sauces. They add complexity to soup bases when combined with leeks, onions, and garlic. We often strew raw, finely diced shallots over tomato salads and grilled meat. On their own, they are delicious roasted or fried.

Most botanists classify shallots as a variety of the onion, *Allium cepa*, var. *ascalonium*. Ascalon was an ancient Palestinian city, and shallots may have been introduced to Europe as the Ascalonian onion by returning Crusaders in the Middle Ages. Shallots, like onions and garlic, grow during the cool months of winter and spring, and mature in the summer. The sweetest, tenderest shallots come to market in midsummer. Shallots are available from storage at other times of the year, but gradually lose quality in the spring.

Shallots grow as a cluster of small, teardrop-shaped bulbs, loosely held together at the base. Most types have brown to reddish brown thin, papery skins, which cover the compact bulbs. The much less common small gray shallot has tougher, gray-brown skin, and although harder to peel, is superior in flavor. There are other uncommon varieties grown by allium specialists, but they are all used interchangeably with the common red shallot.

Shop for firm shallots, with dry, crinkly skins. Don't buy those that are sprouting or that show signs of mold. Buy only as many as you are likely to use in a week or so, unless you have an airy, cool, dry place for storing them. Newly harvested shallots with green tops still attached are sometimes available at farmer's markets. These delicious shallots are very perishable.

To prepare shallots, first cut off the tops and any straggly roots. Peel them with a small, thin-bladed paring knife. Shallots that will be cut up are easier to peel if they are first cut in half lengthwise. Shallots should be diced carefully with a very sharp knife. If they are chopped roughly, they will get a little smashed and exude more of their juices, making them more susceptible to oxidation and the development of off flavors. Diced or sliced shallots to be used in a vinaigrette or wine sauce can be prepared hours ahead of time, if they are kept in a non-corroding bowl covered with the vinegar or wine that will be used in the sauce.

Shallots can be temperamental while growing, but they don't take up much space and may be worth experimenting with, especially the uncommon varieties. They are subject to rot from too much water, so plant with the top third of the bulb above ground in well-drained soil. One sprouting bulb will produce a cluster of new shallots. It is also a treat to be able to harvest shallots like green onions, before they are completely mature.

GLAZED SHALLOTS

To roast shallots, peel them and cut them into halves or quarters so they are all roughly the same size. Toss with a dash of balsamic vinegar, a drizzle of good olive oil, and a sprinkling of salt, and put them in a heavy-bottomed, ovenproof dish just big enough to hold them in a single layer. Roast them, uncovered, in a 350° to 400°F. oven, stirring occasionally for even caramelization, until they have a deep brown glaze and are tender inside, 15 to 30 minutes. Roasted shallots can be served with grilled or roasted meat, either left in wedges or chopped fine and mixed with rinsed and chopped capers and chopped parsley. When they are to be served with baked or grilled fish, roast the shallots with Champagne vinegar.

SHALLOTS

Shallot Flan

1 tablespoon unsalted butter	*Salt and pepper*
12 shallots	*Nutmeg*
½ cup half-and-half	*Optional: Glazed Shallots*
2 eggs	*(opposite)*

Preheat the oven to 275 °F. Butter four ramekins.

Peel the shallots and cook them in a small pot of salted boiling water for 10 minutes, or until very soft. Drain.

Heat the half-and-half. Purée the shallots in a food processor or a blender with the warm half-and-half and the eggs. Strain the purée through a fine sieve. Season lightly with salt, pepper, and freshly ground nutmeg. Pour the mixture into the ramekins and place them in a baking dish. Place the dish on an oven rack and pour enough hot water into the dish to come halfway up the sides of the ramekins. Bake, uncovered, for 1 hour. Check for doneness with a toothpick—it should come out dry. Remove from the oven and let stand for 5 minutes before serving. Serve this flan with a grilled steak garnished with Glazed Shallots, if you like.

Serves 4.

Note: Young green garlic can be substituted for shallots in this recipe. Slice the bulbs and tender portion of the stalks and stew, covered, in a little butter and water until soft. Purée and proceed as above.

Shallots with Balsamic Vinegar

20 shallots	*Salt and pepper*
2 tablespoons unsalted butter	*Balsamic vinegar*
1 pinch sugar	

Peel the shallots. Sauté them in butter with the sugar, season with salt, and cook uncovered for 5 minutes over medium heat, turning them frequently. When the shallots have browned, turn down the heat and cook partially covered for 30 minutes, stirring from time to time. When the shallots are tender and well browned, grind some pepper over them, add more salt if necessary, and add a few drops of the balsamic vinegar.

Serves 4.

Deep-fried Shallots

Peel shallots and slice them ⅛ inch thick. Separate them into rings and soak them in half buttermilk and half milk for at least an hour. In a deep-fryer or a deep pot, heat peanut oil or pure olive oil to 365°F. Drain the shallots and toss them in flour, shake them in a sieve to remove excess flour, and fry in small batches until golden brown. Drain and salt; serve as a garnish for grilled steak or fish or for vegetable purées.

Sherry Shallot Vinaigrette

Shallot vinaigrettes are used all the time at the restaurant, with different combinations of vinegars, or lemon or orange juice. The following two examples offer a general guide to proportions, one for a combination of vinegars and one for vinegar and lemon juice.

2 shallots
2 tablespoons balsamic vinegar
1 tablespoon red wine vinegar

1 tablespoon sherry vinegar
½ teaspoon salt
⅓ cup extra-virgin olive oil

Peel and dice the shallots and put them in a small bowl with the vinegars and salt. Stir and let the mixture sit for 10 to 30 minutes. Whisk in the olive oil.

Makes about ¾ cup.

Lemon Shallot Vinaigrette

2 small shallots
2 tablespoons Champagne
vinegar

2 tablespoons lemon juice
½ teaspoon salt
⅓ cup extra-virgin olive oil

Peel and dice the shallots very fine. Put them in a small bowl with the vinegar, lemon juice, and salt. Stir and let the mixture sit for 10 to 30 minutes. Whisk in the olive oil.

Makes about ¾ cup.

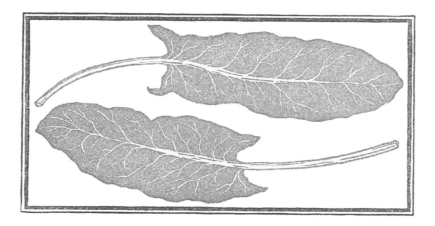

SORREL 🌿

Season: Spring, summer, and fall

Sorrel is such a hardy and undemanding plant, and so useful and pretty at the same time, that it belongs in every kitchen garden. The attractive clumps of leaves growing a foot or two high can be tucked away in a corner of the garden, ready to provide a delicious harvest of lemony-tasting greens.

Two kinds of sorrel are commonly cultivated. Garden sorrel, *Rumex acetosa*, is generally taller, with long narrow leaves. French sorrel, *R. scutatus*, is considered the choicer of the two because of its broader, fleshier leaves. But the distinction is not of great importance. Both kinds can be easily recognized by their pale green, sword-shaped leaves. And both kinds are equally delicious, deriving their sharp, lemony character from the oxalic acid found in the leaves.

The English have added sorrel to spice up mixtures of salad greens since the early eighteenth century at least. But at Chez Panisse, we prefer to use sorrel as the French do, in soups and in butter sauces for fish. The tart flavor of sorrel also has an affinity for potatoes.

Sorrel leaves can be harvested from early spring through fall, although the largest and lushest production is in spring. When the plants start to bloom in summer, leaf production declines as more energy goes into seed production. However, the time of year has little effect on cooking quality.

Sorrel at the market should be pale to medium green and look very fresh. Reject any that is wilted or that has translucent watery spots on the leaves. Keep sorrel in a plastic bag in the refrigerator, as you would other leafy greens, and use it within a day or two. To prepare sorrel for cooking, strip the leaves from the tough stems and rinse them in a large basin of cold water. Lift the leaves out of the water and drain thoroughly before cooking. When cooked, fresh green sorrel turns a distinctive olive drab. This is not unattractive, but some cooks add a little puréed spinach to dishes with puréed sorrel to brighten the color.

A few clumps of sorrel in the garden will give abundant harvests in the spring. The leaves can be cut repeatedly from the plants without decreasing their vigor. Removing the flowering stalks in the summer will increase leaf production into the fall.

POTATO AND SORREL GRATIN

About 24 large sorrel leaves
3 tablespoons unsalted butter
3 pounds russet or Yukon Gold
*   potatoes*
Salt and pepper
Nutmeg

2 cups milk, cream, or stock, or
*   a combination*
¼ cup grated Gruyère cheese
2 tablespoons grated Reggiano
*   Parmesan cheese*

Preheat the oven to 375°F. Butter a large gratin dish.

Wash, stem, and coarsely chop the sorrel leaves. Melt 2 tablespoons of the butter in a sauté pan, add the sorrel, and cook until the leaves are completely wilted and have turned olive green. Transfer to a plate.

Peel and slice thin the potatoes. Layer half the potatoes in the gratin dish, season well with salt and pepper, and grate a little nutmeg over them. Spread the cooked sorrel evenly over the potatoes. Make another layer with the rest of the potatoes and add enough milk to almost cover them. Season again with more salt, pepper, and nutmeg. Dot the surface with the remaining tablespoon of butter and sprinkle with the grated cheese. Bake about 1 hour, until the surface is nicely browned and the liquid is almost completely absorbed.

Serves 6 to 8.

SORREL SOUP

1 medium boiling potato	*1 cup chicken stock*
1 medium yellow onion	*1 large bunch sorrel*
1 small carrot	*(about 1 pound)*
4 tablespoons unsalted butter	*¼ cup cream or half-and-half*
1 sprig thyme	*Parsley*
Salt and pepper	*Optional: 2 ounces smoked*
2⅓ cups water	*bacon*

Peel and dice the potato, onion, and carrot. Melt the butter in a 3- or 4-quart saucepan and add the diced vegetables and the thyme. Pour in ⅓ cup water, cover, and stew gently for about 15 minutes, with the lid slightly ajar. Season with salt and pepper, add 2 more cups water and the chicken stock, bring to a simmer, and stew another 15 minutes with the lid ajar, until the potato is soft and easily mashed with a spoon.

Meanwhile, wash and stem the sorrel, and chop the leaves into a rough chiffonade. When the vegetables are done, add the sorrel, and return the soup to a simmer. Turn off the heat, cover, and let stand for 5 minutes.

Purée the soup in a blender and pass through a medium-mesh sieve into a stainless steel bowl. Stir in the cream; taste and adjust the seasoning; let the soup cool to room temperature.

Chop enough parsley fine to make about 1 tablespoon. If you choose to garnish the soup with bacon, fry it now, chop it fine, rind removed, and then pound it to a paste in a mortar. Mix it together with the chopped parsley. Warm the soup without boiling, pour into a warm tureen, and stir in the bacon and parsley paste, or garnish with the chopped parsley alone.

Serves 4.

Sorrel Sauce

About 24 large sorrel leaves *Salt and pepper*
2 shallots *Lemon juice*
½ cup heavy cream

Wash the sorrel in plenty of cold water. Remove the stems and drain well. Cut the sorrel into a rough chiffonade.

Peel and dice the shallots and put in a nonreactive pot with the cream. Bring to a boil, reduce the heat, and simmer for 5 minutes. Add the sorrel and cook for another 3 minutes. Season with salt and pepper and a squeeze of lemon juice. Sorrel sauce can be puréed. Serve it with fish, chicken, or potatoes.

Serves 4.

Note: Another way to make a sorrel sauce is to add a chiffonade of sorrel to a beurre blanc at the last minute.

SPINACH &

Season: Year-round; best in spring and fall

The crisp, emerald-green leaves of spinach disappear from Chez Panisse menus only briefly, in midsummer. The rest of the year we use it often, as indeed it is used everywhere in the United States, where it is the most widely grown green for the table. Generally oval, sometimes heart-shaped, the leaves of spinach grow in a small bunch, or rosette, on relatively short stems. On some varieties the leaves have a heavy and crinkly texture, typical of the so-called savoy types, such as Bloomsdale. More common are such flat-leaved varieties as Melody or Wolter, which are both equally delicious. The size of spinach leaves is not an indication of their quality. The largest leaves can be the most succulent, having been produced in a rapid flush of growth by a healthy plant. Tiny leaves may have been languishing on a plant past its prime or may be the result of early picking from young plants.

We use spinach in soups, either whole or puréed; as a topping for piz-zas, both cooked and raw; in salads, both cold, and warm and slightly wilted; and as a vegetable side dish, either quickly sautéed or long-cooked. Spinach is the "green" in green pasta. As a rule, the small tender leaves are best for eating raw or in salads, while the largest, thickest leaves are best for cooking.

Because it is grown so widely throughout the country, spinach is found in markets year-round. However, the best spinach grows during periods of cool and even temperatures, typically spring and fall. In California and other favored areas, fall-sown spinach is harvested throughout the winter. Midsummer is the hardest time to find good spinach.

Large-leafed spinach is usually sold by the bunch, while the less mature, or "baby," leaves for salad are sold in bulk, by the pound. In either case, choose crisp, fresh leaves that have an intense green color. Avoid wilted or yellowing leaves and long tough stems. Small leaf-picked spinach wilts quickly after harvest, so be particularly careful to buy only the freshest spinach for salads. Perfectly fresh spinach at the height of the season will be crunchy and clean-tasting. Over-the-hill spinach can have an unpleasant minerally quality that becomes even stronger with cooking.

The leaves can be stripped from spinach as follows. Grasp an individual plant by its base with one hand. With the other hand, grasp one leaf at a time and gently but firmly pull it from the stem. Continue until all the spinach has been stripped. The stems can be saved and added to soups or vegetable stocks. Leaf-picked spinach needs only the occasional ragged stem trimmed off.

Since even a tiny bit of grit can be very unpleasant, all spinach should be carefully washed just before use. Fill a large basin with cold water and plunge the spinach leaves into the water, swishing them around with your hands to help dislodge the sand and dirt. Allow the grit to sink undisturbed to the bottom of the basin, and then carefully lift the spinach out of the water with your hands or with a large strainer. Repeat this process until you see no grit at the bottom of the basin. Drain the spinach in a colander and proceed with the recipe.

Under the best cool weather conditions, spinach can be harvested just six weeks after the seeds are planted, so it makes a quick, attractive home crop. Plant it in earliest spring in areas that will later be occupied by warm weather transplants. You can also sow a fall crop in the little spaces that always seem to be left over at the end of the summer.

ANTIPASTO SPINACH

Remove the large stems and wash the spinach in cold water. Drain and cook in boiling salted water briefly, until just done. Drain and cool quickly under cold water. Drain and press very dry, squeezing dry in a towel if necessary. Chop the spinach roughly and dress lightly with fruity olive oil, salt and pepper, and lemon or vinegar. Serve at room temperature as part of an antipasto plate, garnished with hard-cooked egg and anchovy, or with prosciutto.

SPINACH SALAD

Wash and spin dry tender young spinach leaves. Dress with a garlic and red wine vinaigrette or a Lemon Shallot Vinaigrette (page 262), and garnish generously with sieved hard-cooked egg and baguette croutons (see Garlic Croutons, page 160).

WARM SPINACH SALAD

Wash and dry very fresh spinach leaves. Medium, slightly more substantial leaves are better for this salad than very delicate tiny ones. Prepare some lardons of bacon and fry them crisp. Save the rendered fat. Oil and toast small croutons (see Garlic Croutons, page 160). Marinate diced shallot in sherry vinegar with a pinch of salt. Whisk in olive oil to taste, keeping the dressing rather sharp.

Put the leaves in a stainless steel bowl and toss with the dressing. Mix in the bacon and croutons and season with pepper. Put the bowl over a pan of simmering water and toss continuously with tongs while the salad heats. Remove when the leaves are just wilted and serve immediately on warm plates.

Alternatively, dress the salad with the shallots and vinegar, omitting the olive oil. Put the rendered fat in a small pan and heat it very hot. Heat the salad with the croutons and bacon over the simmering water, pour over the hot fat, toss until just wilted, and serve.

Note: This is also an excellent way to make a salad with dandelion leaves.

SPINACH AND YOGURT RAITA

This makes a savory accompaniment for Saffron Rice (page 319) with grilled chicken or lamb. For a decidedly Indian flavor, add cumin seeds "popped"—heated in a dry pan until they pop and release their aroma.

1 bunch spinach   *2 cloves garlic*
   (about ¾ pound)   *Salt and pepper*
1 pint yogurt   *1 lemon*

Wash and stem the spinach. Wilt in water, or steam, briefly. Let it cool and drain. Squeeze the water out and chop it fine. Add the spinach to the yogurt along with the garlic, peeled and mashed, salt and pepper, and the grated zest and juice of the lemon.

Makes 2½ cups.

SPINACH ROMAN STYLE WITH RAISINS AND PINE NUTS

Find the freshest pine nuts you can. Pine nuts turn rancid quickly, so taste before you buy. Toast the pine nuts in a dry sauté pan or in the oven, until they are golden brown and aromatic.

Put a handful of raisins in a bowl, just cover with boiling water, let stand 10 minutes or so until plump, and drain. Heat a large sauté pan, pour in just enough pure olive oil to coat the bottom of the pan, heat the oil, and add the cleaned and dried spinach. When the spinach has collapsed and wilted, add the raisins and the toasted pine nuts. Toss and warm through, and season with salt and pepper—and a splash of balsamic or sherry wine vinegar, if you wish—and serve.

Note: The same ingredients make a good warm salad. Make a dressing of shallots, balsamic vinegar, and extra-virgin olive oil. Put a stainless steel bowl over simmering water, add the spinach and enough dressing to coat the leaves, and when the spinach begins to wilt, add the raisins and toasted pine nuts, season, and serve. Diced apple or fresh figs are good in this salad instead of raisins.

Spinach Soup

1 onion	*½ cup parsley leaves*
1 clove garlic	*2 bunches young spinach*
1 small carrot	*(about 1½ pounds)*
2 tablespoons olive oil	*2 sprigs fresh tarragon*
4 cups chicken stock	*2 tablespoons crème fraîche*

Peel the onion and garlic, and slice thin. Peel the carrot and dice fine.

In a large pot, stew the onion, garlic, and carrot in the olive oil, covered, until soft and translucent. Add the chicken stock, bring to a boil, and simmer uncovered for about 15 minutes.

Prepare a large bowl half filled with ice, and a smaller bowl, preferably stainless steel, that will fit inside it and rest on the ice.

Wash the parsley and spinach and add them to the pot with the chicken stock and other vegetables. Shut off the heat and allow the soup to stand, uncovered, for 5 minutes, no longer. Immediately purée the soup in a blender and pour it through a medium-mesh strainer into the bowl in the ice bath. Stir the soup slowly with a spoon or spatula until it has cooled to room temperature and then remove it from the ice. Quick cooling preserves the color of the soup.

Chop enough tarragon to make about 1 tablespoon and stir it into the crème fraîche. To serve the soup, reheat it to just below a boil and garnish each bowl with a teaspoon of the crème fraîche.

Serves 6.

SQUASHES, SUMMER ❧
See Zucchini and Other Summer Squashes (page 309)

SQUASHES, WINTER &

Season: Fall through late winter

The winter squashes are the fruits of four different species of the gourd or cucumber family, the *Cucurbitaceae*. They are mostly annual plants, with long-stemmed running vines and with broad leaves, which bear both male and female flowers on the same plant. The male, or staminate, flowers are sometimes picked in bloom for cooking in the summertime; the female, or pistillate, flowers produce the fruits that are left on the vine to ripen and that are used in the fall and winter.

Winter squashes are distinguished from summer squashes more by the time of their harvest and use than by any botanical differences. The summer squashes are eaten when the fruit is immature and soft; winter squashes, after the rind has hardened and when their darker (usually orange) flesh is much sweeter. All the summer squashes belong to exactly the same species as the acorn and Delicata winter squashes: *Cucurbita pepo*, a species that also includes the familiar orange pumpkins. Butternut squash belongs to the species, *C. moschata*. The Hubbard squashes, the turban squashes, and the kabocha squashes, among many others, belong to *C. maxima*. The least common winter squash species, *C. argyrosperma*, includes the cushaw squashes, which thrive only in southern climates.

The varieties we use most often at Chez Panisse are butternut squash, acorn and Delicata squash, some of the Hubbards and kabochas, and sugar pumpkins. Winter squashes can be served diced and sautéed as a lightly browned accompaniment to main courses; in a soup—baked first, slightly mashed, simmered in chicken stock with onions and herbs, and garnished with shavings of Parmesan; in a gratin, tossed with a persillade, drizzled with olive oil, and slowly baked; in gratins with potatoes, flavored with bacon; in onion and squash panade—layered with toasted levain bread, flavored with sage and Gruyère cheese, moistened with stock or water, and baked; in risotti, with thyme and white truffles; or as a simple purée enriched with butter.

Winter squashes are harvested in the fall, and are available from October to March. The midseason fruit is usually best. Many winter squash improve after a few weeks of storage after harvest. Very late season fruit is sometimes fibrous with large, very developed seed cavities. In general, though, winter squash quality is fairly constant throughout the season, due to its even texture and water content. At the market, look for heavy, hard-skinned squash with no blemishes or bruises. Skin color varies considerably according to variety, from the creamy tan-orange of butternut squash to the mottled gray-blue of some kabocha squash. Flesh color can be brilliant deep orange or various shades of yellow or green. Its texture should be firm and smooth.

Winter squashes should not be refrigerated. Uncut and whole, they can be kept for months in a cool place, 50° to 60°F. We prefer to use them within several weeks after their harvest, however.

To prepare acorn squashes, split them in half lengthwise and remove the seeds with a spoon, scraping the seed cavity to remove as much of the fibrousness as possible. Put the halves cut side down on a buttered or oiled baking sheet and bake the squashes for about 1¼ hours, until soft. The flesh can then be scooped out, or the squashes can be left intact and served as a simple vegetable on their own, with a little more melted butter. (Acorn squash seeds can be roasted and salted the way pumpkin seeds are.)

A butternut squash should be cut in two at the point where the squash becomes bulbous and round. The bulbous end contains the seed cavity, and should be cut in half and seeded like an acorn squash, then peeled of its hard skin with a sharp knife. Peeling the tight, hard skin of most squashes requires force, so be careful to keep your fingers out of the way of the knife blade. The neck can be peeled whole or cut in half, whichever is easier. The peeled flesh can then be cubed, diced, or sliced.

Winter squashes are easily grown in a home garden, but they require a good deal of space for their vines to spread out. In urban gardens, vines are sometimes trained up vertical frames and the fruits cradled in cloth slings tethered to the frames to support the weight.

274

Oven-roasted Squash with Garlic and Parsley

Choose a favorite winter squash—butternut, acorn, kabocha, Hubbard—and peel and seed it. Cut into 1-inch chunks and toss with olive oil, salt, and pepper. Spread the chunks evenly on a baking sheet and roast at 375°F. for 40 minutes, until tender throughout and lightly browned, stirring occasionally with a spatula to prevent burning.

Peel and chop very fine a few cloves of garlic and sauté in olive oil for just a minute, being careful not to brown. Toss the squash with the garlic and a handful of chopped parsley, taste and adjust the seasoning, and serve.

Note: You can also toss in chopped garlic with the squash before roasting, but in order not to burn the garlic, add a splash of water when you put the squash in the oven, and stir the squash more often as it roasts.

Winter Squash Purée

*2 pounds butternut, Delicata, or
  acorn squash
Salt and pepper
4 cloves garlic*

*6 sage leaves
¼ pound unsalted butter
¾ cup milk*

Preheat the oven to 400°F.

Cut the squashes in half lengthwise. Scoop out the seeds, season the flesh with salt and pepper, and fill the cavities with the garlic cloves, peeled, and the sage leaves. Place the squashes skin side down, in a shallow ovenproof dish, and add just enough water to barely cover the bottom, to prevent burning. Bake for about 45 minutes, or until completely tender. Allow to cool. Remove and discard the garlic and sage.

In a small saucepan, melt the butter in the milk over a low flame. Scoop the squash flesh out of the skin and put through a food mill or a ricer. Whisk in the milk and butter to give a soft texture to the purée. Taste and adjust seasoning.

Serves 4 to 6.

DELICATA SQUASH, POTATO, AND CELERY ROOT PURÉE

*2 Delicata squashes
  (about 1 pound)*
Olive oil
Salt and pepper
5 sprigs fresh thyme
4 cloves garlic

4 russet potatoes
1 medium celery root
1 cup cream
1 bay leaf
4 tablespoons unsalted butter

Preheat the oven to 375°F.

Split the squashes in half lengthwise and scrape out the seeds and pulpy fiber with a spoon. Brush the squashes with olive oil and season with salt and pepper. Put 1 sprig of the thyme and 1 clove of garlic in the cavity of each squash half, and bake on a baking sheet, cut side down, for about 40 minutes, until completely tender.

Peel the potatoes, cut them into medium chunks, and put them in a pot of salted water. Bring to a boil and simmer for about 30 minutes, until tender.

Peel the celery root, cut it into small chunks, and put them in a pot of water. Bring to a boil and simmer for about 30 minutes, until tender. In another saucepan heat the cream, the remaining sprig of thyme, the bay leaf, and the butter. Bring to a simmer, turn off the heat, and let the mixture steep.

When the potatoes are done, drain them and spread them out to dry on a baking sheet for about 10 minutes. When the celery root is done, drain it and pass it through a food mill or ricer. When the squash is done, remove it from the oven and discard the garlic and thyme. Scrape the flesh from the skin with a spoon. Put the squash, potatoes, and celery root purée through a food mill into a pot. Add more or less of the seasoned butter and cream mixture, depending on the desired consistency. Adjust the seasoning, reheat, and serve.

Serves 8.

OVEN-ROASTED PUMPKIN PURÉE

Choose a sugar pumpkin that is dense and heavy for its size. Cut it in half horizontally. Scrape out the seeds and place the halves cut side down on a baking sheet. Sprinkle with a few tablespoons of water and roast in a preheated 350°F. oven for 1 hour, until the pumpkin collapses and is tender through. Remove from the oven and cool. Scrape the flesh from the skin and purée. Season with salt and pepper, and with a bit of butter or cream, if you like. Serve as a savory vegetable with grills or roasts, or use the purée, unseasoned, to make fresh pumpkin pie.

ROASTED PUMPKIN SOUP

1 sugar pumpkin	*4 cloves garlic*
(about 3 pounds)	*1 quart chicken stock*
Olive oil	*Optional: unsalted butter*
Salt and pepper	*4 slices bread*
2 sprigs thyme	*2 tablespoons butter, melted*

Preheat the oven to 350°F.

Split the pumpkin and scrape out the seeds and pith, oil the cut surfaces with olive oil, and season generously with salt and pepper. Place the halves cut side down on a baking sheet, with a sprig of thyme and 2 unpeeled cloves of garlic tucked underneath each seed cavity. Roast in the oven for 45 minutes, or until completely tender. When the pumpkin is cool enough to handle, scoop out the flesh (or peel off the skins) and add the pulp to a soup pot along with the roasted garlic, squeezed out of its skin. Mash them together with a heavy wire whisk or a wooden spoon, add the chicken stock, and heat to a simmer. Taste and correct the seasoning. For a richer soup, add a little butter at this point.

While the pumpkin is baking, make black pepper croutons: Cut the slices of bread into ½-inch cubes and toss them in the melted butter; salt, spread on a baking sheet, and roast in a medium oven until brown and crisp; generously grind black pepper over them as soon as you take them out of the oven.

Serves 4.

WINTER SQUASH, CHANTERELLE, AND RED WINE PANADE

5 onions	*2 pounds acorn or butternut*
Olive oil or duck fat	*squash*
6 cloves garlic	*1 pound chanterelles*
2 bay leaves	*Salt and pepper*
12 sprigs thyme	*10 slices stale country-style*
1 cup red wine	*bread*
3 quarts chicken stock	*About 3 ounces Reggiano*
	Parmesan cheese

Begin by stewing the onions, peeled and sliced thin, over medium heat, in about ¼ cup of olive oil, duck fat, or a combination. When they have begun to soften, add the garlic cloves, also peeled and sliced thin; the bay leaves; and the thyme. Continue to cook the onions until they just begin to brown, 20 to 30 minutes. Add the red wine and reduce by half. Add the stock and simmer for 30 minutes.

Meanwhile, peel and seed the squash and cut it into ⅛-inch-thick slices. Clean, slice, and sauté the chanterelles in a few tablespoons of olive oil until they brown. Salt and pepper them, and add to the simmering stock.

In a sauté pan over medium heat, lightly brown the slices of bread in more olive oil or duck fat.

Preheat the oven to 375°F. and assemble the panade: Cover the bottom of a large casserole with half the bread slices and gently ladle in enough broth (including the onions and chanterelles) to cover. Make a single layer of the sliced squash on top and ladle in more of the broth, to cover. Make a layer with the rest of the bread, add more broth so that the top layer of bread is well soaked through, and finish by grating the Parmesan over the top to cover lightly. Bake, covered, for 45 minutes; then uncover and bake for about 45 minutes more, until well browned. To serve, scoop the panade into bowls and ladle more of the hot broth around it.

Serves 8 to 10.

Note: A simpler panade can be made with squash, onions, and chicken stock. Use the same method of layering stewed onions, sliced squash, and toasted bread and proceed as above. If you like, use a mixture of Gruyère and Parmesan cheeses.

Butternut Squash Pizza

*1 butternut squash
   (about 1 pound)*
Olive oil
Salt and pepper
2 cloves garlic
Pizza dough for 1 pizza

¼ cup grated mozzarella cheese
¼ cup grated Gruyère cheese
12 sprigs parsley
20 sage leaves
½ lemon

Preheat the oven to 400°F.

Slice off the top of the squash about ½ inch under the stem and slice just enough off the bottom to remove the remnants of the withered flower stem; be careful not to cut into the seed cavity. Split the squash in half crosswise just above the bulge. Stand each half end up and carefully cut away all the skin. Cut each portion in half lengthwise and scoop the seed and fiber from the lower half with a spoon. Cut the quarters crosswise into ¼-inch slices. The upper portions will yield half-moon slices, and the lower sections elongated C shapes.

Brush the slices with olive oil, season with salt and pepper, and arrange them in one layer on a baking sheet. Roast in the oven for 30 to 60 minutes, checking from time to time. The roasting time will vary according to the sugar and moisture content and the density of the squash. It is done when lightly browned and tender to the touch.

Meanwhile, peel and chop fine the garlic and add to about ¼ cup olive oil. When the squash slices are done, remove from the oven. Put a pizza stone in the oven and boost the heat to 450° to 500°F.

Roll out a circle of pizza dough, brush with the olive oil and garlic, and sprinkle evenly with the mozzarella and Gruyère. Arrange the slices of cooked squash over the cheese. Bake the pizza for about 10 minutes, until the crust is browned and the cheeses have melted.

While the pizza is baking, chop the parsley leaves. Fry the sage leaves briefly in hot olive oil, then drain them on an absorbent towel. When the pizza is done, garnish with the sage leaves, the chopped parsley, and a squeeze of lemon.

This is a very rich pizza, and is best served in small portions, as an appetizer.

Makes one 12-inch pizza.

Squash Ravioli with Fried Sage

The flavors of sage and sweet squash have a natural affinity for one another. When whole sage leaves are quickly fried in olive oil until crisp, or cut and fried in butter, their pungent taste becomes subtle instead of overpowering.

1 medium acorn or butternut squash (about 1 pound) or 1 small sweet pumpkin
Salt and pepper
½ lemon
1 sprig thyme
2 sprigs parsley
1 bunch fresh sage

2 tablespoons unsalted butter
½ cup grated Reggiano Parmesan cheese
5 sheets fresh pasta, rolled out to 6 by 24 inches (about 1 pound, or a 2-egg recipe)
Peanut oil
Extra-virgin olive oil

Preheat the oven to 375°F.

Cut the squash in half lengthwise and scoop out and discard the seeds. Lightly season the inside with salt and pepper and place the squash halves cut side down on a lightly oiled baking sheet. Bake for about 1 hour, or until the squash can be pierced easily with a sharp knife.

While the squash is baking, grate or chop fine the zest of the lemon. Chop the thyme and parsley and 3 or 4 leaves of the sage.

When the squash is cool enough to handle, scoop out the flesh and purée in a food processor or pass it through the fine disk of a food mill. Measure 2 cups of the squash purée. If there is extra, save it to add to a soup or a potato and celery root purée. If the squash purée seems at all watery, you must dry it out, or it will make the ravioli soggy. Dry out the purée by cooking it slowly in a small sauté pan over medium heat. Stir the purée frequently until it is a thick paste. Remove from the heat and stir in the butter, chopped herbs, half the Parmesan, and the lemon zest. Season with salt and pepper. If the purée seems overly sweet, add a few drops of lemon juice. Allow the purée to cool thoroughly.

Prepare the pasta dough by rolling out the 6 by 24-inch sheets about twice as thin as you would for a regular noodle. (Keep in mind that the dough will be folded over on itself to form the ravioli.) Either fill a pastry bag with the squash purée or use a tablespoon to fill the ravioli.

Place a sheet of pasta on a floured surface and squeeze or spoon about 1 tablespoonful of filling for each ravioli along the length of the dough, just below the center of the sheet, spacing the mounds about 2 inches apart. You should be able to fit 6 spoonfuls on a sheet. Using an atomizer, lightly mist the entire sheet of pasta with water. Lift the 2 top corners of the pasta and fold it in half over the filling. Be careful not to press down on the pasta and seal the edges just yet. Very lightly tap each mound of filling to spread it out a bit. Starting at one end of the pasta, gently but firmly press around each mound of filling, pressing out the air as you go. The goal is to have each ravioli completely sealed without any pockets of air. Use a pastry wheel or a sharp knife to cut the ravioli apart, trimming their edges to about ½ inch. Put the finished ravioli on a lightly floured cookie sheet and refrigerate if you aren't going to cook them right away.

Heat about ½ inch of peanut oil in a small sauté pan until it is hot but not smoking. Drop the remaining sage leaves, a few at a time, into the oil and fry them until the leaves are just beginning to get crisp but have not begun to brown at all, 5 to 10 seconds. (If the sage overcooks, it will be bitter.) Remove them with a slotted spoon and drain on paper towels.

To cook the ravioli, bring a large pot of salted water to a boil, reduce the heat to a simmer, and carefully drop the ravioli into the pot. Simmer gently for 3 to 5 minutes. Check for doneness by tearing off a little piece and eating it. Scoop the ravioli out of the water with a slotted spoon and place them on a warm serving platter. Drizzle a little extra-virgin olive oil over the ravioli, scatter the fried sage leaves over, and sprinkle with the rest of the Parmesan. Grind some pepper over them if you like, squeeze a little lemon juice over, and serve. The ravioli can also be served in a chicken or vegetable broth, garnished with fresh chopped herbs.

Serves 6.

SAGE AND BUTTERNUT SQUASH RISOTTO

*1 medium butternut squash
  (about 1 pound)
About 24 sage leaves
Salt and pepper
7 to 8 cups chicken stock
1 medium onion*

*5½ tablespoons unsalted butter
2 cups Arborio rice
½ cup dry white wine
½ cup grated Reggiano
  Parmesan cheese, plus extra
  for garnish*

Carefully peel and clean the squash and dice it into very small cubes. Put the diced squash in a heavy-bottomed pot and cook with a few whole leaves of sage, salt, and 1 cup of the chicken stock. Cook until tender, but not too soft, about 5 to 10 minutes. Meanwhile, chop 6 sage leaves fine and cut the onion into small dice.

Heat the rest of the chicken stock and hold at a low simmer. In another, heavy-bottomed saucepan, heat 3 tablespoons of the butter, add the chopped sage, and cook for a minute or so; add the onion and continue to cook over medium heat until it is translucent, about 5 minutes. Add the rice and a pinch of salt and cook over low heat for about 3 minutes, stirring often, until the rice has turned slightly translucent. Turn up the heat and pour in the white wine. When the wine has been absorbed, add just enough hot stock to cover the rice, stir well, and reduce the heat.

Keep the rice at a gentle simmer and continue to add more stock, a ladle or two at a time, letting each addition be absorbed by the rice. While the rice is cooking, sauté the remaining sage leaves in butter until crisp.

After 15 minutes, the rice will be nearly cooked. Stir in the cooked squash, the rest of the butter, and the cheese. Continue cooking for 3 to 5 minutes. Taste for texture and consistency, adding a little more stock if needed. Adjust the seasoning. When done, serve in warm bowls and garnish with extra cheese and the sautéed sage leaves.

Serves 6 to 8.

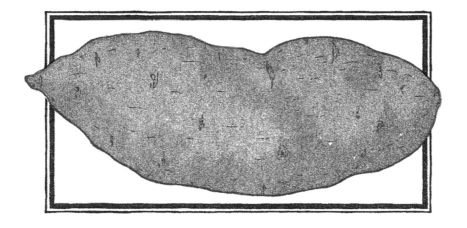

SWEET POTATOES 🍠

Season: Late fall through winter

The fleshy tubers most people call sweet potatoes or yams are related neither to Idaho bakers nor to true yams. They are members of the morning glory family, which you might guess from seeing their purple-tinted, heart-shaped leaves. Sweet potatoes are native to the American tropics. The first recorded mention by Europeans dates from Columbus's fourth voyage to the New World, when sweet potatoes were observed being consumed in the West Indies.

The types that form tubers with dry, mealy flesh are usually called sweet potatoes, and the ones with moister, denser flesh are usually called yams in the market, but they are all one botanical species, *Ipomoea batatas*. Sweet potatoes are shaped like very fat cigars, with tapering ends. The slightly rough and bumpy skin ranges in color from pale tan to a dusty red or purple, depending on the variety. The skin of the Garnet yam can be very dark red. The color of the flesh varies from the almost pure white of the Japanese sweet potato to the deep orange flesh of the Garnet.

Sweet potatoes are in season during the colder months of the year, so we often use them then, alone or accompanying other winter vegetables. Baked in their skins and mashed, they add a rich, spicy flavor to squash purées, and a little sweetness to mashed potatoes. Cubed and sautéed in clarified butter, they are satisfyingly crunchy and tasty as a complement to duck or pork. They can also be julienned and deep-fried, or baked with other root vegetables.

Because of their tropical origins, sweet potatoes grow most prolifically in those parts of the Southern states that a have long, warm growing season. After harvest, they continue to develop sweetness and flavor during several weeks of storage. The best sweet potatoes come to market from late fall through late winter. It is important to look sweet potatoes over carefully in the market, since they can spoil quickly. Shun those with blemishes or any signs of bruising. Instead, choose sound, medium sweet potatoes that are thick and heavy for their size. Squeeze them gently and choose only those that are firm. Skip the spindly ones.

Don't plan on keeping sweet potatoes for more than a few days at home. Any needless handling causes bruising and shortens their shelf life. Remember their tropical origins and keep them at a cool room temperature with good air circulation, not in the refrigerator.

The easiest way to cook sweet potatoes is simply to roast them in their skins. After they have cooled slightly, their skins can be peeled off with your fingers; any bits of skin still clinging to them can be sliced off with a paring knife. Or peel your sweet potatoes before cooking, with a small, sharp knife, and then slice, dice, or julienne them. Cook them shortly after peeling, because they oxidize and start to turn brown quite rapidly.

Because of the beauty of their vines, sweet potatoes are welcome in many a Southern garden. They require light, well-drained, sandy soil and a warm, sunny exposure. Even given the right growing conditions, they may not be practical for everyone, however, because they take up a good deal of space.

Sweet Potatoes with Lime and Cilantro

This recipe is an eye-opener to those who find sweet potatoes cloyingly sweet and unappealing. It is very fine served with Spinach and Yogurt Raita (page 270) and grilled fish.

Bake the sweet potatoes whole, in their skins, until tender, about 1 hour. When done, slit open the skin, and scoop out the flesh onto a serving dish. Season with salt, dot with a few pieces of butter if you like, squeeze fresh lime juice over, and shower with cilantro leaves.

Sweet Potato Purée with Roasted Garlic

1 head garlic	*Salt and pepper*
2 pounds sweet potatoes	*2 cups milk*
2 pounds russet potatoes	*¼ to ½ cup extra-virgin olive oil*

First roast the garlic: Wrap the head in foil, put in a preheated 400°F. oven and bake for 30 to 40 minutes, or until completely soft. (Test with the tip of a knife.) When cool, cut the top free from the head, separate the cloves, and set aside.

Peel and quarter the sweet potatoes and russet potatoes. Put them in a pot with a steamer insert. Season with a teaspoon of salt and steam over medium high to high heat until cooked, about 20 minutes. Drain, add the unpeeled roasted cloves of garlic, and purée through a food mill, using the fine disk. Return the purée to the pot and reheat over low heat. Scald the milk in a separate saucepan and add from 1 to 2 cups to the potatoes, depending on how dry they are. Then add the extra-virgin olive oil to taste, and season with salt and pepper. Serve immediately or keep warm in a double boiler.

Serves 6 to 8.

Sweet Potato Purée with Comice Pear

4 to 5 medium sweet potatoes	*1 sprig thyme*
1 Yellow Finn or russet potato	*1 bay leaf*
4 tablespoons unsalted butter	*1 firm, ripe Comice pear*
1 to 1½ cups milk or half milk	*Salt and pepper*
and half cream	

Peel and dice the sweet potatoes. Bring them to a rolling boil in salted water and cook until tender. Peel and dice the potato and cook separately in boiling salted water. Both the sweet potatoes and the other potatoes must be fully cooked, or the purée will not be smooth.

While they are cooking, melt the butter in the milk (or milk and cream), add the thyme and bay leaf, and steep for about 15 minutes so the milk will be flavored by the herbs. Peel and core the pear and cut into small dice. Pass the potatoes and sweet potatoes through a food mill. Strain out the herbs and add enough of the flavored milk to the purée to achieve the consistency you want. Gently fold in the diced pear, and season to taste with salt and pepper.

Serves 6 to 8.

SWISS CHARD ❧
See Chard (page 91)

THYME ❧
See Herbs (page 172)

TOMATOES 🏵

Season: Summer

The first ripe, locally grown tomatoes still come as a shock. They stimulate all the senses at once, and place us firmly in summer. And they are a reminder of how far agriculture has drifted away from seasonality. When tomatoes are available in the supermarket year round, we lose that keen anticipatory yearning for the juiciness of summer. Instead, we accept a pale approximation of a tomato, a tomato completely severed from our daily reality, grown by farmers thousands of miles away.

In our part of the country, tomatoes are a late summer crop. In other areas, where spring nights are warmer, local tomatoes arrive in the farmer's markets by midsummer. In any climate, the local tomatoes are best when they are most abundant (and also least expensive). Tomato season ends with the first frosts or cold rains of fall.

Almost all of the tomatoes in the market, from small cherry tomatoes to huge beefsteak types, belong to the species *Lycopersicon esculentum.* The exception is the tiny currant tomato, *L. pimpinellifolium,* which is no more than half an inch in diameter and is more closely related to the wild tomatoes still found in Central and South America, the ancestral home of all modern tomatoes.

The first tomatoes we get, toward midsummer, are the cherry types. Two favorites are the intensely sweet, highly flavorful red Sweet 100 and the dark orange Sungold. (By comparison, yellow cherry tomatoes and small red and yellow pear tomatoes are often mealy and lack flavor.) We use cherry tomatoes in salads, with green beans, shell beans, and basil; halved and dressed with herbs and vinaigrette as a sauce for the first fresh tomato pastas of the season; or to garnish a pizza along with cilantro and jalapeño peppers.

In our area, the most flavorful of the mid-season, main-crop tomatoes is the medium, red Early Girl. This popular variety bears well in areas with cool nights. But there are literally hundreds of varieties of large, round, red tomatoes, and others may be better adapted to the local growing conditions of other parts of the country. Talk to the growers at your local farmer's market, and ask especially about any heirloom varieties they might be growing.

We were introduced to the many colors of the tomato spectrum by the Chino family. For over a decade, every summer they have been sending us tomatoes in all sizes and all colors: red, orange, yellow, green, purple, brown, and even white. Now at many farmer's markets (at least in California) you can find the green and amber-striped variety Green Zebra, the bright orange Valencia and Golden Jubilee, and the brilliant yellow Taxi and Lemon Boy. One of our simplest and best salads in the summer is made up of thin slices of these variously colored and flavored tomatoes, dressed with extra-virgin olive oil and a little balsamic vinegar.

Peeled, seeded, and diced, tomatoes go into fish soups, fresh shell bean gratins, vegetable ragouts, and pasta. Sometimes in a whimsical mood we make tomato "cheeks" by cutting round slices from the outside of whole peeled tomatoes, and using them to surround a slice of poached or grilled fish with brilliant color.

Regardless of variety, size, or color, the best tomatoes are fully ripe, but not necessarily vine ripened. Experts say the very best way to ripen them is to pick them off the vine just as their color is starting to change from orange to red, and to keep them inside for four or five days, ideally at 59° to 70°F. This will maximize their sugar and acid content, which actually decreases if the fruit is left on the vine to finish ripening. Nor should they be left to ripen on a sunny windowsill. Normal indoor light is best.

At the market, most of the tomatoes you buy in season will be ripe already. Good ones will feel heavy for their size and will have a good balance of sweet and tart flavors; firm flesh that is neither crisp nor mealy; and a smooth, unblemished skin. When you cut into them, they are full of juice. Tomatoes for a salad should have tender skins if they are not going to be peeled.

Never store tomatoes in the refrigerator; cold temperatures kill their flavor. Keep them at room temperature. Perfectly ripe ones may keep only a day or two, but less ripe ones should keep for a few days to a week. If you find yourself with too many ripe tomatoes at once, make them into a quick sauce.

To prepare tomatoes for a salad, rinse and dry them carefully. Tough-skinned ones should be peeled. To peel tomatoes, drop them into boiling water for about fifteen seconds, just long enough to loosen the skin. Scoop them out of the boiling water and cool them in icy cold water to prevent the outer layer of flesh from cooking and softening. Then cut out the stem end with a small knife; the skin will easily slip off. Some recipes call for seeded tomatoes: Cut the peeled tomato in half horizontally and squeeze out the seeds and juice; if the tomato half needs to remain intact, you can coax the seeds out of their cavities with the help of a finger or the handle of a spoon. Except when you stuff them, whether or not you bother to seed tomatoes is largely a matter of taste.

Tomatoes may be the vegetable most commonly grown in home gardens. If you grow them yourself, you can be assured of a fresh-picked, ideally ripe fruit. One cherry tomato plant will sometimes produce enough fruit for a small household, but you will probably need at least six plants of the slicing types. Ask your neighbors and local farmers about varieties well suited to your area.

TOMATO SALAD

This is one of the best tastes of summer: tomatoes in season, ripe, juicy, and full-flavored. When tomatoes are plentiful, this salad is on the menu every day, varying slightly with the many possible garnishes. There is usually a mix of tomatoes of different colors, sizes, and flavors. Garlic croutons are always present—slices of levain bread or torn-up bite-size pieces, oiled, toasted, and rubbed with garlic while still warm from the oven. They are best mixed in with the tomatoes so that they absorb the juices.

Choose the best tomatoes you have that are fully ripe but not too soft. Slice large tomatoes in wedges or slices, cherry tomatoes in half. Moisten with balsamic vinegar (how much will depend on the sweetness and acidity of the tomatoes), season with salt and pepper, and drizzle generously with fine olive oil. Mix gently to keep the tomatoes intact and garnish with any of the following, singly or in combination: basil leaves, torn, cut into a chiffonade, or left whole; garlic croutons; slices of fresh mozzarella or the tiny bocconcini mozzarellas; sliced red onion; brandade and tapenade croutons.

GREEK SALAD

Combine sliced cucumbers, red onions, tomatoes, crumbled feta cheese, and black olives, and dress with fruity olive oil, roughly chopped marjoram or oregano, and black pepper.

CHAMPAGNE TOMATO SALAD

Macerate finely diced shallot in Champagne. Slice tomatoes, arrange them on a platter, sprinkle with the shallot, season with salt and pepper, and pour a little Champagne over all. Serve immediately.

PAN BAGNA

Summer on the French Riviera wouldn't be complete without this popular sandwich. It is a simple vegetable salad served in a bun, but its successful preparation demands a few obligatory elements. First and foremost, the bun: Ideally it is made of white bread, the size of an open hand, and it must have a fairly dense crumb and a soft but tenacious crust (especially for the bottom half, which will absorb all the juices). Any kind of white bread with a good crust will do—a baguette or an Italian loaf, for example. (If the crust is too hard, wrap it tightly and store overnight to soften it.) Focaccia is a good choice, too, if it's not too crumbly.

Slice the bun in half horizontally and drizzle as much olive oil on the inside of the bottom part as you see fit. Cover with a thick layer of sliced juicy tomatoes. Salt them and add a layer of sliced cucumbers, a few strips of bell pepper, and more salt. Top with slices of hard-boiled egg and pepper to taste. Finish with two or three fillets of anchovies and a few pitted niçoise olives. Close with the other half of the bun, and let it rest for half an hour, if you can; this sandwich should be eaten slightly soggy.

Of course you can change some of the ingredients, grill the bun, rub it with garlic, add a layer of rocket. Just use your imagination, but make sure you use enough olive oil and tomatoes to make it a *pan bagna*.

TOMATO AND BASIL BRUSCHETTA

Slice large, ripe tomatoes into thick slices and season well with salt and pepper. Fry thick slices of crusty country bread in a heavy skillet in ⅛ inch of olive oil until they are golden brown on both sides (or grill the bread over a fire). As the bread fries, you will need to add more oil to keep the pan from going dry. Remove the bread slices from the pan and drain them briefly on a towel. Rub the bread slices generously with garlic. Top each slice of bread with a thick tomato slice and a basil leaf, and season with salt and pepper. Drizzle a little extra-virgin olive oil over the tomatoes and serve.

GARDEN TOMATO AND GARLIC PASTA

As for all simple dishes, each of the ingredients for this sauce must be absolutely delicious. The sauce goes well with any kind of pasta, but long, thin noodles, such as spaghetti, spaghettini, or cappellini, are perhaps the nicest for this sauce.

3 ripe tomatoes
3 cloves garlic
1 small bunch parsley or basil
    (about ¼ pound)
½ cup fruity extra-virgin
    olive oil
¾ pound pasta
Salt and pepper

Cut out the stem ends and dice the perfectly ripe tomatoes. Peel and chop the garlic and chop the leaves of the parsley or basil. Have all the ingredients prepared and ready by the stove. Put the pasta on to cook in rapidly boiling salted water.

Heat the olive oil in a heavy-bottomed skillet until quite hot but not smoking. Throw the garlic into the oil. Right away, before the garlic starts to brown, add the tomatoes and stir; they will probably splatter a little. Add the parsley or basil and cook just a minute or two, until the tomatoes are warmed through and have started to relax. Season to taste with salt and pepper, and toss with the cooked pasta.

Serves 4.

ROASTED TOMATO SAUCE

An interesting way to deepen the tomato flavor of a simple sauce is to roast the tomatoes first. We often cook the tomatoes in the wood-burning pizza oven during the less hectic hours between lunch and dinner service. Roasted tomato purée can be made into sauce, as follows, or added to sautés, soups, and sauces for other dishes.

2 pounds ripe tomatoes
¼ cup olive oil
1 large yellow onion
1 medium leek
1 small carrot
1 head garlic

1 bay leaf
1 sprig thyme
1 small bunch basil
(about ¼ pound)
Salt and pepper

Preheat the oven to 350°F.

Cut out a cone at the stem end of the tomatoes to remove the core, and cut the tomatoes into quarters. Toss with half the olive oil. Put the tomatoes in a baking dish and roast them, uncovered, for 30 minutes, stirring a couple of times to encourage even cooking. The tomatoes are cooked when the flesh is very soft and the skin separates easily from the flesh.

Peel and slice the onion. Trim, wash, and dice the leek. Peel and dice the carrot. Cut the head of garlic in half horizontally.

Heat the remaining olive oil in a stainless steel or other nonreactive pot (aluminum reacts with the acid in tomatoes and spoils the flavor). Add the vegetables and the garlic and cook the vegetables over medium heat until completely soft, about 10 minutes. Add the roasted tomatoes and the herbs. Simmer, stirring frequently to prevent scorching, until the flavors come together, for 30 to 45 minutes. Pass the sauce through a food mill and adjust the seasoning with salt and pepper.

Makes about 1 quart.

Tomato and Cantal Cheese Galette

This is an hors d'oeuvre tart typical of many served at the restaurant, usually with a salad of spicy greens. Some other tart combinations are caramelized onions and potato, onion confit and grilled chicory, and wild mushrooms. A galette also makes an excellent light supper.

Cantal is an aged cheddar-style cheese from the southwestern mountains of France, with a mild nutty flavor. Typical American cheddars are too sharp to use as a substitute for it.

½ recipe Galette Dough (page 320)	*Salt and pepper*
3 large, ripe tomatoes	*1 bunch fresh basil*
2 medium yellow onions	*8 ounces Cantal cheese*
Extra-virgin olive oil	*1 egg yolk*
	2 tablespoons heavy cream

Roll out the pastry dough to a circle about 12 inches in diameter. Place it on a baking sheet without sides, lined with parchment paper, and chill in the refrigerator. Cut out the stem end of the tomatoes and slice them ⅛ inch thick. Set aside on a towel to drain. Peel and slice thin the onions and sauté them in olive oil until softened. Season with salt and pepper and a handful of the basil leaves, chopped. Let cool completely.

Preheat the oven to 375°F.

Take the tart shell out of the refrigerator and sprinkle the dough with half the cheese, grated. Spread the cooled onions over the cheese, leaving a 1-inch border around the edge. Put a layer of whole basil leaves on top of the onions. Arrange the tomato slices, slightly overlapping, on top. Season with salt and pepper, sprinkle over the rest of the cheese, grated, and drizzle generously with olive oil.

Working around the circle of dough, fold the edge of the dough up and over to make a shell around the filling; brush the dough with the egg yolk and cream, whisked together with a fork. Bake for 50 minutes to 1 hour on the bottom rack of the oven, until the bottom of the crust is well browned. Cover with foil if the tart is browning too quickly.

Take the tart out of the oven and immediately slide it off the baking sheet and parchment paper and onto a cooling rack. (If you leave the tart on the pan, it will steam and get too soft.) Garnish with the rest of the basil leaves, cut into a chiffonade, drizzle with more olive oil, slice, and serve immediately as a first course, alone or with a garden salad.

Serves 8.

TOMATO, ONION, AND POTATO GRATIN

1 medium yellow onion	*1 tablespoon chopped thyme*
2½ pounds red or Yellow Finn	*leaves*
potatoes	*3 tablespoons extra-virgin*
1½ pounds tomatoes	*olive oil*
2 cloves garlic	*2 tablespoons white wine*
Salt and pepper	*1½ cups chicken stock*

You will need a 9-inch square or oval gratin dish with 2-inch sides. Peel the onion, cut it in half lengthwise, and slice it as thin as possible. Peel and slice the potatoes ⅛ inch thick, and hold in cold water until ready to use. Cut out the stem end of the tomatoes and slice them ⅛ inch thick. Peel the garlic and slice thin.

Preheat the oven to 375°F. Lightly oil the gratin dish and distribute the onion slices evenly over the bottom. Season with salt and pepper. Drain the potatoes and arrange half of them over the onions, overlapping like shingles. Season with salt and pepper and half of the thyme. Make a layer of the tomato slices on top of the potato slices, salt and pepper them, and sprinkle with the rest of the thyme and the garlic slices. Finish with a final layer of overlapping potatoes and more salt and pepper. Drizzle with the olive oil and the white wine, and add enough chicken stock to come two thirds of the way up the sides of the gratin. (You may need to add more liquid later, but you must allow for the juice the tomatoes will give off.)

Cover with foil and bake for 40 minutes. Uncover and press down on the mixture, flattening it to ensure that the top layer of potatoes is moistened. The liquid will emulsify somewhat as it continues to cook. Bake uncovered for another 40 minutes, or until a knife pierces through easily and the top is golden brown. Serve either warm or at room temperature.

Serves 6 to 8.

Italian Tomato and Bread Soup (Pappa al Pomodoro)

2 small onions
4 to 6 cloves garlic
½ to ¾ cup extra-virgin olive oil
Salt
2 pounds very ripe tomatoes

1 small bunch basil
*   (about ¼ pound)*
2 to 2½ cups bread crumbs
Reggiano Parmesan cheese

Peel and dice the onions and peel and chop the garlic. Sauté the onions in about ½ cup of the olive oil until soft. Add the garlic and some salt and cook a few minutes more.

Make sure you choose very ripe tomatoes, or the soup may be too acidic. Core and chop them roughly. When the onions and garlic are done, remove and set aside one third of the mixture. Add the tomatoes to the remaining onion mixture, along with the basil stems (reserving the leaves), and cook for about 15 minutes to make a nice tomato sauce. Pass through a food mill and return to the pan.

Add the reserved onions and garlic to the tomato sauce. Over very low heat, stir in about 1½ cups of the bread crumbs. (The best bread crumbs to use for this are from light, white Italian-style bread that is fairly dry and finely crumbled.) After 10 minutes, turn off the heat and let the soup sit for 10 minutes. As the bread crumbs absorb liquid, the soup will slowly thicken. The dryness and density of the bread crumbs, the soupiness of the tomatoes, and your own personal preference will dictate how much bread to add. The denser the crumbs, the longer the soup takes to thicken and the less you will need. If you have very dense bread, make finer crumbs and cook the soup more slowly. If the soup thickens too much, thin it out with a little water.

Chop a handful of the reserved basil leaves and stir them into the soup, with a little more olive oil if you like, and adjust the seasoning. Serve hot or cold, garnished with a thread of olive oil, grated Parmesan, and a whole basil leaf if you wish.

Serves 6.

CHILLED TOMATO SOUP

4 pounds ripe tomatoes   *2 stalks celery*
2 tablespoons salt   *3 shallots*
1 small cucumber   *White wine vinegar*

Cut the tomatoes in quarters, put them in a bowl, add all the salt, and mix well. Peel and seed the cucumber, clean the celery, and peel the shallots. Cut them all into fine dice. Put the shallots in a small bowl, add just enough of the vinegar to cover, and set aside.

After about half an hour the salt will have softened the tomatoes. Mash them with a wooden spatula and work them through a food mill to obtain a thick tomato juice. Add the shallots, celery, and cucumber. Season to taste with salt and vinegar. (Use balsamic vinegar if the tomatoes need a little sweetness.) Refrigerate over ice and serve well chilled.

Serves 4 to 6.

Note: You can use different-colored tomatoes—for example, Early Girls, yellow Taxis, and Green Zebras—and prepare them in separate batches. Then pour them carefully into the same bowl for a tricolor soup that will also allow you to appreciate the distinctive flavor of each kind of tomato.

A richer, spicier version can be made by adding olive oil and mashed garlic to the tomato base, and by garnishing the soup with diced hot and bell peppers.

PASTA WITH TOMATO CONFIT

Allow about 2 tomatoes per serving. Make a bed of basil leaves in the bottom of an ovenproof dish that will hold the tomatoes snugly in one layer. Peel and core the tomatoes and place them core side down on the basil. Lightly salt and pepper. Pour in enough extra-virgin olive oil to come halfway up the sides of the tomatoes. Bake for 1½ hours in a preheated 350°F. oven, until the tomatoes are soft and lightly caramelized and have infused the oil with their perfume. Season to taste and serve spooned over cooked and drained fresh noodles.

BAKED EARLY GIRL TOMATOES

Choose small Early Girl tomatoes (or Stupice, Carmello, Green Zebra, or large red cherry tomatoes) that are 2 to 3 inches in diameter and perfectly ripe. Core them, score the bottoms, and parboil for 30 seconds in boiling water, until the skins just begin to peel away from the flesh. Scoop out the tomatoes, put them in a bowl of ice water and let them chill for 5 minutes. Peel off the skins and place the tomatoes in a shallow gratin dish. Drizzle extra-virgin olive oil and splash a little balsamic vinegar over the tomatoes and sprinkle evenly with chopped parsley. Intersperse thin slices of garlic among the tomatoes and strew sprigs of thyme around the dish. Season liberally with salt and pepper. Bake the tomatoes uncovered in a preheated 400°F. oven for 35 minutes or so. They will be browned but still intact.

FRESH TOMATO JUICE

Wash about 4 pounds of ripe tomatoes and cut out their stem ends and any blemished parts. Cut the tomatoes in half and put them into a stainless steel saucepan. Cover, bring to a boil, and simmer until the tomatoes are soft and juicy, about 30 minutes.

Strain the juice through a sieve into a pitcher, shaking the strainer to force a little of the pulp through. For thicker juice, let the juice stand so the thicker juice settles, and pour off the clear liquid. Pass the unstrained pulp, skins, and seeds through a food mill twice to make a purée. For very thick juice, add the purée to the strained juice in the pitcher.

TURNIPS &

Season: Fall through spring

Turnips (*Brassica rapus*) are available throughout the year, but the sweetest and most tender come to market only when growing conditions are most temperate, in the spring and fall. The freshest young turnips have only a mild suggestion of the heat associated with some of their cousins in the mustard family, such as radishes or rocket. The tops of young turnips are tender enough to steam or stir-fry for cooked greens.

Like radishes, turnips come in many shapes and colors. Varieties are often divided into two categories, Japanese and French. You may be familiar with the round, white Japanese varieties, usually called Tokyo, as well as with the more tapered French types with purple shoulders, such as Purple Top. However, our friends the Chinos have introduced us to turnips with brilliant red skins and pearly white flesh, turnips that are pale yellow both inside and out, and skinny, foot-long tapered turnips with rosy-purple tops. There are also varieties grown only for their greens.

Rutabagas are not simply large, yellow turnips but a different species, *Brassica napus*. They are best in late fall and winter after a period of cold weather, when their true sweetness and flavor have developed. They are used much like large, starchy turnips.

Sweet, young turnips are especially welcome at the restaurant in the late fall, when the summer's vegetables are a fading memory. Steamed turnips add a background of delicate spiciness to vegetable ragouts and Moroccan tagines. When roasted with other vegetables, such as carrots, celery root, and parsnips, their flavor adds balance. We often make gratins combining turnips with potatoes, and we frequently mash chunks of larger turnips into purées, with potatoes and celery root. Pickled

turnips are a wonderful foil for roast duck or pork. Even large and starchy turnips are completely transformed when they are made into a turnip confit—thinly sliced and sautéed slowly in a little duck or goose fat until they are well browned and perfectly tender.

Because turnips thrive when it is uniformly cool, without much fluctuation of temperature, they are at their best in spring and fall. Drought and heat cause them to become tough and bitter. Even under the best of conditions, turnips develop thicker skins and stronger flavor as they grow. Early spring and fall are the times to look for the tiny turnips that are best for steaming whole, with their tops still attached. Later in the season they may have to be peeled and cut up before cooking. In winter you may find only large, topless turnips that have been held in storage.

At the market choose turnips that feel firm and smooth. Their tops should look fresh and green. Avoid turnips with yellowing or wilted tops: these are signs that they have been stored too long, and they inevitably will have lost sweetness. In particular shun the ones whose tops appear to be bolting, because they will surely be woody. Big, topless turnips should be firm, and the cuts where their tops were chopped off should look fresh.

The preparation of turnips for cooking depends on their type and maturity. The very smallest, tender-skinned ones need only a thorough washing of roots and tops before cooking to rid them of any traces of sand. Larger, thicker-skinned turnips will need to have their tops cut off (the greens can be saved to be cooked separately), and they will need to be peeled. When peeling the largest turnips, pare off the outermost eighth of an inch or so of flesh along with the peel; it may be tough and fibrous.

Because they mature quickly, turnips are good candidates for the home garden. They can be used to fill in places in your garden that would otherwise be vacant in early spring or at the end of summer. Some of the Tokyo turnips will be ready for harvest in less than a month. Try planting some of the varieties with unusual shapes and colors, too. The long, tapered Hinona-kabu, for example, does well when sown in late summer.

CARAMELIZED TURNIPS

Preheat the oven to 425°F.

Turnips that are sufficiently young and tender need only be rinsed and dried before cooking; older purple-top turnips will need to be peeled. Cut the turnips into halves, or quarters if they are small. Big ones should be cut in half lengthwise and the halves sliced into wedges.

Toss the turnips in a bowl with a generous splash of olive oil and salt and pepper. Spread them out in an even layer on a baking sheet and roast them for about 10 minutes, then toss them once (if tossed or turned more frequently, they tend to break apart as they become tender). Roast for 5 minutes more and check for doneness—depending on the water content of the turnips, they can take from 15 to 30 minutes. The turnips are done when they are fork tender and nicely caramelized.

TURNIP AND POTATO GRATIN

5 medium Yellow Finn or russet potatoes	*Butter*
	Salt and pepper
10 medium turnips	*2 cups heavy cream*

Preheat the oven to 375°F.

Peel and slice the potatoes ¼ inch thick, with a knife or on a mandolin, and put them in a bowl of cold water to prevent them from discoloring.

Peel the turnips if their skin is tough and slice them ¼ inch thick. Butter the sides and bottom of a 9 by 12-inch baking dish. Drain the potatoes and pat them dry. Layer the potatoes and turnips alternately in the baking dish, seasoning each layer with salt and pepper. Pour in enough of the cream, or half cream and half chicken stock, to barely cover the vegetables. Bake uncovered for 40 minutes. Rotate the dish periodically for even browning.

Serves 6 to 8.

BRAISED BABY TURNIPS AND CARROTS

A very simple stewing is all that is wanted for very tiny and delicate turnips and carrots. Wash and trim the vegetables. Both should be tender enough to make peeling unnecessary. Trim off the carrot tops but leave a half inch or so of the stalks. Leave the tender turnip greens attached, trimming off only the leaves that are wilted or damaged. Put the young roots in a saucepan with a little butter and water, and stew gently, covered, until softened but not overcooked. Season with salt and pepper and serve. This is especially nice if you have a variety of carrots of different shapes and colors.

TURNIP AND TURNIP GREEN SOUP

1 yellow onion	½ teaspoon chopped thyme
1 clove garlic	leaves
1 tablespoon olive oil	1 small piece prosciutto or
1 tablespoon unsalted butter	smoked bacon
2 bunches young turnips with	8 cups rich chicken stock
greens (about 2½ pounds)	Salt and pepper
1 bay leaf	Reggiano Parmesan cheese

Peel and slice the onion and garlic thin. Put in a nonreactive pot with the olive oil and butter and 1 tablespoon water and stew, covered, until they are soft and translucent. Trim off the stems and greens from the turnips and reserve the greens. If the turnips are very young and tender, it is unnecessary to peel them. Trim off their roots, slice the turnips thin and add them to the pot. Stew them for a few minutes, until they begin to soften. Add the bay leaf, thyme, prosciutto or bacon, chicken stock, and salt and pepper. Cover and simmer over low heat for about ½ hour.

Wash the turnip greens and cut them into ½-inch-wide strips and stir them into the soup. Simmer the soup for another 10 minutes or so, until the greens are soft and tender. Garnish the soup with a few curls of shaved Parmesan.

Serves 8.

Note: Water or vegetable stock may be substituted for the chicken stock, and the prosciutto omitted for a meatless version of this soup.

YOUNG TURNIP AND SWEET POTATO SOUP

2 leeks	6 bunches small young turnips
1 medium onion	with greens (2 to 3 pounds)
4 tablespoons unsalted butter,	2 russet potatoes
plus 1 teaspoon	1 small sweet potato
Salt and pepper	2 quarts chicken stock

Remove the coarse outer leaves and dark green tops from the leeks, rinse thoroughly, and dice. Peel and dice the onion. Sauté the leeks and onion over medium heat in the butter and cook until soft. Season with salt and pepper.

Trim the greens from the turnips. Reserve the greens of 2 bunches to garnish the soup, and save the rest for another meal. Peel and dice the turnips and potatoes. If the turnips are tender, it is not necessary to peel them. Add the turnips and potatoes to the onions and leeks and stew gently for 5 minutes, stirring to prevent sticking. Add the chicken stock and simmer until the potatoes and turnips are fully cooked, about 15 minutes.

Purée in a blender until smooth or pass through a food mill. Season to taste with salt and pepper.

Wash the reserved turnip greens and chop roughly. Sauté over high heat in the teaspoon of butter until just wilted. Purée the greens in a blender or pass through a food mill. Serve the soup warm and add a spoonful of the puréed greens to each bowl. Stir the greens into the soup to turn it pale green.

Serves 6 to 8.

WATERCRESS AND GARDEN CRESS 🦋

Season: Spring and fall

Watercress grows wild in streams in North America, and it is easily grown under cultivation. But depending on when and where it grows, it can be sweet, spicy, and tender, or it can be inedible. The best watercress is young watercress, just gathered from the farm or from the stream, in the cooler months of the year.

In addition to true watercress, *Nasturtium officinale,* there are other cresses we like to use. Garden cress, *Lepidium sativum,* has a similar peppery flavor and leaf shape, but it is more tender, without the crunchiness of watercress. One cultivar of garden cress, with finely cut leaves, is known as peppergrass or curly cress. Land cress and upland cress are the names of yet another species, *Barbarea verna,* which is very similar to garden cress.

All these plants are members of the mustard family. They grow quickly and develop their sweet, spicy flavor, without becoming impossibly hot or bitter, only when they have cool temperatures and a steady supply of water. Therefore the best cress is to be found in the spring and fall.

When we have beautiful watercress, we put a little bouquet of it—raw and undressed—on the plate with meat or fish. It is particularly good with lamb, duck, and smoked salmon. The sweetest, mildest watercress or garden cress is also good in salads, both alone and mixed with other greens. We make a purée of watercress soup that is a refreshing, brilliant green concentration of watercress flavor. (A watercress purée can be swirled into leek and potato soup, adding color and another dimension of flavor.)

Once harvested, all kinds of cress lose their sweetness quickly, leaving only the hot, bitter flavor components. It is essential to taste cress before you buy it. Choose watercress with small leaves and thin stems, avoiding any that may be flowering. The tiny flowers are attractive, but bolting watercress is extremely peppery and bitter.

While watercress is usually sold bunched, garden cresses are usually sold as cut leaves. Choose cress that has small, fresh-looking leaves. Don't buy any that has formed stalks, which indicates bolting.

Use fresh cress as soon as possible. Wash, dry, and refrigerate cress as you would a delicate lettuce.

To prepare watercress, pull off and discard any large roots that may still be attached; any wilted or discolored leaves; and the heavier stalks, saving only the tiny roots (which are perfectly edible), the healthiest leaves, and the tender stems. Wash and drain just before use. Garden cress needs only a quick sorting through for any yellow or wilted leaves, and a rinse.

Watercress can be grown in any home garden with an ample water supply. It can be grown in flats or pots, and the tiny sprigs can be harvested for a garnish when they are no more than two inches high. You can transplant and encourage watercress to naturalize in permanently wet places in your garden. Garden cress grows very quickly and can be sown in any odd corner not needed for other crops; it can be harvested in two weeks.

CURLY CRESS AND BLOOD ORANGE SALAD

Because this salad is so simple, its success depends on the quality of its two main ingredients. The cress should be tender and not too peppery; the blood oranges should be sweet and tangy.

2 small shallots
1 tablespoon Champagne
  vinegar
Juice of 1 blood orange
¼ teaspoon salt

3 tablespoons extra-virgin
  olive oil
4 blood oranges
3 handfuls curly cress, washed
  and dried
Black pepper

Peel and dice the shallots fine and put them in a small bowl with the Champagne vinegar, orange juice, and salt. Let the mixture sit for 10 minutes and then whisk in the olive oil.

With a sharp paring knife, trim off the top and bottom of each orange. Pare off the rest of the peel, making sure to remove all the pith while wasting as little of the orange as possible. Slice crosswise into ¼-inch rounds.

Arrange the orange slices on a large serving platter. Sprinkle the sprigs of curly cress on top. Drizzle the dressing evenly over the entire salad and grind a little black pepper over it. Serve immediately.

Serves 6.

WATERCRESS SALAD WITH BELGIAN ENDIVE AND APPLE

3 bunches small-leaved
  watercress (about 2 pounds)
2 Belgian endives
1 apple
Juice of 1 lemon
1 tablespoon Champagne
  vinegar

2 tablespoons Dijon mustard
Salt and pepper
4 tablespoons olive oil
Optional: 1 tablespoon heavy
  cream

Wash the watercress and remove any large stems. Dry and put in the refrigerator. Remove any damaged outer leaves from the endives. Quarter them and cut away the core. Cut the endive quarters lengthwise into long strips.

Peel and quarter the apple. Cut out the core from the apple quarters, slice them thin, and cut the slices into julienne.

Make a vinaigrette in a salad bowl by whisking together the lemon juice, vinegar, mustard, and salt and pepper. Let stand for a few minutes, then whisk in the olive oil. Add the watercress, endive, and apple to the bowl and toss thoroughly to coat everything with the vinaigrette. Taste, and correct the seasoning. If the vinaigrette is too sharp, add the heavy cream.

Serves 4.

WATERCRESS SOUP

2 bunches watercress	*4 cups chicken stock or water*
(about 1 pound)	*A few parsley leaves*
1 yellow onion	*A few tarragon leaves*
1 clove garlic	*Salt and pepper*
2 tablespoons olive oil	*Crème fraîche*

Pick through the watercress and discard any thick stems.

Peel and slice the onion and garlic thin and stew them in the olive oil, covered, until soft and translucent. Add the chicken stock, bring to a simmer and cook, uncovered, for 10 minutes. After 5 minutes, add the parsley. Have ready a large bowl half filled with ice and a smaller bowl, preferably stainless steel, that will nest inside it and rest on the ice.

Remove the soup from the heat, add the watercress and tarragon, and allow the soup to stand for 5 minutes, no longer. Immediately purée the soup in a blender and pour it through a medium-fine sieve into the bowl on ice. Stir the soup until it is at room temperature, then remove it from the ice and season to taste with salt and pepper.

Reheat the soup to a simmer just before serving; do not boil it. Ladle the soup into bowls and garnish lightly with lines of lightly salted crème fraîche streaked on the surface.

Serves 6.

Note: This recipe also makes excellent spinach soup: just substitute tender young spinach for the watercress.

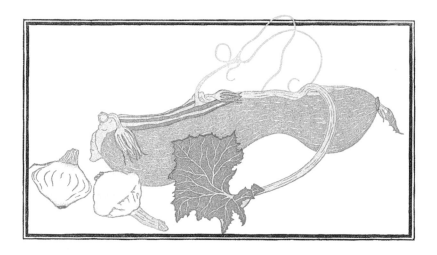

ZUCCHINI AND
OTHER SUMMER SQUASHES &

Season: Summer

The season for summer squash is, of course, summer. We use summer squash from the time the first blossoms appear on the plants in late spring until the first cold days of fall.

The familiar dark green zucchini, the round scalloped pattypan, and the slightly warty, pale yellow crookneck are all immature fruit of *Cucurbita pepo*. This species includes many cultivated varieties of squash and pumpkins. (See Squashes, Winter, page 273.) The summer squash varieties we serve most often include the yellow pattypan called Sunburst and both green and yellow zucchini. We also use Cocozelle, which has shallow ridges of green and white, and Ronde de Nice, a round green variety the size of a tennis ball. Tromboncino is an unusual Italian variety that is thin, sinuous, and pale green, and which has dense, tasty flesh that is good sliced thin and eaten raw.

We often serve the first squash blossoms fried, with late-spring vegetables. Later in the summer, squash blossoms are stuffed with ricotta, steamed, and served in a broth with basil and tomatoes or corn. A chiffonade of squash blossoms makes a colorful garnish for corn soup.

The squash fruits themselves start to appear in the summer. This is the season for squash gratins with cream and Parmesan and for squash *tians* with onions, garlic, tomatoes, and eggplant. Diced squash and corn, seasoned with hot chilies, is wonderful with whole-wheat pasta. And ratatouille must have summer squash in it.

Ideally, squash blossoms should be used the day they are picked. The male flowers, those without tiny squashes attached to them, are generally preferred for stuffing. If you can't use them right away, put the stems in water, as with any other cut flower. The freshest blossoms should be vibrant orange, not bruised, and wide open. Blossoms even one day old will have closed up and the petals will begin to stick together. At this point they are difficult to stuff, but may still be good in soup or cut up in chiffonade.

The skin of a summer squash should be tender enough to be pierced easily with a fingernail. Choose squashes with bright color that are heavy for their size. Avoid the largest squashes on the pile; they will tend to be watery and seedy. Also avoid any squashes that are starting to wrinkle, or show bruises. Because the skins of summer squashes are very tender, a few surface scratches are almost unavoidable.

Unless you are sure of the origin of your squashes, they should be rinsed and dried with a towel before using. Otherwise, rub any dust off with a damp towel. Trim the stem and flowering end with a knife before proceeding with the recipe. Squashes that have been cut for later use can be covered with a damp towel and refrigerated for several hours.

Summer squashes are well known for their abundance in home gardens. If you grow some of your own, make a point of harvesting many of their blossoms, and try the more unusual varieties to share with neighbors. Most zucchini and pattypan plants are quite compact, and the Italian Tromboncino types grow well on trellises.

STUFFED SQUASH BLOSSOM SAUTÉ

Open the blossoms wide and check for bugs. Inside each blossom place a piece of mozzarella cheese about the size of your thumb and a pinch of chopped herbs (basil, parsley, marjoram, etc.). Close the petals snug around the stuffing, twisting the ends together. Quickly dip each blossom, one by one, first in beaten egg, and then into fine corn flour, or masa harina. Fry the blossoms in hot olive oil, without crowding, in a cast iron pan, turning them over as they brown. Drain on towels and serve hot sprinkled with a little salt.

SUMMER SQUASH BLOSSOMS STUFFED WITH RICOTTA

½ pound ricotta cheese
1 large egg
1½ tablespoons melted butter
About ½ cup grated Reggiano
   Parmesan cheese
¼ teaspoon salt

1 tablespoon flour
8 squash blossoms
Butter
A few sage leaves
Optional: Chicken broth

Any summer squash blossoms will do for this dish, including the blossoms that have tiny squashes attached.

To prepare the stuffing, beat the ricotta, egg, butter, Parmesan, and salt together until smooth. Taste for seasoning; the mixture should be fairly highly seasoned. Stir in the flour and set aside.

Check inside the blossoms for any critters; as we all know, insects love flowers. Fill the clean blossoms with the stuffing. The easiest way is with a pastry bag; otherwise, a spoon will do. Fill them about three quarters full and gently squeeze the petals together at the top.

Poach them in gently boiling water until the filling is set, about 6 minutes. You can feel the doneness by gently squeezing the blossoms: they are done when you feel resistance all the way through. Drain them and put them on a serving platter. Garnish with melted butter that has had chopped sage gently heated in it, or serve them in bowls with chicken broth boiled with butter and sage (1 tablespoon butter for each cup of broth) poured over the squash blossoms.

Serves 4.

SUMMER SQUASH WITH GARLIC AND HERBS

Choose a mixture of very fresh squashes: yellow crookneck, green and yellow zucchini, and little pattypan squash. Trim and slice or cut into julienne. Sauté in olive oil in a sauté pan until tender and just beginning to brown. Add a generous amount of freshly chopped garlic and basil or marjoram, and season with salt and pepper. Cook just a minute more, until the garlic releases its aroma; squeeze over a bit of lemon juice, and serve.

Summer Squash and Squash Blossom Risotto

¼ pound summer squashes
6 tablespoons unsalted butter
6 squash blossoms
1 medium onion
7 to 8 cups chicken stock
2 cups Italian rice (Arborio,
   Carnaroli, Baldo)
⅓ cup white wine

Salt and pepper
1 tablespoon chopped sage
1 tablespoon chopped marjoram
1 tablespoon chopped savory
½ cup grated Reggiano
   Parmesan cheese, plus more
   for garnish

Cut the squashes (a variety of baby ones is nice for color and flavor variation) into small cubes, wedges, or half-circles, depending on their sizes and shapes. All the pieces should be bite size, so they will fit easily on a spoon.

Heat about 2 tablespoons of the butter in a heavy sauté pan, and sauté the squash over lively heat until golden brown. Slice the squash blossoms into thin slices, cutting from tip to stem, using all of the blossom.

Peel and dice the onion and cook in about 2 tablespoons of the butter in a heavy-bottomed pot. In another pot, warm the stock and keep it at a very low simmer.

When the onion is soft, add the rice and cook for a couple of minutes. Add the white wine and cook, stirring, until the wine has been nearly absorbed. Season well. Begin to add ladlefuls of stock, about a cupful at a time, letting each addition be almost all absorbed by the rice before adding the next. Be sure not to let the rice stick and scorch. It should cook over medium-low heat, and should never be allowed to dry out.

After about 10 minutes, when the rice begins to soften but is still just a bit hard in the center, stir in the cooked squash, the squash blossoms, and the herbs. After 2 minutes more, stir in the rest of the butter and the Parmesan. Add more stock if needed, but in small amounts, keeping in mind the consistency you want to achieve. It should be loose and a little saucy, but not soupy. Adjust the seasoning. When done, serve in warm bowls with a generous dusting of Parmesan as a garnish.

Serves 6 to 8 as a first course; serves 4 to 6 as a main dish.

Zucchini Fritters

1 pound small green zucchini
Salt and pepper
1 clove garlic
1 small bunch chives

Zest of 4 lemons
1 tablespoon potato starch
1 egg
2 tablespoons olive oil

Grate the zucchini and salt them. Let stand for 30 minutes in a colander. Squeeze the zucchini dry with your hands or wring it out in a towel.

Peel and chop the garlic fine, chop fine about 1 tablespoonful of the chives, and grate the zest from the lemons.

In a large bowl, combine the zucchini with the garlic, chives, lemon zest, the potato starch, and the egg, lightly beaten. Heat the olive oil in a nonstick sauté pan over medium heat. For each fritter, pour a generous tablespoonful of the zucchini batter into the pan. They will look like little pancakes. Turn them over after about 3 minutes, or when golden. Cook 2 minutes more on the other side. Drain on paper towels.

Serves 4.

Summer Squash and Corn Pasta

4 to 6 small summer squashes:
    zucchini, scallop, crookneck
5 to 6 ears sweet corn
2 cloves garlic
½ jalapeño pepper
3 tablespoons olive oil

Salt and pepper
1 handful cilantro leaves
2 tablespoons unsalted butter
4 tablespoons water
1 pound fresh, thin fettuccine
½ lemon

Cut the squashes into small dice. Cut the corn kernels from the cobs. Peel and chop the garlic fine and chop the jalapeño fine. Sauté the squash in the olive oil until tender and a little brown; season with salt and pepper. Add the corn, garlic, and jalapeño to the squash. Continue cooking a few minutes more. Finely chop the cilantro, reserving some leaves for garnish. Add the cilantro, butter, and water to the pan. Taste, and correct the seasoning. Boil the fettuccine, add it to the pan, and toss all together. Add a squeeze of lemon if the corn is very sweet. Serve immediately, garnished with the reserved cilantro leaves.

Serves 4.

Ratatouille

<table>
<tr><td>1 large eggplant</td><td>6 to 12 cloves garlic</td></tr>
<tr><td>Salt</td><td>Extra-virgin olive oil</td></tr>
<tr><td>3 onions</td><td>Optional: hot pepper flakes</td></tr>
<tr><td>3 red bell peppers</td><td>1 large bunch basil</td></tr>
<tr><td>4 summer squashes</td><td>(about ½ pound)</td></tr>
<tr><td>5 tomatoes</td><td></td></tr>
</table>

Cut the eggplant into ½-inch cubes. Salt it liberally and leave it to drain in a colander.

Peel and cut up the onions, and cut up the peppers, squashes, and tomatoes, keeping them all separate. Everything should be cut into pieces about the same size as the cubed eggplant. Smash and peel the garlic and chop it coarsely. Press down on the eggplant to extract more water and dry it.

In a heavy-bottomed pot, heat some of the olive oil and gently fry the eggplant until golden. Drain and reserve. Add more olive oil to the pot, and over medium-low heat start sautéing the onions. When they are soft and translucent, add the garlic, optional hot pepper flakes, and a bouquet garni consisting of the bunch of basil wrapped tightly with string, reserving a handful of the basil leaves for a garnish. Stir for a minute, toss in the peppers, and cook for a few minutes; next add the squash and cook a few minutes more, and then add the tomatoes. Cook for about 10 minutes, stirring occasionally. Finally add the eggplant, and cook 15 to 25 minutes more, until everything is soft and the flavors have melded together. Remove the bouquet of basil, pressing on it to extract all its flavors, and adjust the seasoning with freshly chopped basil leaves, salt, and a bit of fresh extra-virgin olive oil and fine-chopped garlic, if needed. Serve warm or cold. The dish tastes even better the next day.

Serves 8.

Note: Another method of making ratatouille is to fully cook all the vegetables separately, and to combine them with the tomatoes, herbs, and seasonings just before serving. This makes for a very beautiful dish; the vegetables don't break down, and the shape and color of each remain intact.

ZUCCHINI AND TOMATO GRATIN

1 yellow onion
Olive oil
Salt and pepper
1 small branch thyme

1 bunch fresh basil
(¼ to ½ pound)
6 to 8 medium slicing tomatoes
10 small green or yellow zucchini
Balsamic vinegar

Peel and slice thin the onion and sauté it in olive oil until soft and translucent. Season with salt and pepper; add the leaves of the thyme and basil, stripped from their stems and chopped. Cut out their stem ends and cut the tomatoes into ¼-inch slices. Trim the zucchini and cut them into ¼-inch-thick slices on the diagonal.

Spread the onion and herbs on the bottom of a 9 by 12-inch gratin dish or glass baking dish. Make a row of partially overlapping tomato slices. Season lightly with salt and pepper, and if the tomatoes are not very sweet, with a sprinkling of balsamic vinegar. Overlap the first row of tomato slices with zucchini slices, season with salt and pepper, and drizzle with a little olive oil. Continue making alternate rows of zucchini and tomatoes until they are used up.

Press down on the vegetables slightly, drizzle a little more olive oil over, and bake, uncovered, for 30 to 45 minutes, until the vegetables are fully cooked and the gratin has started to brown. If the top appears to be drying out while it bakes, tip the dish slightly and with a spoon collect some of the pan juices and use them to moisten the top.

Serves 6.

PASTA WITH ZUCCHINI, WALNUTS, AND PESTO

Trim and julienne some zucchini or other summer squashes, and sauté in olive oil until tender and starting to brown. Season with salt and pepper. Cook fresh noodles and add to the pan with a ladle of the pasta water or some chicken stock; some toasted walnuts, roughly chopped; and pesto sauce. Turn off the heat and toss well, taste for seasoning, and serve with grated Parmesan.

APPENDIX 🌢

These recipes are odds and ends. Although not really vegetable recipes, they either complement many of the preceding dishes or are indispensable to them.

TAPENADE

This is our version of the traditional Provençal olive and anchovy paste. There are others, some without anchovies, some perfumed with orange rind. Spread it on hors d'oeuvre garlic croutons; flavor vegetable ragouts with it; use it as a sauce for grills of all kinds.

2 cups niçoise olives
2 salt-packed anchovies
1 clove garlic
Salt

2 tablespoons capers
2 teaspoons lemon juice
⅓ cup extra-virgin olive oil

Pit the olives. Rinse and fillet the anchovies. Peel and smash the garlic with a pinch of salt. Chop the olives, anchovies, garlic, and capers together to make a coarse paste. (Or use a food processor.) Put the paste into a bowl, add the lemon juice and olive oil, and mix until they are completely incorporated.

Makes 2½ cups.

Note: If you are interested in curing your own olives, a concise and excellent method is to be found in *Lulu's Provençal Table,* by Richard Olney.

Picholine Olives Braised with White Wine and Lemon

Picholine olives are pale green, fruity olives from southern France that are traditionally cured in wood ashes.

9 ounces picholine olives   *One 2-inch piece lemon zest*
¼ cup water   *A few sprigs thyme*
¼ cup dry white wine   *1 bay leaf*

Put all the ingredients in a nonreactive pan and cover tightly. Braise in the oven at 375°F. for 1 hour. Allow the olives to cool in their juice. Pit the olives (or not) and serve as an hors d'oeuvre or as an accompaniment to roasted new potatoes, dandelion salad, sautéed or braised fennel, or dishes that would be complemented by the olives' savory citric taste.
     Serves 6.

Flavored Oils

Olive oil can be flavored with spices and herbs in two different ways. A lighter-tasting olive oil can simply be puréed with fresh herbs such as parsley, cilantro, or basil. Or extra-virgin olive oil can be infused over very low heat with strongly flavored herbs, such as wild fennel, thyme, rosemary, or sage; with spices such as fennel, cumin, coriander seed; or with flavorings such as red pepper flakes or lemon or orange peel. Flavored oils taste best if they are used right away, but they can be stored, refrigerated, for a few days. Do not store any longer, however, because dangerous anaerobic bacteria may survive and multiply in homemade infused oils.

To make an oil flavored with puréed herbs, first wash the herbs, drain in a colander, and dry thoroughly in a salad spinner. Purée the leaves in a blender with an equal volume of pure, light-bodied olive oil.

To infuse extra-virgin olive oil with stronger flavorings, either grind the herb or spice seed or chop the fresh herbs, then cover with 6 to 8 times their volume of extra-virgin olive oil. (Neither pepper flakes nor citrus peel need be chopped.) Set the oil in a very warm spot for 3 to 4 hours—over an oven pilot or near a very low flame. Or heat the oil over a low flame until it is distinctly warm to the touch, pour it over the flavoring, and let it stand at room temperature 3 to 4 hours before use.

SAFFRON RICE

The reason this method is useful to know is that rice made this way can be made ahead and kept warm over a little steam without getting sticky or mushy.

2½ cups basmati rice	1 big pinch crumbled
1½ tablespoons unsalted	saffron threads
butter	2 quarts water
¼ cup milk	1 tablespoon salt

Gently rinse the rice in cold water until the water runs clear. Soak the rice for 30 minutes in cold water. Butter a large heavy saucepan with a tight-fitting lid with about half the butter. In a separate pot melt the rest of the butter over low heat and add the milk and saffron.

Preheat the oven to 400°F. In a large pot, bring the water and salt to a rolling boil. Add the rice, cover, and cook for 7 minutes. Immediately drain the rice and put it in the buttered saucepan. Pour the butter, milk, and saffron mixture over the rice, cover tightly, and bake in the oven for 15 minutes.

Remove and taste for seasoning—it may need more salt. Let the rice rest, uncovered, for 5 minutes, then fluff with a fork. Serve with braised lamb or chicken, sautéed shrimp, or the Spicy Broccoli Vegetable Sauté (page 52).

Serves 6 to 8.

Note: For many more basmati rice recipes, see *An Invitation to Indian Cooking*, by Madhur Jaffrey.

TOASTED BREAD CRUMBS

Preheat the oven to 300°F. Pare off the crust from stale levain bread or other country-style bread. Shred the bread into small pieces and either chop it by hand or in a food processor, or leave in rough chunks depending on their use. Toss with a pinch of salt and a little olive oil to coat the bread. Spread the crumbs on a baking sheet in a thin layer. Put the sheet in the oven and bake until golden brown, about 30 minutes, tossing every 10 minutes.

Galette Dough

This pastry differs from a regular short crust in the proportion of butter to flour and in the way the butter is blended into the dough. Some of the butter is left in relatively large pieces, which makes for a crisper pastry. This pastry is suitable for both sweet and savory tarts.

2 cups flour	⅓ cup ice water
½ teaspoon salt	1 egg yolk
¼ teaspoon sugar	1 tablespoon cream
6 ounces unsalted butter	Optional: sugar

Combine the flour, salt, and sugar (the sugar helps the pastry brown). The butter should be cool—not cold and hard, but not too soft, either. Cut half the butter into the flour mixture and work it in lightly until the dough is roughly the texture of cornmeal. Add the other half of the butter in marble-size chunks. Work it into the dough very briefly, leaving the butter in unevenly incorporated bits. Lightly fork in the ice water just until evenly moistened. Divide and gather the dough into two balls, cover separately with plastic wrap, and knead very lightly through the plastic wrap, forming the dough into two even disks.

Refrigerate the dough and let it rest at least 1 hour. It can be kept for a day in the refrigerator and can be frozen for longer. Allow time outside the refrigerator for the dough to warm until it is just soft enough to be rolled out.

Roll each disk out on a floured surface to a 12-inch circle about ⅛ inch thick. Transfer to a parchment-lined baking sheet. Complete the tart with a savory or sweet filling, or refrigerate until ready to fill. Typically a single thin layer of vegetables or fruit fills the shell. If the filling is too thick, the pastry bottom does not brown well.

Fold the outside inch or so of dough over the filling to enclose it, and brush the outside crust with beaten egg yolk mixed with a little cream; for sweet tarts sprinkle the edge with sugar. Bake the tart at 400°F. on the bottom shelf in the oven, or place the baking sheet directly on a hot pizza stone in the oven. Bake for about 45 minutes, until the bottom is browned and crisp.

Makes enough dough for two 10-inch tarts or 1 large tart.

Farro

Farro is the Italian word for emmer, or two-grained spelt, a kind of wheat known botanically as *Triticum dicoccum.* We were introduced to farro by John Meis, an American who makes his home in Tuscany, and who is the author of *A Taste of Tuscany.* Serve farro with a spring vegetable ragout, accompanied with Parsley and Toasted Almond Salsa (page 175); use it in soups—the Chickpea and Farro Soup (page 99), for example; add it to cannellini beans in a gratin; or serve it with roast meats.

2 quarts water	*2 cups farro*
1 onion	*Salt*
1 carrot	*Olive oil or butter*
Bouquet garni: thyme sprigs and bay leaves	

Bring the water to a boil in a big pot with the onion and the carrot, peeled, and the bouquet garni. Simmer for about 15 minutes. Meanwhile, rinse the farro in three to four changes of water. Remove any black kernels of grain (they are very bitter). Add the farro to the boiling water, salt generously, bring back to a boil, and simmer uncovered for 40 minutes to 1 hour, depending on the dryness of the grain. Check after 40 minutes; the farro kernels should be slightly popped open and soft but still chewy. Drain, remove and discard the aromatic vegetables and the bouquet, and toss the farro with olive oil or butter. Taste and add more salt if necessary.

Serves 4.

Vegetable Stock

We make an all-purpose vegetable stock to use in all the ways chicken stock might be used—in vegetable ragouts, pastas, soups, and sauces—but when a light and meatless broth is wanted.

Start with a piece of kombu. (Kombu is a dried seaweed that imparts both flavor and body to the stock. The type we use comes in flat, cut pieces about 6 inches square and about ⅛ inch thick. A piece about 3 inches square would do for 3 to 4 quarts of broth.) Soak the kombu for about an hour in as much tepid water as you intend to use for the stock, remove it, and set aside to be added later.

Trim and dice or slice thin leeks, celery, carrots, and onions. Exact proportions are not important, but it is better if you go lightly on the sweeter vegetables—carrots and onions. In a stockpot, sauté the vegetables in butter until softened and lightly browned. Add some chopped garlic and then pour in the kombu water. Add parsley stalks, thyme, bay leaves, and peppercorns, and bring to a simmer. Lower the heat, add the piece of kombu, and cook at just below a simmer for an hour. (Cooking at higher heat will make the stock too gelatinous.) Strain, and it is ready to use. Salt just before using, depending on the preparation; the saltiness of the seaweed varies. If you like, darken the color of the stock with a little soy sauce.

BIBLIOGRAPHY

Allen, Oliver E. *Gardening with the New Small Plants.* Boston: Houghton Mifflin, 1987.

Araldo, Josephine, with Robert Reynolds. *From a Breton Garden: The Vegetable Cookery of Josephine Araldo.* Berkeley, Calif.: Aris Books/Addison-Wesley, 1990.

Bayless, Rick, and Deann Bayless. *Authentic Mexican.* New York: William Morrow, 1987.

Bertolli, Paul, with Alice Waters. *Chez Panisse Cooking.* New York: Random House, 1988.

Boulud, Daniel. *Cooking with Daniel Boulud.* New York: Random House, 1993.

Bras, Michel, with Alain Boudier and Christian Millau. *Le Livre de Michel Bras.* Rodez, France: Editions de Rouergue, 1991.

Brennan, Georgeanne. *Potager: Fresh Garden Cooking in the French Style.* San Francisco: Chronicle Books, 1992.

Bugialli, Giuliano. *The Fine Art of Italian Cooking.* New York: Times Books, 1977.

Campbell, Susan. *Cottesbrooke: An English Kitchen Garden.* London: Century Hutchinson, 1987.

Castelvetro, Giacomo. *The Fruit, Herbs and Vegetables of Italy.* New York: Viking, 1989.

Clarke, Ethne. *The Art of the Kitchen Garden.* New York: Alfred A. Knopf, 1987.

Creasy, Rosalind. *Cooking from the Garden.* San Francisco: Sierra Club Books, 1988.

———. *Earthly Delights.* San Francisco: Sierra Club Books, 1985.

David, Elizabeth. *Elizabeth David Classics.* New York: Alfred A. Knopf, 1980.

Dille, Carolyn, and Susan Belsinger. *Herbs in the Kitchen: A Celebration of Flavor.* Loveland, Colo.: Interweave Press, 1992.

Giobbi, Edward. *Eat Right, Eat Well—The Italian Way.* New York: Alfred A. Knopf, 1985.

Gray, Patience. *Honey from a Weed.* New York: Harper & Row, 1987.

Grigson, Jane. *Good Things.* London: Penguin Books, 1971.

———. *Jane Grigson's Vegetable Book.* New York: Atheneum, 1978.

———. *The Mushroom Feast.* New York: Alfred A. Knopf, 1991.

de Groot, Roy Andries. *From the Auberge of the Flowering Hearth.* New York: Bobbs-Merrill, 1973.

Hamady, Mary Laird. *Lebanese Mountain Cookery.* Boston: David R. Godine, 1987.

Harris, Lloyd J. *The Book of Garlic.* Berkeley, Calif.: Panjandrum/Aris Books, 1974.

Harris, Valentina. *Recipes from an Italian Farmhouse.* New York: Simon & Schuster, 1989.

Hom, Ken. *Ken Hom's Vegetable and Pasta Book.* London: BBC Books, 1987.

Jabs, Carolyn. *The Heirloom Gardener.* San Francisco: Sierra Club Books, 1984.

Jacobs, Susie. *Recipes from a Greek Island.* New York: Simon & Schuster, 1991.

Jaffrey, Madhur. *An Invitation to Indian Cooking.* New York: Random House, 1973.

———. *Madhur Jaffrey's Far Eastern Cookery.* New York: Harper & Row, 1989.

Jeavons, John. *How to Grow More Vegetables.* Berkeley, Calif.: Ten Speed Press, 1974.

Jenkins, Nancy Harmon. *The Mediterranean Diet Cookbook.* New York: Bantam, 1994.

Kamman, Madeleine. *Madeleine Kamman's Savoie*. New York: Atheneum, 1989.

Kasper, Lynne Rossetto. *The Splendid Table*. New York: William Morrow, 1992.

Kennedy, Diana. *Mexican Regional Cooking*. New York: Harper & Row, 1978.

Khalsa, Baba S. *Great Vegetables from the Great Chefs*. San Francisco: Chronicle Books, 1990.

Kourik, Robert. *Your Edible Landscape—Naturally*. Santa Rosa, Calif.: Metamorphic Press, 1986.

Kraus, Sibella. *Greens: A Country Garden Cookbook*. San Francisco: Collins, 1993.

Lanza, Anna Tasca. *The Heart of Sicily*. New York: Clarkson N. Potter, 1993.

Larkcom, Joy. *Oriental Vegetables: The Complete Guide for the Gardening Cook*. New York: Kodansha International, 1991.

———. *The Salad Garden*. New York: Penguin, 1984.

Lewis, Edna. *In Pursuit of Flavor*. New York: Alfred A. Knopf, 1988.

Lyte, Charles. *The Kitchen Garden*. Sparkford, England: The Oxford Illustrated Press, 1984.

Madison, Deborah. *The Greens Cookbook*. New York: Bantam, 1987.

———. *The Savory Way*. New York: Bantam, 1990.

Marshall, Lydie. *A Passion for Potatoes*. New York, HarperCollins, 1992.

Meis, John Dore. *A Taste of Tuscany*. New York: Abbeville, 1993.

Meyer, Danny, and Michael Romano. *The Union Square Café Cookbook*. New York: HarperCollins, 1994.

Ogden, Shepherd, and Ellen Ogden. *The Cook's Garden: Growing and Using the Best-Tasting Vegetable Varieties*. Emmaus, Pa.: Rodale Press, 1989.

Olney, Richard. *Lulu's Provençal Table*. New York: HarperCollins, 1994.

———. *Provence the Beautiful Cookbook*. San Francisco: Collins, 1993.

——— . *Simple French Food*. New York: Simon & Schuster, 1970.

Organic Gardening and Farming, the editors of. *Unusual Vegetables: Something New for This Year's Garden*. Emmaus, Pa.: Rodale Press, 1978.

Peirce, Pam. *Golden Gate Gardening: The complete guide to year-round food gardening in the San Francisco Bay Area & Coastal California*. Davis, Calif.: agAccess, 1993.

Phillips, Roger. *Wild Food*. Boston: Little, Brown, 1986.

Romer, Elizabeth. *Italian Pizza and Hearth Breads*. New York: Clarkson N. Potter, 1987.

Rossant, Colette, and Marianne Melendez. *Vegetables: Growing, Cooking, Keeping*. New York: Penguin Books, 1991.

Sahni, Julie. *Classic Indian Vegetarian and Grain Cooking*. New York: William Morrow, 1981.

Schneider, Elizabeth. *Uncommon Fruits and Vegetables: A Commonsense Guide*. New York: Harper & Row, 1986.

Schwartz, Arthur. *Soup Suppers*. New York: HarperCollins, 1994.

Simeti, Mary Taylor. *Pomp and Sustenance*. New York: Alfred A. Knopf, 1989.

Tanis, David. *Corn: A Country Garden Cookbook*. San Francisco: Collins, 1995.

Thompson, Sylvia. *The Kitchen Garden*. New York: Bantam, 1995.

———. *The Kitchen Garden Cookbook*. New York: Bantam, 1995.

Tolley, Emelie, and Chris Mead. *Cooking with Herbs*. New York: Clarkson N. Potter, 1986.

Waldron, Maggie. *Potatoes: A Country Garden Cookbook*. San Francisco: Collins, 1993.

Waters, Alice. *Chez Panisse Menu Cookbook*. New York: Random House, 1982.

———, with Bob Carrau and Patricia Curtan. *Fanny at Chez Panisse*. New York: HarperCollins, 1992.

———, with Patricia Curtan and Martine Labro. *Chez Panisse Pasta, Pizza, and Calzone*. New York: Random House, 1984.

Wells, Patricia. *Bistro Cooking*. New York: Workman, 1989.

Wolfert, Paula. *The Cooking of the Eastern Mediterranean*. New York: HarperCollins, 1994.

———. *Couscous and Other Good Food from Morocco*. New York: Harper & Row, 1973.

INDEX 🐚